T0385466

OUT OF THE DARK NIGHT

OUT OF THE DARK NIGHT

ESSAYS

on

DECOLONIZATION

ACHILLE MBEMBE

Columbia University Press

New York

Columbia University Press
Publishers Since 1893
New York   Chichester, West Sussex
cup.columbia.edu

Achille Mbembe, *Sortir de la grande nuit* copyright © 2010 Éditions
La Découverte

Library of Congress Cataloging-in-Publication Data
Names: Mbembe, Achille, 1957 author. | Mbembe, Achille,
1957– Sortir de la grande nuit. English.
Title: Out of the dark night : essays on decolonization / Achille Mbembe.
Description: New York : Columbia University Press, 2021. | "The English edition
of this book does not exactly correspond to what was published in French as
Sortir de la grande nuit in 2010, and different passages date from different times
of writing and have different translators. Daniela Ginsburg translated the
material that came from *Sortir de la grande nuit*. Portions of the new material is
based on work featured in my essay "Future Knowledges and Their Implications
for the Decolonizing Project," in *Decolonisation in Universities: The Politics of
Knowledge*, edited by Jonathan Jansen and published by Wits University Press in
2019"—page viii. | Includes bibliographical references.
Identifiers: LCCN 2020045271 (print) | LCCN 2020045272 (ebook) |
ISBN 9780231160285 (hardback) | ISBN 9780231500593 (ebook)
Subjects: LCSH: Postcolonialism—Africa. | Africa—Politics and
government—1960– | Africa—Social conditions—1960–
Classification: LCC JQ1875 .M42313 2021 (print) | LCC JQ1875 (ebook) |
DDC 325.3096—dc23
LC record available at https://lccn.loc.gov/2020045271
LC ebook record available at https://lccn.loc.gov/2020045272

Cover image: © Sarah Calhoun

CONTENTS

6 AFROPOLITANISM

EPILOGUE: THE POLITICS OF THE FUTURE WORLD

ACKNOWLEDGMENTS

This book is the fruit of long conversations with Françoise Vergès. It repeats, sometimes verbatim, reflections, developed over the course of the past ten years between Africa, France, and the United States, in the form of journal articles (*Le Débat, Esprit, Cahiers d'études africaine, Le Monde diplomatique*), course notes, seminars, workshops, and interventions in the African press and other international media. I would like to express my gratitude to those who have provoked, encouraged, nourished, and welcomed these reflections: Pierre Nora, Olivier Mongin, Jean-Louis Schlegel, Michel Agier, Didier Fassin, Georges Nivat, Pascal Blanchard, Nicolas Bancel, Annalisa Oboe, Bogumil Jewsiewicki, Thomas Blom Hansen, Arjun Appadurai, Dilip Gaonkar, Jean Comaroff, John Comaroff, Peter Geschiere, David Theo Goldberg, Laurent Dubois, Célestin Monga, Yara El-Ghadban, Anne-Cécile Robert, Alain Mabanckou, and Ian Baucom.

This work was written during my long stay at the Wits Institute for Social and Economic Research (WiSER) in Johannesburg, where I benefited from the support of my colleagues Deborah Posel, John Hyslop, Pamila Gupta, Irma Duplessis, and Sarah Nuttall. I also benefited from discussions at the Johannesburg Workshop in Theory and Criticisim (JWTC), directed by Kelly Gillespie, Julia Hornberger, Leigh-Ann Naidoo, Eric Worby, Tawana Kupe, and Sue van Zyl. François

Gèze, Béatrice Didiot, Pascales Iltis, and Johanna Bourgault, from Éditions La Découverte, have marvelously accompanied the process of the book's making and have not hesitated to share their intuitions.

The English edition of this book does not exactly correspond to what was published in French as *Sortir de la grande nuit* in 2010, and different passages date from different times of writing and have different translators. Daniela Ginsburg translated the material that came from *Sortir de la grande nuit.* Portions of the new material are based on work featured in my essay "Future Knowledges and Their Implications for the Decolonising Project," in *Decolonisation in Universities: The Politics of Knowledge,* edited by Jonathan Jansen and published by Wits University Press in 2019.

INTRODUCTION

Those who, each day, pitch camp farther off from their
birthplace, those who, each day, haul in their boat on
other banks, know better, day by day, the course of
illegible things; and tracing the rivers towards their
source, through the green world of appearances they
are caught up suddenly into that harsh glare
where all language loses its power.

—SAINT-JOHN PERSE, "SNOWS"

Half a century ago, most of humanity was living under the yoke of colonialism, a particularly primitive form of racial despotism. Colonialism was itself but one dimension of a long history, that of imperialism, "the ruthless drive for dominance" which periodically seized metropolitan states, leading them to trample over the sovereignty of other political communities. Historians identify three waves of active imperialism in modern European history. The first, argues C. A. Bayly, "was marked by the Iberian and Dutch conquests in the New World and Asia between 1520 and 1620." The second occurred "between about 1760 and 1830 when European empires first seized substantial territory in south and south-east Asia, raced ahead in north America and Australasia, marked out the near east and southern Africa as spheres of dominance, and brought the Atlantic slave system to its peak." The third age of imperialism "culminated with the Partition of Africa after 1878, the Russian conquest of central Asia and the battle for concessions in China."[1] In the case of Britain, the empire was defined by conquest as well as by trade and settlement. British power and influence were exerted simultaneously in all quarters of the globe. The global nature of imperial activity in turn raised questions about the ways in which "alien non-Protestant and non-Christian peoples should be governed within the empire," and "concerns about the effects upon the metropolis of the 'despotism' and 'tyranny' that were being imported from Britain's empire of conquest in the east."[2]

The liberation of part of humanity from the yoke of colonialism constitutes a key moment in the history of our modernity. That this event left almost no mark on the philosophical spirit of our time is in itself hardly an enigma. Not all crimes necessarily engender sacred things. Certain crimes in history have resulted in nothing but stains and profanity, the splendid sterility of an atrophied existence: in short, they show the impossibility of "making community" and rewalking the paths of humanity. Can it be said that decolonization was precisely the spectacle par excellence of the impossible community—rife with spasmodic convulsion and futile static noise? This book will only indirectly tackle this question, the complete and detailed history of which remains to be written.

Its central object is the wave of African decolonizations during the twentieth century. I will not be retracing their history or studying their sociology—even less their typology. Such work has already been done and, with few exceptions, there is very little to add to it.[3] Even less will I be assessing the results of independences. If decolonization was an event at all, its essential philosophical meaning lies in an *active will to community*—as others used to speak of a will to power. This will to community is another name for what could be called the *will to life*. Its goal was to realize a shared project: to stand up on one's own and to create a heritage. In our blasé age, characterized by cynicism and frivolity, such words might cause only snickers. But at the time of decolonization, many were ready to risk their lives to affirm such ideals. These ideals were not pretexts for avoiding the present or shirking action. To the contrary, they acted as catalysts, and served to orient becoming and to impose a new redistribution of language and a new logic of sense and life through praxis.[4] Colonization was perceived as neither a destiny nor a necessity as the decolonized community tried to establish itself on its ruins. It was thought that by dismembering the colonial relationship, the lost name would resurface. The relation between what had been, what had just happened, and what was coming would be reversed, making possible the manifestation of one's own power of genesis, one's own capacity for articulating difference and for expressing a positive force.

In addition to the will to community, there was the will to know and the desire for singularity and originality. Anticolonial discourse had, for the most part, espoused the postulate of modernization and the ideals of progress, including where it criticized them either explicitly or implicitly. This critique was animated by the quest for a future that would not be written in advance, one that would mix together received or inherited traditions with interpretation, experimentation, and new creation to leave this world and go toward other possible worlds. At the heart of this analysis was the idea that Western modernity was imperfect, incomplete, and unfinished. The Western claim to epitomize the language and forms in which any human event could arise, and even to have a monopoly on the very idea of the future, was only a fiction. The new postcolonial world was not condemned to imitate and reproduce what had been accomplished elsewhere.[5] Because history was being produced in a unique way each time, the politics of the future—without which there would be no full decolonization—required the invention of new images of thought. This was only possible if one committed oneself to a long apprenticeship in signs and their modes of encounter with experience—an apprenticeship in the time specific to the sites of life.[6]

Does the mixture of realities that prevails today invalidate these propositions and take away their historical density, their actuality? Was decolonization—if such an open concept can actually mean anything—nothing but a fantasy without substance? Was it ultimately only a noisy accident, a crack on the surface, a little chink on the outside, the sign of a future bound to go astray? Does the colonization/decolonization duality have only one meaning? As historical phenomena, isn't one reflected in the other, implicated in the other, like two sides of the same mirror? These are some of the questions this book will endeavor to examine. One of its theses is that decolonization inaugurated a time of branching off toward innumerable futures. These futures were by definition contingent. The trajectories followed by the newly freed nations were partly the consequences of internal struggles within the societies under consideration.[7] These struggles were themselves shaped both by the old social forms and economic structures inherited from colonization and by the techniques and practices of government of the new postcolonial regimes. In most cases, these struggles resulted in the implementation of a form of domination that has been described as "domination without hegemony."[8]

For many, the postcolonial moment, properly speaking, began with an experience of decentering. Decolonization—especially where it was granted rather than won—instead of acting as an intensive sign forcing the formerly colonized to think by and for themselves, rather than being the site of a renewed genesis of meaning, took on the appearance of an encounter with oneself through effraction: it was not the result of a fundamental desire for freedom, something the subject gives him- or herself, something that becomes the necessary source of morality and politics, but was rather an exteriority, something seemingly lacking any power of metamorphosis. As form and figure, act and relation, colonization was in many regards a coproduction of colonizers and colonized. Together, but from different positions, they forged a past. But having a past in common does not necessarily mean sharing it. Here I examine the paradoxes of "postcolonialism" in a former colonial power, France, that decolonized without self-decolonizing (chapter 3). I focus on the disjunctions and ramifications of the gesture of decolonization in the present, especially from the point of view of an apparent inability to write a shared history on the basis of a shared past (chapter 4).

In chapters 2 and 5, I tackle what is considered the central paradox of decolonization: *sterile extraction* and *repetition* on the one hand, and *indefinite proliferation* on the other (terms that are borrowed from Gilles Deleuze).[9] In fact, one of the processes set in motion in the aftermath of decolonization was the destruction of the state form and the institutions inherited from colonization—a destruction sometimes patient and underhanded, sometimes chaotic.[10] The history of this demolition as such has not yet been grasped in its singularity. The new independent entities, henceforth more or less free vessels (in fact, heterogeneous grafts of at first glance incompatible fragments and, in the long run, conglomerations of societies), resumed their course. At great risk. The overlap of successive dramas, unpredicted ruptures, and foretold declines continues against the backdrop of a formidable asthenia of the will. In some places, change takes on the contours of repetition; elsewhere, it takes the form of inconsequential flashes, and still elsewhere, it appears as dissolution and a plunge into the unknown and unpredicted: the impossible revolution.

But the will to live remains. An enormous work of reassemblage is somehow or another underway on the African continent. Its human costs are high. It goes as deep as structures of thought. Through the postcolonial crisis, a reconversion of the mind has taken place. Destruction and reassemblage are so tightly connected that, isolated from each other, these processes become incomprehensible. Next to the world of ruins and what has been called the "house without keys" (chapter 5), an Africa in the process of synthesizing itself, in a mode of disjunction and redistribution of differences, is taking shape. The future of this Africa-in-circulation will be shaped by the force of its paradoxes and its unwillingness to submit (chapter 6). This is an Africa whose social framework and spatial structure are now decentered, and which goes in the direction of both the past and the future—an Africa whose spiritual processes are a mixture of a secularization of consciousness, a radical immanence (care for this world and care for the moment), and an apparently unmediated plunge into the divine, an Africa whose languages and sounds are deeply creole, an Africa that accords a central place to experimentation, an Africa in which astonishingly postmodern images and practices of existence germinate.

Something fertile will spring from this *Africa-glebe*, this immense tilled field of matter and things: something capable of opening onto an infinite, extensive, and heterogeneous universe, a wide-open universe of multiplicities and pluralities.[11] A name has been found for this *African-world-to-come*, whose complex and mobile fabric slips constantly out of one form and into another and turns away all languages and sonorities because it is no longer attached to any language or pure sounds, this body in motion, never in its place, whose center moves everywhere, this body moving in the enormous machine of the world: that name is Afropolitanism.

1

PLANETARY ENTANGLEMENT

Writing about Africa in 1830–1831, this is what Hegel had to say:

> The peculiarly African character is difficult to comprehend, for the very reason that in reference to it, we must quite give up the principle which naturally accompanies all our ideas—the category of Universality. In Negro life, the characteristic point is the fact that consciousness has not yet attained to the realization of any substantial objective existence—as for example, God, or Law—in which the interest of man's volition is involved and in which he realizes his own being. . . . The Negro . . . exhibits the natural man in his completely wild and untamed state. We must lay aside all thought of reverence and morality—all that we call feeling—if we would rightly comprehend him. There is nothing harmonious with humanity to be found in this type of character.[1]

Hegel then went on promising himself not to mention Africa again, for "it is no historical part of the World; it has no movement or development to exhibit." What we properly understand by Africa, he concluded, "is the Unhistorical, Undeveloped Spirit, still involved in the conditions of mere nature."[2]

HEGELIAN MYTHOLOGY

More than a century after Hegel's verdict, Robert Kaplan authored a portrayal of that same continent in the February 1994 issue of the US-based *Atlantic Monthly*. The Cold War had just ended and most of the Western world was triumphantly riding on the crest of a wave of optimism. Celebrating this triumph—that of the West and of what he called the Western *idea*—Francis Fukuyama suggested in 1989 that "what we may be witnessing is not just the end of the Cold War, or the passing of a particular period of postwar history, but the end of history as such." By "the end of history as such," he did not simply mean the end point of humankind's ideological evolution. More fundamentally, he meant the reconciliation of the market principle and the idea of freedom, and "the universalization of Western liberal democracy as the final form of human government."[3]

Yet, projecting himself to the day and times after history had ended, he could only see melancholia and sadness, a profound nostalgia for the Hegelian world:

> The end of history will be a very sad time. The struggle for recognition, the willingness to risk one's life for a purely abstract goal, the worldwide ideological struggle that called forth daring, courage, imagination, and idealism, will be replaced by economic calculation, the endless solving of technical problems, environmental concerns, and the satisfaction of sophisticated consumer demands. In the post-historical period there will be neither art nor philosophy, just the perpetual caretaking of the museum of human history.[4]

As Fukuyama wrote his epitaph to history, Africa was in the midst of a spectacular collision. While Apartheid and white minority rule were coming to a formal end in South Africa, a genocide of cataclysmic pro-portions was unfolding in Rwanda. The apotheosis of long years of strug-gle on the one hand, self-destruction on the other. Declining per capita incomes and production, low levels of savings and investment, slow growth in agricultural production, failing export earnings, strangled imports and unserviceable foreign debt burdens—all plagued most of sub-Saharan Africa.

In his scenario for the twenty-first century, Kaplan argued that West Africa in particular was becoming "the symbol of worldwide demo-graphic, environmental, and societal stress, in which criminal anarchy emerges as the real 'strategic' danger. Disease, overpopulation, unpro-voked crime, scarcity of resources, refugee migrations, the increasing erosion of nation-states and international borders, and the empower-ment of private armies, security firms, and international drug cartels are now most tellingly demonstrated through a West African prism."[5] In Kaplan's political geography—just as in Hegel's a century earlier— "West Africa" became the epitome of those regions of the world where central governments were withering away, tribal and regional fiefdoms were on the rise, and war had turned pervasive. West Africa, he argued, "is reverting to the Africa of the Victorian Atlas. It consists now of a series of coastal trading posts . . . and an interior that, owing to violence, volatility and disease, is again becoming . . .'blank' and 'unexplored.' It is Thomas Malthus, the philosopher of demographic doomsday, who is now the prophet of West Africa's future. And West Africa's future, even-tually, will also be that of most of the rest of the world . . . in an age of cultural and racial clash."

This apocalyptic view of Africa's future was echoed in 2000 when, building upon Hegelian tropes once again, the influential financial weekly the *Economist* declared that Africa was a "hopeless continent." In a famous editorial, it conjured up images of destitution, failure and despair, floods and famine, poverty and pestilence, brutality, despotism and corruption, dreadful wars and plunder, rape, cannibalism, ampu-tation, and even the weather to suggest that Africa's future was defi-nitely doomed. Foreign aid workers, peacekeeping missions, humani-tarian agencies, and the world at large could well give up, so deeply "buried in their cultures" were the reasons for so much human misery, it concluded.[6]

As the twenty-first century unfolds, it is gradually seeping into the minds of many that to a large extent our planet's destiny might be played out in Africa. From a philosophical and cultural point of view, this *planetary turn of the African predicament* takes us far away from the Hegelian myths, which, for too long, have colonized Africa's imagination of the world and the world's imagination of Africa. On the continent itself, older senses of time and space and notions of history based on linear approaches to development and progress are gradually being replaced by newer senses of futures founded on open narrative models. There are many who increasingly believe that, through self-organization and small ruptures, we can actually create myriad "tipping points" that may lead to deep alterations in the direction that both the continent and the planet take.

Yet to write the world from Africa, or to write Africa into the world or as a fragment thereof, is an exhilarating and, most of the time, perplexing task.[7] As a name and as a sign, Africa has always occupied a paradoxical position in modern formations of knowledge. On the one hand, the region has provided most of our modern disciplines with some of their foundational categories.[8] From anthropology to political economy, from poststructuralism to psychoanalysis and postcolonial theory, the continent has been the purveyor of some of the most compelling concepts, without which modern criticism would be utterly poor.[9]

DENATIONALIZATION

On the other hand, it has been largely assumed that "things African" are residual entities, the study of which does not contribute anything to knowledge of the world or of the human condition in general.[10] Predicated on a narrow definition of what "Africa" stands for in the history of human thought, this assumption has in turn led to too restricted a conception of what knowledge is all about and whom it is supposed to serve. Today, the overwhelming belief is that, coupled with science and technology, market capitalism and "humanitarian" interventions will sort out most of the continent's problems. Complex social structures and processes such as war, mass poverty, joblessness, disease, and illiteracy are treated as if all of these are purely technical matters and the human subjects implicated in these dramas have no histories. History itself has been reified in a set of abstractions, and the sense of being at the edge of a future so palpable in the immediate aftermath of colonialism and Apartheid has quickly vanished.[11]

As radical changes have unfolded, each requiring ever more complex modes of explanation and understanding, ignorance has been harnessed as a resource, enabling knowledge to be deflected, obscured, or concealed in a way that has increased the scope of what remains unintelligible.[12] Throughout the twentieth century, the region has witnessed a surge in problem-oriented research that has become attractive to governments and private funding agencies because of its putative relevance to "real-world" challenges.[13] Funding scarcity, in turn, has led numerous scholars to work as NGO entrepreneurs and consultants, to stockpile short-term research contracts, and to shift rapidly from one topic to another, a practice that increases the atomization of knowledge rather than the thorough understanding of entire fields.

The research-for-hire financed by philanthropic organizations and development agencies favors the collection of large data sets. It privileges the production of quantitative indicators over critical analyses. Buttressed by an explicit and at times unqualified commitment to instrumentalism and social empiricism, it mainly treats Africa as a crisis-prone entity. The crisis itself is understood simply in technicist terms as an event that calls for a technical decision. Needless to say, this kind of research has not resulted in as big of an improvement in knowledge as might have been expected.[14] Nor has it made any space for theorization. Nowhere have we witnessed the kind of cultural ferment and intellectual innovation that would have allowed scholars, critics, and artists to cut across the customary boundaries separating philosophy, history, aesthetic criticism, political theory, and theology, not to mention science and technology, or even metaphysics.

Yet, as the new century unfolds, many increasingly acknowledge that there is no better laboratory than Africa to gauge the limits of our epistemological imagination or to pose new questions about how we know what we know and what that knowledge is grounded in. Recent ethnographic studies of the region have shown how to draw on multiple models of time so as to avoid one-way explanatory shortcuts, how to open a space for broader comparative undertakings, and how to account for the multiplicity of the pathways and trajectories of change.[15] In fact, there is no better terrain than Africa for a scholarship that is keen to describe novelty and originality, multiplicity, singularity, and complexity, and is mindful of the fact that the ways in which societies compose and invent themselves in the present—what we could call the creativity of practice—are always ahead of any knowledge we can ever produce about them.[16]

In their book *Theory from the South*, Jean and John Comaroff have amply demonstrated that the challenges to critical social theory are nowhere as acute as they are in the Southern Hemisphere, perhaps the epicenter of contemporary global transformations—in any case the site of unfolding developments that are contradictory, uneven, contested, and for the most part undocumented.[17] Here, fundamental problems of poverty and livelihood, equity and justice are still, for the most part, unresolved. A huge amount of labor is still put into eliminating want, repairing that which has been broken, making life possible, or simply maintaining it. People marginalized by the development process live under conditions of restlessness, uncertainty, and great personal risk.[18] They permanently confront a threatening environment in conditions of virtual or functional superfluousness.[19] In order to survive, many are willing to gamble with their lives and with those of other people.[20]

This is a deeply heterogeneous world of flows, fractures and frictions, accidents and collisions. Power relations and the antagonisms that shape late, deregulated capitalism are redefined here in ways and forms not seen at earlier historical periods.[21] Contemporary forms of life, work, property, production, exchange, languages, and value testify to an openness of the social that earlier descriptive and interpretive models can no longer account for.[22] New boundaries are emerging, while old ones are being redrawn, extended, or simply abandoned.[23] The paradoxes of mobility and closure, of entanglement and separation, of continuities and discontinuities between the inside and the outside, the local and the global, or of temporariness and permanence pose new challenges to critical thought and intellectual inquiry.[24]

These processes have coincided with the redrawing of the global intellectual map—a shift that started during the era of decolonization.[25] Besides traditional northern Atlantic research institutions and centers of learning, alternative circuits of circulation (South/South, North/East, South/East) have emerged during the last quarter of the twentieth century.[26] This worldwide dissemination of thought has been buttressed by a worldwide circulation and translation of texts, a highly productive invention and reappropriation of concepts, and the denationalization of the great academic debates.[27] Whether the denationalization of the humanities and academic discussion has brought a truly global perspective to conventional Western theory and criticism remains to be seen.[28] At the very least, it is now recognized that the world can be studied from everywhere and anywhere.[29] Major transformations in the way in which we think about the histories of the world are underway.[30] In this context, any inquiry into the place of Africa—and by extension the global South—in theory is necessarily an interrogation concerning the experience of the world in an epoch when "the planet is no longer as large as it once was."[31]

THEORY TODAY

Theory has been not only the name of the West's attempt at domesticating contingency, but also the way in which the West has distinguished itself from the "Rest." To be sure, social theory formally recognizes a common ontological domain of human sociality. Yet, it can also be seen "as one particularly modern form of posing questions that are not altogether different from those the natural law tradition has been raising."[32]

Historically, natural law emerged with an explicit set of ideas about human nature. Whether it is possible to abide by the universalistic aspirations of social theory without replicating the metaphysical and normative implications of its Western origins is a question many are no longer willing to postpone.[33] Nor can we postpone a critical reappraisal of modern social theory's deep investment in human reason as the ultimate guarantor of a detached scrutiny of the natural and social world. The segregation of human rationality and the division of the mind between an unconscious grounded in the biological (and thus subject to its own laws) and an autonomous reason lodged in consciousness are at the core of modern Western humanities. It is this segregation that allows modern human sciences to think of reason both as the repository of interpretation and free will and as the sovereign instrument of self-knowing in the pursuit of perfection. Is this kind of philosophical anthropology valid for every single human culture or region of the planet?[34]

The foundation of the modern university itself and the current geopolitics of knowledge at the planetary level rest, to a certain extent, on a Yalta-like division of the world between the global North, where theory is done, and the "Rest," which is the kingdom of ethnography.[35] In this global cartography, the functions of marginal regions of the world are to produce data and to serve as the test sites of the theory mills of the North. To be sure, theory (at least among the Western Left) has always been many things at the same time. It has always been an investigation into the conditions and limits of knowledge. But the task of theory, at least in the human sciences, has also always been to ask, what characterizes our present and our age? In other words, it has been about deciphering one's own time and taking responsibility for one's own fate.

Obviously, then, theory was always conceived as a political intervention, something somewhat beyond "criticism" as such, that is, "a certain kind of reflection on language and literature that garnered the tag 'deconstruction' in the 1970s."[36] What gave theory its edge was its presupposed capacity both to transform the existing structures of power and to imagine alternative social arrangements. In this sense, theory was always understood to be a means of struggle—which allows Michael Hardt to reduce it to a form of "philosophical and political militancy."

Whatever the case, critical theory emerged in Western Europe between the late nineteenth and early twentieth centuries in response to transformations in the economy, society, and culture.[37] At stake in these transformations was a change in the character of the capitalist economy and the liberal political order. This was indeed a time of multiple transitions—out of a notionally liberal nineteenth century and into an era of monopoly formations, imperialist adventurism, and late-modern forms of conquest and colonization, an era of the blurring of the boundaries (already then) between private and public spheres, an era of the displacement of skilled artisanship by the serialized processes that would ultimately lead to Fordism, an era of the subversion of traditional structures in the world of work, and an era of the collapse of utopian revolutionary hopes.

These processes had a profound impact on the nature and forms of cultural critique, from sociology (its interest in questions of modernity, rationalization, capitalism, and the relationship of ideology to these phenomena) to developments in philosophy, theology, law, science, aesthetics, literature, film, and comparative mythology. Witness, for instance, the Frankfurt School's interest in the withering away of the culture of autonomous individuality and how it paved the way for the expansion of the state—an expansion that, for Adorno, Horkheimer, and Marcuse, encouraged a conformist and manipulative culture industry that nurtured a regressive subordination to bureaucratic administration and allowed for the emergence of what Marcuse in particular called "the one-dimensional man."[38]

There is no agreement today about what theory is and what distinguishes it from "criticism."[39] As with science itself, theory today refers to a heterogeneous population of individual themes, fields, and subfields, at times without any discernible convergence toward a grand synthesis.[40] It covers a wide variety of practices—from (1) methods of questioning the truth of authority to (2) techniques to reveal the figures of power that operate in dominant discourses, institutions, or social processes to (3) ways of investigating the limits of human reason and judgment.[41] Furthermore, over the last quarter of the twentieth century, there has been "something of a flight from theory, a re-embrace both of methodological empiricism and born-again realism; also a return to the ethical and the theological"[42]—to which should be added the growth of versions of popular science that have produced "a ready public for arguments that seek to reduce human nature to biology."[43]

The brain sciences (neurobiology, psychopharmacology, biological psychiatry, brain imaging), for instance, have thrown into disarray older accounts of the human and of the mind. Novel preoccupations with feelings, thinking, belief, and intentions have led to renewed efforts to read the mind at the very moment when biometric devices of all kinds attempt to measure and visualize body data.[44] Theorizing subjectivity, estrangement, otherness, and self-division as both socioculturally constituted and experiential, embodied, and singular in the wake of a radically altered biomedical and biotechnological landscape has become the new challenge. When subjectivity is framed and analyzed in predominantly cognitive or sociorational terms, the task is to account for the affective and for emotional experience without drifting toward neurobiological reductionism.[45]

The increasing theoretical confidence of theology and biology has resulted in the story of "being human" becoming more and more conflated with the story of "human nature."[46] A renewed faith in material causes has been spearheaded by the extraordinary discoveries in genetics during the past half century. Explanations of human psychological properties, beliefs, and actions that emphasize genes and brains while excluding thoughts have become prominent. "We have seen the rise of a molecular and neuromolecular style of thought that analyzes all living processes in body and brain in terms of the material properties of cellular components: DNA bases, ion channels, membrane potentials and the like," writes Nikolas Rose.[47] Instead of meaning originating in learned associations between words and events, embodiment theorists, for instance, nowadays suggest that "a person infers the meaning of an action when a relevant motor circuit that stimulates the action is activated."[48] A profound distrust of invisible, immaterial processes has ensconced the belief that every action, thought, and feeling is determined by a brain state that is the product of a person's genes.

The "flight from theory" has left a vacuum in which evolutionary theory, sociobiology, cognitive sciences, genetics, and neurosciences have flourished.[49] The resurgence of broadly behavioral accounts of human life and actions has far-reaching consequences for how we understand and intervene in human rationality.[50] These disciplines are annexing core humanities questions of intentionality, agency, memory, sexuality, cognition, and language.[51] They reassert a domain of inquiry that focuses not so much on the modes of production of the historical and the social as on "the place of human beings in the universe." To a certain extent, their goal is to produce a theory of how "history" is humanly produced as an essence, and not as openness-to-contingency.

This notwithstanding, insights from genomics and neuroscience have opened up the workings of our bodies and our minds to new kinds of knowledge and intervention.[52] Human memory, interiority, consciousness, and emotional and cognitive development are increasingly understood as scaffolded by various kinds of cultural and technological resources.[53] To account for the subject and the body in contemporary surgical culture requires a journey through experiences of bodily remaking or catastrophes (amputation, prosthetization, phantom limbs), through the provisional coming together of disparate parts, and through the cosmetic surgical transformations that nurture the belief that one's body is mutable.[54] Untying human identity nowadays is akin to opening it up as a space in which multiple and powerful organizational forces and energies collide—the organic, the biological, the cultural, the linguistic. Humans are where biology, nature, and culture converge and collide.[55] "In fact, their collision constitutes our identity as a unique species of being."[56]

Meanwhile in the United States in particular, or at least in certain sectors of the traditional humanities and social sciences, theory is nowadays haunted by melancholia.[57] Thanks partly to deconstruction and psychoanalysis, the idea that "there is neither truth nor facts" has gained a lot of traction. This is a time, too, when history itself tends to be understood either as memory or as representation. The idea that there is no truth is filling many with real terror. To this should be added the feeling that critique has "run out of steam."[58] We keep making the same gestures when everything else has changed around us, says Bruno Latour. We keep fighting enemies long gone, and we are ill equipped in the face of threats we have not anticipated and for which we are thoroughly unprepared. In short, we are at the ready, but one war late. How do we get out of this impasse? By "renewing empiricism," says Latour; by getting closer to facts, cultivating a "stubbornly realist attitude" in relation to what he calls "matters of concern." Latour's crusade is mainly directed against "deconstruction," which he would like to replace with something he calls "constructivism." For Mary Poovey, on the other hand, "we now need to move beyond theories of representation" (what she calls "language-based theories") to "consideration of social processes." According to her, this project requires the formation of "alliances with practitioners in the social and natural sciences"—as if the human and natural worlds were not, to a large extent, organized into discrete series of signals and messages that invite recognition and interpretation, a certain way of coming to terms with language and with representation.

In the eyes of many, critique is overrated. In any case, it is no longer a tool needed for the kinds of situations we now face. For Karen Barad, it has become too easy—a practice of pure negativity—especially in these times when a commitment to reading with care no longer seems to be a fundamental element of critique. Barad calls for a method of reading that looks for "differences that make a difference"—a practice of diffraction.[59] The entanglement of matter and meaning calls into question the set of dualisms that separates matters of fact from matters of concern and care.[60] The current division of labor is such that the natural sciences are assigned matters of fact (and nature) and the humanities matters of concern (and values, meaning, and culture). The cordoning off of concerns into separate domains elides the resonances and dissonances that make the entanglements visible. The world, she argues, must be accounted for as a whole rather than as comprising separate natural and social realms and agencies.[61]

Yet, most of the assumptions concerning the death of theory can be contradicted. In the wake of poststructuralism, critical theory extensively relied on theories of the subject and of subjectivity in its effort to

account for the operations of power, the production of human difference, or the constitution of the social.[62] Today the centrality of human
subjectivity in the discourse of theory is challenged in various philosophical projects, from speculative realism, new materialisms, and
actor-network theory to object-oriented ontology. It is more and more
understood that humans are part of a very deep history that is older than
the existence of the human race. This history of entanglement with multiple other species requires that the reality of objects be rethought
beyond human meanings and uses, in their "thingness" and in their
"animate materiality." Matter, on the other hand, has morphogenetic
capacities of its own. It is not an inert receptacle for forms that come from
the outside, or are imposed by an exterior agency. Concepts of agency
and power having been extended to nonhumans, conventional understandings of life must be called into question. To be a subject is no longer to act autonomously but to share agency with other subjects that have
also lost their autonomy.[63]

Rather than theory having died, what we have witnessed is its displacement. Abstract theory has never had such a hold on the material
and social reality of the world as it does today. The particular power of
economic abstraction is a case in point. Theory is always a particular
theory of the world. More than in the most recent past, that world is constructed by invisible entities like finance capital and abstract singularities like derivatives—a business, says Nigel Thrift, "that uses theory as
an instrumental *method*, as a source of *expertise* and as an *affective register* to inform an everyday life that is increasingly built from that theory."[64] The power and effectiveness of abstractions depend not so much
on whether their depiction of the world is accurate as it does on their
capacity *to constitute a world*.[65] This is indeed the case when "idealized
apprehensions of the world produced through theory" end up being held
up "as desirable states of being" to which social, economic, political, or
cultural life should conform.[66] As a practice that flows from abstraction
to action, theory becomes a guideline or a template that operates on different scales and registers.

On the other hand, theory has been displaced into myriad *critical
practices*, some of which are flourishing, alongside new forms of public

and politically committed intellectual work.[67] Some of these critical practices are direct responses to an emphatic moment of urgency that itself seems to have rekindled the utopia of the radically new. They are also facilitated by rapid transformations in contemporary media.[68] The sensibilities, ethos, interiors, and public lives of most people today are determined more and more by television, cinema, DVDs, the Internet, computer games, and technologies of instant communication. Critical intellectual practices today are those that are capable of writing themselves within a frame of immediacy and presence, those that are able to locate themselves in nodes that attract other texts, forms of discourses that have the potential to be forwarded, redistributed, quoted, and translated in other languages and texts, including video and audio. Such is the case in contemporary visual art, film, video, literature, culinary arts, fashion, or Internet applications where, the sampling and recombining of preexisting material having become the norm, the old distinctions between original and copy, difference, repetition, or simulation are crumbling.[69] The result is not only a transformation in the language of knowledge itself, but also a *displacement* of theory, the kind of disarray in which it finds itself these days.

The stakes are rendered even higher as a result of various key transformations in contemporary life. The biggest challenge facing critical theory now is arguably the reframing of the disciplines and critical theory in light of contemporary conditions and the long-term sustainability of life on Earth.[70] An epoch-scale boundary has been crossed within the last two centuries of human life on Earth. We have entered a new geological epoch characterized by massive and accelerated human-induced changes to the Earth's climate, land, oceans, and biosphere. The transnational regime of petrochemical extraction and petroagriculture is the chief engine of the Anthropocene. Coupled with six billion humans and "twelve billion interconnected machines," their "omnipresent neurological and cognitive partners," it has "destabilized all notions of physical limits at any scale, astronomical, planetary, biological, or atomic."[71]

The scale, magnitude, and significance of these changes have a deep impact on the future evolution of the biosphere and on Earth's environmental life support system. If to survive the ecological crisis means to work out new ways to live with the Earth, then alternative modes of being human and inhabiting the world are required. The new ecological awareness forces us to recover an appreciation of human limits and the limits of nature itself.[72] Anthropocentrism—that is, the belief in the possibility of human mastery over all matter and the privileging of human existence as determining the actual and possible qualities of both thought and being—has thus become the object of a renewed philosophical critique.[73] So have the age-old nature/culture and human/animal divides as well as the opposition between an instrumentalist attitude toward nature and what has been taken to be the "nature worship of the primitive."[74] The extent to which new modes of being human are prefigured in contemporary arts, technology, and natural and environmental sciences is increasingly at the core of ongoing projects to rethink knowledge itself. As interfaces become a central part of contemporary life, boundaries between the human body, tools, and machines are reconsidered while the endless dynamism and flexibility of our relations to new technological artifacts are more clearly highlighted than ever before.[75]

A second challenge stems from the alliance between technology, capital, and militarism, with the aim of achieving what the late French critic André Gorz called "ectogenesis." In his mind, the term *ectogenesis* did not simply imply the separation of science and politics from morality and aesthetics. It also stood for the attempt to industrialize the (re)production of humans in the same way that biotechnology is industrializing the (re)production of animal and plant species.[76] Furthermore, as Derek Gregory suggests, "nature" itself is now the medium through which military and paramilitary violence is conducted. The militarization of nature and the naturalization of war are part of a dialectic in which "earthly, vibrant matter shapes the contours of conflict" and is in turn shaped by the latter.[77]

Such a planetary pursuit of pure power and pure profit without any goal other than power and profit themselves—a power indifferent to any ends or needs except its own—is driven by capital's attempts to transform life itself into a commodity in an age when all beings and species are only valued in terms of their availability for consumption.[78] The degree to which capital today is adept at exploiting this constitutional consumability of beings and species represents a major inflection point in the history of humanity. It radically redefines the very nature of "the human" and forces us to revisit the categories by which we used to conceive of social life. If indeed the possibility of our experience of the world pivots precisely on the question of availability and consumability, what then remains of nature, politics, and the social?

Not very long ago, we conceived of the world as a huge arithmetic problem—a world in which, as Simmel reminds us, things and events were part of a system of numbers.[79] We acted as if it were a world whose deep secrets could be revealed and harnessed if we subjected it to rigorous procedures of calculation, formalization, classification, and abstraction.[80] Today, our world is one in which the human body and indeed life itself are more and more part of a vast system of "info-signs" and electronic codes.[81] It is a world governed by electronic reason, one in which an important dimension of technological development is converting the human body into information (from DNA testing to brain fingerprinting to neural imaging to iris or hand recognition). Thanks to recent advances in robotics, perception, and machine learning, a new generation of incorporeal, invisible, and powerful autonomous systems that rival or exceed human intelligence and capabilities has emerged, ushering in what is now referred to as a "second machine age."[82]

Everyday environments are filled with "ever more kinds of information, in ever newer formats of technology, used in ever more activities of life."[83] An expanding array of sensors monitors various aspects of our physical world, while various interface designs (windows, frames, facades), networked objects, and positional traces connect us to "screens of ever more sizes, in ever more places." A consequence of the proliferation of display possibilities is the significant alteration not only of traditional modes of perception and subjectivation, but also of traditional definitions of what visual practice is all about, of what "matter" consists of, and of what qualifies as "human."[84]

The long twentieth century has also seen the emergence of a general phenomenon that might be called image-capitalism. Image-capitalism is a form of capitalism in which the image is not simply taking over the calculative functions previously associated with numbers; rather, the image has become a *techno-phenomenological institution*. The circuits from affect to emotions and from emotions to passions and convictions are, more than ever before, attached to the circulation of images meant to stimulate desire, the connection of affect and capital serving to reconfigure not only "the everyday," but also the physical, political, and psychic conditions of embodiment in our time. Any attempt to theorize culture today must therefore attend to these new pathways of capital.

Furthermore, capitalism today has the features of a huge computational formation. The market is now a stand-alone world constituted in opposition to the material and embodied life-world. In contemporary high-frequency trading, for instance, embodied, physical transactions and transmission capabilities have been replaced by automated trading technologies and behaviorally enhancing components that allow the market to perform globally and at an unprecedented speed onscreen.[85] As suggested by David Berry, it is restructuring through certain computational interventions in the wider economy.[86] Time is understood not only to unfold; nowadays, it is literally streaming. If not so long ago vision was taken as a Romantic aspect of subjective perception and sensory experience, today the visual field itself is increasingly mathematical. Algorithmic images not only use mathematics to program and set the conditions of possibility for the perceptual field. Algorithmic models of perception also determine what can or cannot be seen and therefore known, just as they recalibrate the relationship between visual imaging and truth, or the role of automated machines in the production of human knowledge.[87]

In turn, contemporary technologies of the image and the convergence of visual, digital, and consumer cultures have helped to propel belief structures and practices of affect that accord a preeminent role to faith and conviction, sometimes in lieu of reason and calculation. Moreover, they have transformed what is taken for "fact" (evidence, the real) and altered the basis of our sensory experience and the connections of human beings to otherwise incomprehensible phenomena. The impact of these transformations in terms of contemporary conceptions of material causality, or in terms of the ways in which we fill the space between truth, fiction, and imagination, has been immeasurable. This might help explain the troubling psychic presence of the image to the real, its capacity for double reality, its power to replace the inanimate with the animate, and its anarchic unruliness. The image's uneasy status as a double of the real and its power to excise time have their origins in a deep anxiety about what constitutes the real—an anxiety that has become a cornerstone of contemporary life. But what gives such power and value to the image at the start of the twenty-first century is the fact that it keeps the human person in circulation. It traces the shadow of the human subject and creates an exact transcription of his or her presence, based on the image cast by his or her shadow. It captures and preserves permanently what we know to be a transient form or a fleeting life and existence.

Meanwhile, liberal political principles (liberty, equality, the rule of law, civil liberty, individual autonomy, and universal inclusion) have been overtaken by neoliberal rationality and its criteria of profitability and efficiency.[88] As a result of the colonization of everyday life by market relations, the worship of wealth and the workings of a mode of production that depends on the destruction of the natural foundations of life, our work, our needs, our desires, our fantasies, and our self-images have been captured by capital. An impoverished conception of democracy as the right to consume has triumphed, making it difficult to envisage a different economy, different social relations, different ends, different needs, or different ways of life.[89] This in turn has led to debates about whether humans indeed want "the responsibility of authoring their own lives" and whether they can be expected "to actively pursue their own substantive freedom and equality, let alone that of others."[90]

Finally, the neoliberal drive to privatize all forms of art has resulted in the endless commodification of culture and its permanent translation into spectacle, leisure, and entertainment. This significant development comes at a time when global capitalism itself is moving into a phase in which the cultural forms of its outputs are critical elements of productive strategies.[91] Because the arts and culture have become integral parts of the economic, their capacity to engage critically with the velocities of capital can no longer be taken for granted. Spaces of culture are no longer just aesthetic spaces; they are also commercial spaces. This is one of the reasons why culture is more and more understood as "heritage," "custom," "the ancestral," and it is in this sense that many would like to view it as a set of practices reducible to cash. Identity, on the other hand, is understood as "difference"—religious, ethnic, racial, gender, national.

To be sure, "culture" and "identity" have not lost their affective, auratic, and expressive potentials. But maybe more than ever before, marks of otherness (now called culture, identity, and authenticity) and even meaning itself are more and more exchanged, valued, and allocated as a function of the market.[92] On the other hand, the hypertechnological enframing of the life-world and the growing implication of art and culture in global systems of militarization of consciousness represent major challenges to critical arts practices. In the militarized landscape of our time (with its obsession with surveillance and security), to "demilitarize" culture itself has become a cornerstone of the new humanities.

COLLISIONS AND COLLUSIONS

Everything just mentioned should be read in light of the fact—highlighted by Jean and John Comaroff in *Theory from the South*—that at the present moment, "it is the global South that affords privileged insight into the workings of the world at large."[93] In accounting for the workings of the world, the question therefore is no longer whether the bundle of issues that defined critical theory at its inception—bureaucracy and domination, innovation, originality and singularity, capitalism and its metamorphoses, reification and democracy, art and emancipation—can be of any help in the effort to understand the dramatic changes underway in the global South. It is rather that in accounting for the workings of the world today, "our theory-making ought to be coming from the global South, at least in significant part."[94]

This is where novel ways of articulating politics and culture are in the making. And yet here also the lag between actual social processes and our efforts to make sense of them conceptually is nowhere near to being closed.[95] The effort to produce a sense of stability and permanence in the face of temporariness, instability, and volatility raises new questions concerning the relationship between causality and intentionality, contingency and routine.[96] Many of these changes can no longer be interpreted solely from within orthodox forms of political, social, or cultural analysis. This is also where the question of how emancipatory possibilities can coexist with rapidly widening social differentiations is most acute, where we wonder the most whether the spread of private rights can coexist with the regulative and interventionist state in the name of distributive justice, where contemporary socioeconomic, political, cultural, and ethical questions regarding social criticism, forms of democracy, modes of the secular, forms of normative judgments, and the validity of normative judgments intersect and clash the most with established traditions of critical theory.

The study of Africa has long been (and is still) dominated by two modes of argumentation. The first has been descriptivism. "Descriptivism" is neither a method nor a theory; it is a way of defining and reading African life-forms that simply relies on a series of anecdotes and negative statements, or that simply turns to statistical indices to measure the gap between what Africa is and what we are told it ought to be. This way of reading always ends up constructing Africa as a pathological case, as a figure of lack. It is a set of statements that tell us what Africa *is not*. It never tells us what it *actually is*.

The second is a tradition of detailed, vivid, and richly textured ethnography and historiography of life-forms. Deeply embedded within a tradition of area studies, thick ethnography, interpretive history, and symbolic analysis have become powerful examples of how we should think and write about human agency, as well as what analytical strategies we should deploy in order to describe and interpret specific forms of social life in particular settings. The extent to which this tradition indirectly helped set the stage for the critical debates on the forms and methods of social and historical inquiry that dominated from the mid-1980s to the mid-1990s has unfortunately not been sufficiently recognized.

Indeed, by the time we entered the 1990s, the study of life-forms and life-worlds in Africa had yielded precious gains in at least four major arenas of social life—informality and struggles for livelihood, the question of singularities (rather than of individuality or individuation), the logics of mobility and multiplicity (that is, of unfinished series rather than a calculus of countable collections), and the logics of experimentation and compositional processes.[97] These gains included, for instance, expanded conceptions of rationality and subjectivity that were not limited to that of the rational, individual, self-interested, and risk-averse social actor; the realization that the self or the singular is not only a fiction or artifice or something we come to believe through habit; the discovery that our lives are always in-the-making (the theme of life as potentiality, a process of fragile actualization); and the notion that, in many ways, our lives do acquire a certain unstable consistency, even in the midst of shifts, instability, and volatility.[98]

In the wake of structuralism, and after the demise of certain forms of Marxism, the collapse of theories of modernization, and the crisis of certain forms of world-system analysis, this tradition has engaged, if indirectly, with several key concerns of social theory in the late 1980s and mid-1990s: the matter of form and forces; questions of historical agency; the connections among context, intentionality, and what today we would call subjectivity but in those days was named "consciousness," or even "ideology"; the creativity of practice and the pragmatics of repetition and change; the thorny questions of power and domination and of resistance and liberation; and more generally, the vexing issues of the body and its unfinished yet excessive qualities, of the nature and figures of the political.[99]

During the last quarter of the twentieth century, the best historically and theoretically inclined studies of African life-forms helped us understand that historical and cultural structures are not necessarily mechanical reflections of underlying social and economic structures. In fact, they are equal to them in "ontological" standing. In turn, social and economic structures are themselves as much objective facts (if this means anything at all) as they are the products of the interpretive work of human actors. The best works on Africa have also shown that we can expand our ethnographic reach within Africa without losing the capacity to make general analytical and theoretical points. This can be done if, on the one hand, we take seriously the task of historicizing institutions, practices, and cultural repertoires and if, on the other hand, we take just as seriously the reality of the long-term sedimentation of experience.[100]

The search for alternative acts of thinking requires the exploration of other ways of speaking of the visual, of sounds, of the senses, and it requires thinking as philosophically and historically as possible about the precariousness of life in Africa, the intensive surfaces of power, and the various ways in which events coexist with accidents. Indeed, if the project is to "rethink Africa," or, for that matter, to write the world from Africa or to write Africa into contemporary social theory, then there is no better starting point than the question of time. Time is neither uniform nor homogeneous. Structures of temporality in colonial and post-colonial conditions are thoroughly entangled with the vicissitudes of the affective, with the subjective play of desire and uncertainty.

In such contexts, we can only refer to the abstraction of time as a rhetorical figure. For many people caught in the vortex of colonialism and what comes after, the main indexes of time are the contingent, the ephemeral, the fugitive, and the fortuitous—radical uncertainty and social volatility. Radical changes go hand in hand with various other gradual and subtle shifts that are almost imperceptible, and sudden ruptures are deeply embedded in structures of inertia and the logic of routine and repetition. To account for change in such a context is therefore to account for simultaneity, bifurcation, multiplicity, and concatenation. The task of the critic is therefore to help us think historically and philosophically about the various ways in which events coexist with accidents.

The interrogation of time is very much related to the interrogation concerning the daily amount of labor involved in the production of the sense, if not the illusion, of stability, or continuity, or something like permanence in the face of the known temporariness or volatility of almost all the arrangements of social existence. Indeed, the question of *temporariness* has been central to recent efforts to account for life-forms and life-worlds in Africa.[101] One of the most brutal effects of neoliberalism in Africa during the last quarter of the twentieth century has been the deepening of social inequalities, the privatization of the State, and the radicalization of a condition of temporariness. In his depiction of contemporary Mumbai—which applies *nolens volens* to most of Africa— Arjun Appadurai argues that for the poor, many things in life have a temporary quality: not only physical and spatial resources, but also social, political, and moral relations. The social energy and personal creativity of the poor are devoted to producing a sense of permanence. For many people, the struggle to be alive is the same as the struggle against the constant corrosion of the present, both by change and by uncertainty, as Appadurai rightly argues.[102]

In Africa in particular, temporariness can also be described as the encounter—a very regular occurrence—with what we cannot yet determine because it has not yet come to be or will never be definite. It is an encounter with indeterminacy, provisionality, the fugitive, and the contingent. Temporariness is not simply an effect of life changing rapidly; it also derives from the fact that vast domains of human struggle and achievement are hardly the objects of documentation, archiving, or empirical description—and even less so the objects of satisfactory narrative or interpretive understanding. It has to do with the colossal amount of things we literally do not know.[103] It also has to do with the fact—as shown in the best of current history and anthropology of African life-forms—that uncertainty and turbulence, instability and unpredictability, and rapid, chronic, and multidirectional shifts are the social and cultural forms taken, in many instances, by daily experience.[104]

Then there is the question of labor, which, at least in the history of capitalism in South Africa, cannot be delinked from the histories of race and of the body—a body-commodity that enters into the realm of capital under the paradoxical sign of the *superfluous*. In the history of race and capital in South Africa, the superfluous means, on the one hand, the valorization of black labor-power and, on the other hand, its dispensability—the dialectics of valuation and dissipation, indispensability, and expendability. This dialectics has been radicalized in this neoliberal moment.[105] Capitalism in its present form might need the territory people inhabit, their natural resources (diamonds, gold, platinum, and so on), their forests, or even their wildlife. But does it need them as persons?[106]

Indeed not long ago, the drama was to be exploited, and the horizon of liberation consisted in freeing oneself from exploitation. Today, the tragedy is less in being exploited than in being utterly deprived of the basic means to move, to partake in the general distribution of things and resources necessary to produce a semblance of life. The tragedy is to not be able to escape the traps of temporariness and immediacy.[107] These are also times of high social velocity. In South Africa, for instance, hypermobility is dramatically expressed through the emergence of a black middle class that is hungry to consume, and willing to contract debt to spend on housing, fridges, cars, and all the trappings of a highly consumerist society.[108] Coupled with outright repression, welfare and consumption have, in any case, become the two main technologies of social discipline, if not "pacification," that the government is using in its attempt at demobilizing society. As such, they are critical tools in the making and unmaking of citizenship.[109]

There is no accident without some form of collision, or even collusion. Three such instances of collision and collusion are reshaping the continent. There is, first of all, collision and collusion that occur when privatization has to be carried out in an environment structurally characterized by privation, dispossession, and predation. A second type of collision and collusion occurs when extraction goes hand in hand with abstraction in a process of mutual constitution. After all, the places where capital is most prosperous on the continent today are extractive enclaves, some of which are totally disconnected from the hinterland, in some nowhere that is accountable to nobody except to petro-capital.[110] The third instance of collision and collusion comes in the form of a structural convergence of massive social upheavals, profiteering, and war.[111] Here, in order to create situations of maximum profit, capital and power must manufacture disasters and feed off disasters and situations of extremity that then allow for novel forms of governmentality.[112]

These three instances of collision and collusion epitomize the modalities of Africa's entanglement with global capital. In spite of its uneven incorporation into the world economy, this region does tell us a lot more than we might want to think or hear about the future of global capitalism—and not only in its extractive and at times militarized version, by which I mean the kind of "primitive accumulation" that lies close to, but is not always coincident with, the vast global shadow economy that is dependent on illegal activities like smuggling, drug and people trafficking, and money-laundering, through which trillions of dollars circulate around the globe outside formal legal reckoning. Let's call this extractive economy of unprocessed raw materials the "raw economy."[113]

The logic of *extraction* that underpins this economy of raw materials (diamonds, platinum, gold, oil, cobalt, copper, coltan, vanadium, and other strategic minerals) might not be the same as the logic of deindustrialization that seems to partly characterize Northern economies.[114] But both seem to have quickened the accumulation of surplus populations. Marx used to divide "surplus populations" into three categories: "latent" (made up of those with insecure employment), "floating" (those cycling rapidly in and out of the labor force), and "stagnant" (those only rarely employed).[115] To these three categories we should add a fourth comprising those who *will never* be formally employed. The expansion of capitalism in this new phase of globalization and its transformation into a planetary financial system significantly intensify this process. In fact, it confirms global unemployability and the rise of surplus or superfluous populations as part of what Marx called its "absolute general law." Such a rise itself not only points toward the growing *crisis of reproduction* going on worldwide—a crisis of reproduction that Africa has, to use one of Jean Comaroff and John Comaroff's terms, "prefigured." It also signals a new age of capital when people and things can become the objects of a sudden process of devaluation and expendability. Disposable containers, they are subject to "obsolescence" and can be discarded.

Whether the old categories of "production," "work," "exploitation," and "domination"—and the more recent ones of "bare life" or "naked life," inherited from recent theorizations of sovereignty and the state of exception—suffice to write into theory such planetary recodings of situations of misery, debt, and enforced idleness is open to question.[116] Indeed it is possible today to produce increasing quantities of commodities with decreasing quantities of labor. Labor has ceased to be the great wellspring of wealth. The real economy is becoming an appendage of the speculative bubbles sustained by a finance industry whose novel power resides in its capacity to write and enforce contracts about the future price of assets. In so doing, it does not only turn money into the most abstract form of commodity value; it also refines the art of making money by buying and selling nothing but various forms of money.[117]

The continent's historical experience shows that in order to expand, capitalism paradoxically does not need to absorb everything in its path. It does not need to interiorize everything that was hitherto exterior to it. In fact, it needs to keep producing or generating an exterior. For this to happen, it needs to keep jumping from place to place—hopping, as James Ferguson says.[118] But for the dynamic of expansion to be able to produce its full effects, global capitalism needs massive *racial subsidies* or "discounts." It needs to work through and across different scales of race as it attempts to extract value from—or to mark—people either as disposable or as waste.[119] It needs to produce, order, segment, and racialize surplus or superfluous populations to strategic effect. This takes various forms. One of these is their incorporation into military markets. Significant in this regard is the fact that today, white working-class masculinity has been alienated in the deindustrializing contexts of Euro-America, allowing for an accumulation of "excess masculinity" upon which the military complex is drawing.

To maintain military numbers, unemployed or underemployed whites are not enough. Vast reserves of racially disenfranchised men have been recruited. It hardly matters that some are uneducated. Those with criminal(ized) pasts are granted "moral waivers" that allow them for the first time to join the lower rungs of military ranks and, hence, to gain a semblance of enfranchisement and citizenry. Those who are marked as waste are disenfranchised, or simply spatially confined within the prison-industrial complex.[120] Another form is through cross-border migrant labor. Labor operating in the interstices or the entrails of the global economy is hyperexploited. The racial subsidy is precisely what allows global capital to feel no sense of responsibility for its actions, its crimes against humanity, and the horrendous damage done not only in Euro-America but in the rest of the world as well.

Seen from Africa, global capitalism is moving in two directions. The first is toward increasing exploitation of large parts of the world through what Marx called "primitive accumulation," which, as suggested earlier, is increasingly taking the form of a "raw economy." The other direction is toward squeezing every last drop of value out of the planet by increasing the rate of innovation and inventions, or through an active refiguring of space, resources, and time, or through a planned human intervention in the climate system that would undermine all notions of limitation,[121] or even by boosting difference and inserting that difference into the cycles of reproduction of capital—contracts, but also coercion and racial subsidies.

Significant too is the increasing conflict between market forces and democracy. Democracy should normally imply the rule of the majority. Since the rich in any given society are almost always a minority, democracy in the form of majority rule should—taken to its logical consequences—imply the rule of the poor over the rich. It is also the idea that people have rights that take precedence over the outcomes of market exchanges, and one of the roles of a democratic government is to honor, to some extent, this most human expectation of a life outside the law of the market and the right of property.[122] Historically, the biggest fear of capital has always been that the rule of the poor over the rich would ultimately do away with private property and the "free" play of market forces. Faced with this dilemma, capital would rather abolish democracy in order to save capitalism from a majority dedicated to economic and social redistribution.

It is increasingly apparent that capitalism is not naturally compatible with democracy. For capitalism to be compatible with democracy, capitalism would have to be subjected to extensive political control and democracy would have to be protected from being restrained in the name of market power.[123] Under the emerging international politics of public debt, global capital increasingly requires that the "average citizen" pay—for the consolidation of public finances, the bankruptcy of foreign states, the rising rates of interest on public debt, and, if necessary, the rescue of national and international banks—with his or her private savings, and through cuts in public entitlements, reduced public services, and higher taxation.[124]

The capacity of national states to mediate between the rights of citizens and the requirements of capital accumulation is severely affected. The tensions between economy and society, between market power and democracy, can no longer be handled exclusively inside national political communities. They have become internationalized. Markets are dictating in unprecedented ways what presumably sovereign and democratic states may still do or not do for their citizens. The *preemption— or even suspension—of democracy* by market forces is now propounded as the only rational and responsible behavior in a world in which individual debt, public deficits, and public debt have resulted in the mortgaging of the futures of entire nations and the expropriation of their citizens. Euro-American democratic states—just like African states during the long years of structural adjustment programs—are in danger of being "turned into debt-collecting agencies on behalf of a global oligarchy of investors" and the propertied classes are now firmly entrenched in what looks like "a politically unassailable stronghold."[125]

AFRICA AS A CHINESE QUESTION

In view of the transformations described earlier, an epistemic reorientation is once again needed. The Western ethnocentric tendency to interpret the world and all its socioeconomic, political, and cultural processes from a Euro-American perspective has led to a cul-de-sac. This epistemic reorientation, away from a thousand years of linear history, has been attempted in a number of disciplines in the past (world history in particular), where it has raised various methodological questions not unlike those implied by the Comaroffs' "counter-evolutionary" and "prefigurative" approach.[126]

For instance, should the global system be studied as a single world system? Would it better be described in terms of its many nodes and edges or as a whole that is greater than the sum of its parts? Should we rather understand regions of the world in their own terms, mindful of the fact that they experience separate models of development that may overlap in various ways, but that are nonetheless essentially independent? Or is it that what we need is a horizontally integrative macrohistory, one that seeks the connections between the various events that are happening in regions that have traditionally been considered separate? To what extent does our ability to link events in one region to subsequent events in regions connected with it depend on a close identification of the series of paths that tie the various regions of the world? Under what conditions do simultaneous and momentous events triggered in a particular region of the world lead to similar outcomes and similar implications elsewhere?[127]

Take, for instance, Giovanni Arrighi's *Adam Smith in Beijing: Lineages of the Twenty First Century*. As he himself states in an interview with David Harvey before his death,[128] Arrighi's variety of world-systems analysis had deep African roots—just like some of the most significant social theories of the twentieth century (the story of the work Africa does in twentieth-century theory still needs to be properly told and documented). In fact, some of the key categories Arrighi deployed in his work were forged during his African experience—especially his encounter with "the Africa of the labor reserves" (Samir Amin), that is, the trajectories of accumulation through racialized dispossession in the context of white-settler colonialism in Southern Africa.[129] It was in Southern Africa that he discovered that the full dispossession of much of the African peasantry (so as to provide low-cost migrant labor for agricultural, mining, and manufacturing industries) not only ended up raising labor costs, but hindered the development of capitalism by eliminating the ability of the rural labor force to subsidize its own reproduction and capital accumulation. In this sense, the Southern African experience stands in marked contrast to accumulation without dispossession and associated rural development and industrialization throughout much of East Asia.

It is significant that, having started his attempt to account for the *longue durée* of capitalism and its current crises in Africa, Arrighi ended in East Asia, and in particular in Beijing. To be sure, his project was not necessarily to decenter Euro-American theory or to highlight the plurality of theories that emerge from the processes of decolonization.[130] He ended up in Beijing because China has become the workshop of the world. Euro-America is no longer where the most advanced production facilities are located, although Euro-America is still able to cream off a substantial part of the superprofits created elsewhere. Euro-America depends, more than at any time in its history and nowadays in an increasingly parasitic manner, on the productive labor of others.

Today, some of the most innovative modes of producing value are being relocated southward and eastward. The production of value is one thing. The capture or appropriation of value physically produced elsewhere is another. How surplus value created in newly industrializing nations is captured by deindustrializing ones through transnational production networks, foreign trade, and international finance is key to our understanding of the future of global capitalism. A new space of material relations is being formed between China and Africa. China is now the world's largest consumer of Africa's copper, tin, zinc, platinum, and iron ore, and a large consumer of Africa's petroleum, aluminum, lead, nickel, and gold. Indeed, it might be that if "Euro-America is evolving toward Africa," Africa in turn is likely to evolve toward China rather than toward Euro-America. The need to feed a vast and growing productive capacity compels Chinese capital to source raw materials from all over the world, especially in Africa. The ongoing acceleration and redistribution of global productive forces China is leading will not bypass Africa. Without Africa, China will not be able to indefinitely lend so that America (the globe's most parasitic nation) can buy Chinese and other Asian products and see a sizable portion of its enormous debt written off through the fall of the value of the dollars and treasury bills China holds.

Whatever the case, it has of late been a matter of tacit consensus that *Africa represents the last frontier of capitalism.* It is the region of our world where some of the brutalism of capitalism and some of the most far-reaching formal and informal experiments in neo-liberal deregulation have been taking place. Even more decisively, this is the region of the world where the relationship between transnational extractive projects—which underpin most of Africa's economic growth during the late twentieth and early twenty-first century—and the transformations of contemporary global finance (especially under the sign of clandestine economies, enclave economies, and offshoring) has been the most perversely tested.[131] One important implication of these transformations has been the extent to which they have influenced almost everything from household economics to environmental disruptions to scientific expertise to state governance. Another perhaps even more important implication has been the extent to which these kinds of transnational operations disentangle the production of profit from the place in which the industry happens to find itself while structuring liability and responsibility in such a way that the firms involved can remove themselves from local social, legal, political, and environmental entanglements.

As sites of experimentation, Africa's extractive economies have been deeply involved in—and will keep contributing to—the shaping of key aspects of contemporary financial capitalism. For instance, they have contributed to the remaking of the structures and conditions of corporate activity and what it means to incorporate in the first years of the twenty-first century. The financialization of risks—a key structural feature of contemporary futures markets—has been shaped to a large extent by experiments on the African continent. The current African moment can therefore be characterized as a moment of *acceleration*, and Africa is now perceived as a significant potential source of rising global consumption. As intimated earlier, it is an acceleration toward a capitalism that is mostly disjointed. It consists of a seemingly random collection of disconnected enclaves incongruously linked together in a contrived geography. It is a capitalism of multiple nodal points, of scattered patterns of spatial growth combined with swathes of neglect and decline. This frontier-type of capitalism is mostly extractive. Its expansion in Africa is a key aspect of the world-historical shift in the fortunes of humanity—a shift that is now underway by dint of the rise of China.

The unfolding of capitalism in China is characterized by its "compressed" nature: that is, a fundamental change in national economic structures occurred in the 1970s mainly through (1) a large industrial sector rapidly absorbing low-wage migrant labor for manufacturing for a large-scale export market, and (2) state investment in critical sectors and thus industrial deepening and consequently rising wages, increasing inequalities, and social polarization. A steady stream of migrant labor freed from the countryside as a result of land appropriation, legal or illegal, violent or peaceful, ensued. The flow of rural residents to urban areas was officially regulated through the *hukou* registration system, which required would-be migrants to seek approval from local authorities to move to new areas.

Today, advanced forms of accumulation such as high-value manufacturing, high-value services, and innovation-led economic expansion in a global setting coexist with primitive forms of accumulation and a vast agrarian sector. In addition to contributing to growth and rising incomes, the technological complexity in the structure of China's economy is fast adding to the pool of precarious employment due to the displacement of labor, the hiring of contract labor, and the increasing structural power of capital.[132] Whatever the case, China has, for now, become a far more prominent actor than others in the future-making of Africa, to the point where *Africa is now not only a planetary question, but also and more specifically a Chinese question.*

We cannot stress enough the multiplicity of transformational outcomes arising from China's involvement in Africa. These transformations will run in multiple directions and in complex combinations. China has become the workshop of the world with labor-absorbing, export-oriented manufacturing sectors aiming to upgrade to high-value, capital-intensive manufacturing. The African trajectory is far from being based on export-oriented industrialization. In some regions of the continent, land transfers are on the rise, the result of wholesale expropriation of land by real estate speculators, by large corporations in the natural resource business, and by state-led infrastructure development. But the process of primitive accumulation is far from having acquired the intensity it reached in China. Africa, like China, comprises an urban labor market with informal, casual work and self-employment, along with precarious, short-term, poorly paid, and insecure jobs. This market offers a plethora of low-cost commodities and services. If in China petty commodity producers act as a reserve army that big global and national capital may deploy and exclude when needed to support their worldwide accumulation, such is not the case in Africa.

The planetary library is an attempt at reframing theory in the aftermath of the planetary turn of the African predicament. If the planet and the human constitute themselves through relations between multiple forces, then attempting to simply reimpose an expanded version of human subjectivity to all forms and forces will not suffice. "Desegregating" and disenclaving theory must become a constitutive part of the new agenda.[133] In this regard, the planetary library will of necessity be a theory of the interface. The interface itself must be understood as a form of relation between two or more distinct archival entities. The planetary library will only come into being as these distinct archives are summoned to enter into an active relation with one another. The planetary library project rests on the assumption of the inseparability of the different archives of the world—Édouard Glissant's *le Tout-Monde*. Instead of holding them apart, it will recognize them as assets shared with all humans, nonhuman actors, and self-sustaining systems. It will draw upon each of them while drawing them together. As such, it will be a *theory of the threshold*.

In the meantime, race has once again reentered the domain of biological truth, viewed now through a molecular gaze. A new molecular deployment of race has emerged out of genomic thinking. Worldwide, we witness a renewed interest in the identification of biological differences. In these times of global migrations, many are entertaining the dream of "nations without strangers." Genomics has injected new complexity into the figure of the human. And yet the core racial typology of the nineteenth century still provides a dominant mold through which this new genetic knowledge of human difference is taking shape and entering medical and lay conceptions of human variation.

Fundamental to ongoing rearticulations of race and the recoding of racism are developments in the life sciences. The last quarter of the twentieth century saw the rise of a molecular and neuromolecular style of thought that analyzes all living processes in body and brain in terms of the material properties of cellular components such as DNA bases, ion channels, membrane potentials, and the like. This process started during the first half of the century and gained momentum during the last quarter of the last century and the start of the twenty-first century. This process has been rendered even more powerful by its convergence with two parallel developments. The first is the emergence of the digital technologies of the information age and the second is the financialization of the economy. These two developments have led to two sets of consequences. On the one hand is a renewed preoccupation with the future of life itself. On the other is the new work capital is doing under contemporary conditions. Thanks to the work of capital, we are no longer fundamentally different from things. We turn them into persons. We fall in love with them. We are no longer only persons, or we have never been only persons. We now realize that there is probably more to race than even Hegel ever imagined.

Because race-thinking increasingly entails profound questions about the nature of species in general, the need to rethink the politics of racialization and the terms under which the struggle for racial justice unfolds here and elsewhere in the world today has become ever more urgent. Racism is still acting as a constitutive supplement to nationalism. How do we create a world beyond nationalism? Behind the veil of neutrality and impartiality, racial power still structurally depends on various legal regimes for its reproduction. How do we radically transform the law? Even more ominously, race politics is taking a technogenomic turn. In order to invigorate antiracist thought and praxis and in order to reanimate the project of nonracialism, we particularly need to explore the emerging nexus between biology, genes, technologies, and their articulations with new forms of human destitution. At stake in the contemporary reconfigurations and mutations of race and racism is the splitting of humanity itself into separate species and subspecies as a result of market libertarianism and genetic technology. At stake are also, once again, the old questions of who is who, who can make what kinds of claims on whom and on what grounds, and who is to own whom and what. In a contemporary neoliberal order that claims to have gone beyond the racial, the struggle for racial justice must take new forms.

But simply looking into past and present local and global rearticulations of race will not suffice. To tease out alternative possibilities for thinking life and human futures in this age of neoliberal individualism, we need to connect in entirely new ways the project of nonracialism to that of human mutuality. In the last instance, nonracialism is about more than mere recognition. It is about radical sharing and universal inclusion. It is about humankind's implication in a common that includes nonhumans, which is the proper name for democracy. In this sense, democracy is the antithesis of the rule of the market. The domination of politics by capital has resulted in the waste of countless human lives and the production in every corner of the globe of vast stretches of dead water and dead land.

To reopen the future of our planet to all who inhabit it, we will have to learn how to share it again among humans, but also between humans and nonhumans, between the multiple species that populate our planet. It is only under these conditions that, becoming aware of our precariousness as a species in the face of ecological threats, we will be able to overcome the possibility of outright human extinction opened up by this new epoch, the epoch of the Anthropocene.

2

DISENCLOSURE

I n the end, decolonization became a concept for jurists, historians, and international political economists.[1] This was not always the case. To be sure, such thinkers have reasserted the importance of seeing decolonization not as a "moment" but as a concatenation of complex, uneven, and variegated processes that unfolded over a long span of time. A. G. Hopkins, for instance, has called for a larger view that would relate decolonization to a historic change in the character of globalization.[2] Such a view, he argues, would include states within continental Europe in conventional studies of the imperial crises of the late eighteenth century.[3] It would also add so-called white dominions, the Chinese "informal empire," and the United States to studies of imperialism, colonial rule, and decolonization.[4] Many analysts and critics have shown the extent to which the disentanglement from formal colonial relations fit into wider trends of rethinking and reordering the world at large, a story of experimentation and adjustment that "hardly fits into the temporal dichotomy of a 'before' and 'after.'"[5] Peering into the fissures of history, they have also argued that the outcome of these processes was far from predictable. "The possibilities and constraints of the 'after' were shaped not only by the fact of colonialism, but by the process by which it was challenged, by the responses of the colonial state to those challenges, and by hopes, fears, and traumas unleashed in the course of the struggle."[6]

Yet in the eagerness to refine periodization, to map broad patterns, to establish parametric models, and to combine world-economy and institutional perspectives, the concept of decolonization may have grown philosophically poorer.[7] Decolonization may have been reduced to a set of discontinuous "happenings" and "occurrences" at multiple and often unrelated geographical sites and loci. Its *eventfulness*, singularity, and intensities weakened, its phenomenality may have been diluted. In the process, its multiple genealogies may have been obscured. Its traces and consequences too.

More importantly, in the hands of historians, international relations specialists, and jurists, the concept has lost some of the incendiary tenor and quasi-mystic exaltation that marked its many trajectories.[8] In this minor form, decolonization no longer refers to the "complete overthrow" of structures, institutions, and ideas.[9] It simply designates the transfer of power from the metropolis to former colonial possessions at the moment of independence. This transfer of power was generally either the result of peaceful negotiations and compromises between the political elites of the new independent countries and former colonial powers, or the consequence of an armed struggle that ended foreign domination and led to the colonizers' defeat and eviction and to the repossession of national territories by new autochthonous powers.[10]

THE WORLD AS THE STAGE OF HISTORY

Decolonization, called by many names throughout the nineteenth and twentieth centuries in Africa, was, however, a full political, polemical, and cultural category. In this major form, decolonization was akin to a "struggle for freedom" or, as Guinean anticolonial thinker Amilcar Cabral suggested, a "revolution."[11] Like many before him, by "revolution" he meant three things: first, a violent, almost visceral refusal of all forms of servitude, in particular those practiced in the name of race; second, a carefully calibrated effervescence akin to mystic exaltation and yet totally rational; and third, a promise whose main mode of existence was its futurity. As a set of experiences and praxis, these three features were written and spoken about in a language that even inanimate things and beings could hear. In a word, decolonization was a struggle by the colonized to reconquer the surface, horizons, depths, and heights of their lives. Through this struggle, which demanded immense psychic effort and extraordinary capacities for mass mobilization, the structures of colonization were to be dismantled, new relations between the sacred and the mundane, between the subject and the world instituted, and the possible rehabilitated.[12] Understood from this point of view, the concept of decolonization was a shortcut for departitioning the world and bringing together its scattered fragments and isolated parts.[13] It also referred to the difficult reconstitution of the subject, the disenclosure of the world, and humanity's universal ascent to a "higher life."

However, it very quickly appeared that reconstituting subjects endowed with human bodies, faces, voices, and names of their own was not simply a practical-political task. It presupposed enormous epistemological, psychic, and even aesthetic work.[14] It was understood that in order to free oneself once and for all from colonial alienation, and in order to heal the wounds inflicted by centuries of bioracism and racecraft, it was necessary to know oneself.[15] Knowledge of the self, self-repair, psychic and religious healing, and renewed care for the self became preconditions for detaching oneself from the mental frames, aesthetic discourses, and representations that the West had used to put a stranglehold on the idea of the future.[16] Decolonization itself, as an act of refusal turned into an act of assertion, an act of rebellion turned into an act of refoundation, as sign and Event, was imagined as a kind of relation to the future. The future, in return, was another name for the force of self-creation and invention. To recover this force it was thought necessary to rehabilitate endogenous forms of language and knowledge.[17] They alone would make it possible to grasp the new conditions of experience adequately and render them newly thinkable. It was equally necessary to forge thinking on a world scale: thought capable of taking into account the common history that colonization had made possible. Thus was born postcolonial critical theory, with which the second half of this chapter deals.

The age of imperialism profoundly shaped the modern world. Thanks to various structures of dependence and a mixture of ideological, symbolic, and material forces, outlying regions of the world became subordinated to dominant metropolitan centers. Central to the colonial world was the notion of white superiority. In turn, the dissolution of empires profoundly shaped international politics.[18] Yet, there does not really exist a theory of decolonization as such. In order to explain the facts of colonialism and empire—and, indirectly, the breakdown of Western empires and the entry of non-Western states into the international state system during the twentieth century—many classical approaches have emphasized military, technological, and economic factors.[19] Most explanations of the modern desire to acquire land, territory, and resources through conquest or to forcefully control other societies focus on the metropolis's demand for riches, markets, or jobs. Thus, Lenin, Hobson, and others maintained that the colonies' function in the historical development of capitalism was to absorb surpluses of metropolitan capital, whether in the form of merchandise and money, or in the demographical form of overpopulation.[20] According to this logic, colonies were created and maintained to protect investments. As outlets, they contributed to deferring the crisis of overproduction that threatened the capitalist mode of production from within.[21] From the perspective of dependency theorists, the division of labor and the colonies' coerced and forced specialization in producing raw materials constituted both the form and the content of the colonial relation properly speaking. These raw materials were cheap to produce, thanks to the low cost of labor, which served, as Marx himself pointed out, to raise the rates of profit.[22] According to dependency theories, this division of labor—as well as its corollary, specialization—not only was one of the conditions for developing industrial capitalism; it also put into place the structural conditions of unequal exchange that, since then, have characterized relations between center and periphery.[23] The colonies were thus not external frontiers at all. Far from being mere outlets, they were essential links in the concentration of economic and political resources in the core and, as such, in the global expansion of capitalism (the "becoming-world" [*devenir-monde*] of the capitalist system).[24]

The world-economy perspective highlights a number of structural conditions that affect not only the form of core-periphery linkages, but also the long and unending cycle of world power and prosperity.[25] As David Strang suggests, one such condition is "the presence or absence of a hegemonic state, a state which dominates the world economy industrially, commercially, and financially." On the one hand, it is argued that relative equality among core states "preserves and expands colonial empires by intensifying competition over peripheral areas." On the other hand, the rise of a hegemonic state reduces the amount of competition between them.[26] This was the case with Britain's rise to hegemony after 1763 when the costs and benefits of empire for both European colonial powers and American settler colonies were reshaped, leading to decolonization in the Americas.[27] Britain's industrial dominance was challenged by the United States and Germany in the intensely competitive post-1870 environment. By the end of the Second World War, American hegemony had been cemented. Military and industrial power had shifted away from the major colonial powers. For the first time, an Asian nation (Japan) had successfully reversed Western political expansion. Political ideas and institutions that delegitimized Western imperialism and supported decolonization were in full swing .

Within this context,[28] decolonization is explained in economistic terms. Imperialism is interpreted as the inevitable product of capitalist expansion. Economic stagnation is thought to lead to imperial conquests, while booms reduce interest in colonial holdings. Decolonization is also explained from an institutionalist perspective in terms of the emergence and diffusion of Western models of popular sovereignty. This is what Emerson Rupert called the "turning of the weapons—the ideas, the instruments, the institutions—of the West against itself."[29] Shifting power relations among beneficiaries and those hurt by colonialism are held as key explanatory factors of decolonization. So is the intensification of competition by political liberalization in the metropolis. Colonial imperialism, it is argued, put in place structural conditions for a coerced and unequal exchange between center and periphery. These conditions were such that any possibility of genuine emancipation was stifled from the start. Once these structural conditions were established,

the properly colonial form inevitably became anachronistic. Its maintenance could no longer be justified, and it was able to give way to other,
more efficient, less onerous, and more profitable mechanisms of exploitation and domination. Thus, colonial imperialism was but a moment
in the long history of capitalism: the moment when—through the expropriation of natives, the transformation of the work force into merchandise, the specialization of colonized societies in the production of cheap
raw materials, and political and cultural subjection—the mechanisms
and conditions allowing for the production and reproduction of capital
over the long term were put into place. But the colonial form, as an original form of expropriation whose function was to institutionalize the
regime of unequal and coerced exchange over the long term, was, in the
end, as the French historian Jacques Marseille suggests, a primitive mode
of developing natural and social resources and productive forces. It
became a burden on the metropolitan powers.[30] A decline in the value
of colonial holdings, it is argued, made the cost of occupation prohibi-
tive.[31] This is why the transition to independence and to national sovereignty (that is, to the form of the nation-state) was inevitable—because
it hardly put an end to the economic, political, and ideological subjection of the former colonies. From this point of view, decolonization did
indeed constitute a decoupling, but was nevertheless a *non-Event*. In any
case and above all, it opened the way for neocolonialism, a mode of international relations of force that blends private income and coercion, and
in which violence, destruction, and brutality go hand in hand with a new
form of accumulation by extortion.[32]

Just as there were several ages of colonization, so there were several pathways to decolonization.[33] Historians generally distinguish three ages of
colonialism. The first corresponds to the period of mercantilism. During that time, European powers conquered foreign territories, marked
them, established bonds of subjection with the native populations—
usually legitimized by some ideology of racial supremacy—and then
put these populations to work producing riches from which they

benefited only minimally. The period of mercantilism, inaugurated by what have been called the "great discoveries" and then strengthened by the trade in black slaves, marked a veritable entrance into a new "time of the world." This time was characterized by the crossing of frontiers, the mixing of monies, and the expansion of zones of exchanges and encounters. Of course, fragmentation did not disappear. Even less did differences, hierarchies, and inequalities. But gradually, a relative unity and coherence of the world were constructed. The new forms of transgressing limits set into motion by the development of mercantilism encouraged the transition from an understanding of the world as an enormous surface comprising differentiated blocs to an awareness of the globe as a massive stage where history henceforth unfolded.[34] Colonization and decolonization participate fully in this new age of globality [*mondialité*]. The second age of colonialism was a result of the industrial revolution. If the engine of the first age—which more or less came to an end with independence in the United States and Latin America between the eighteenth century and the mid-nineteenth—was the trade and plantation economy, the second age was characterized by the double imperative of accessing raw materials and developing outlets for industrial products.[35]

The first waves of decolonization in Latin America took place between 1880 and 1890, and then in the 1920s. To a large extent, they were prompted by the collapse of the metropolitan polity. Legitimist revolts had been set off in the Americas subsequent to Napoleon's invasion of Spain and the accession of Louis Bonaparte to the Spanish throne in 1808. During the Napoleonic period, the British navy cut Spain's administrative ties to its colonies and revolts blossomed into independence movements.[36] They coincided with the golden age of pan-Americanism. Pan-Americanism, a political and ideological project, defined itself in opposition to the hegemonic designs of the United States. One of its goals was to end the American policy of intervening in its neighbors' affairs. These waves of decolonization were marked by conflicts: the war between Mexico and the United States (1846–1848), which led to the annexation of half of Mexico's territory; the war for Cuban independence (1895–1898); the Mexican Revolution (1910–1917); and the First World War

(1914–1918). With the exceptions of the old Portuguese possessions of Mozambique and Angola, Africa was the epicenter of the second wave of colonialism. This wave was characterized by *large-scale mining*. It took on different forms and allied demographical considerations along with other considerations of strategy and prestige, and opened the way to what has been called "modern imperialism."[37]

As a historic event, decolonization was one of the turning points in what can be called our late modernity. Indeed, decolonization signaled a planetary reappropriation of the ideals of modernity and their transnationalism. Within the black experience, Haiti represents the first site where this modern idea was embodied. Between 1791 and 1804, slaves and former slaves rose up and created a free state out of the ashes of what, fifteen years earlier, had been the most profitable colony in the world.[38] In its Declaration of Rights of 1795, the French Revolution had affirmed the inalienable nature of people's rights to independence and sovereignty. It was Haiti, the "eldest daughter of Africa,"[39] but also the "eldest daughter of decolonization,"[40] that for the first time gave universal scope to this principle.[41] Through a pure sovereign gesture, black slaves gave flesh and content to the postulate of the equality of all human beings. At the same time, this sovereign gesture was an act of abolition—one whose historical dimension has been commented on many times, yet whose phenomenal character remains to be deciphered. First, the concept of freedom so closely associated with the experience of modernity has meaning only in opposition to the reality of slavery and servitude. And slavery is characterized above all by the experience of scission and the absence of autonomy. Thus, emergence into freedom must pass through the abolition of this scission and the reunification of object and concept. Decolonization, in its primitive sense, begins with the liberation of slaves and their emancipation from a vile, base existence. This emancipation happens through a play of forces anchored in both matter and consciousness. It is a question of abolishing the moment in which the self is constituted as object of the other: only ever seeing itself in and through someone else, only ever inhabiting the name, the voice, the face, and the residence of an other, and the other's work, life, and language. This first abolition aims to end a relation of extroversion.

In Haiti, the insurgent slaves went into combat.[42] It was literally a fight to the death. In order to be born into freedom, they sought the death of their masters. But, by putting their masters' lives in peril, they put their own lives at stake. This is what Hegel, in speaking of servitude and domination, called "trial by death." It is "only through staking one's life that freedom is won, only thus is it proved. . . . The individual who has not risked his life may well be recognized as a *person* but he has not attained to the truth of this recognition as an independent self-consciousness."[43] The transition from damaged consciousness to autonomous consciousness requires that slaves expose themselves and abolish the being-outside-of-self that is precisely their double.[44] The postcolonial history of Haiti shows, however, that this first abolition is not enough to achieve recognition and establish new relations of mutuality between former slaves and former masters. A second abolition is necessary, which is much more complex than the first, which fundamentally represents only an immediate negation. It is no longer simply a matter of abolishing the Other: it is a matter of abolishing oneself by ridding oneself of the part of oneself that is servile, and working to realize oneself as a singular figure of the universal.

But this liberation of slaves precisely did not lead to a *state of mastery*. To the contrary, this emancipation, negation without autonomy, led to reduplication and new forms of servitude—the activities of the Other practiced on and against oneself.[45] In this way, servitude survives the process of abolition. Emancipation having produced the exact inverse of what it wanted, the object-related side of existence remained permanently present. The recovery of the self by the self did not take place.

We observe a somewhat similar process in Liberia, the second place where the ideas of freedom and equality, the principle of African nationality, and a sovereign black political body were established. In Liberia as well, it was a matter of former slaves.[46] In 1807 and 1834, first the slave trade and then the institution of slavery as such were abolished in the British Empire. The Civil War in the United States opened the way to emancipation, and then to the period of Reconstruction in the 1860s.[47] This period was also characterized by religious revival. The cornerstone of the new phase of Protestant evangelism was the will to convert Africa to Christianity. There were prophetic, messianic, and apocalyptic aspects to this phase. Immense hopes were nourished concerning the progress of Africa and the regeneration of the black race. The freed blacks who moved to the colony of Liberia were themselves borne by the memory of Jubilee and the image of Ethiopia, which, it was thought, would soon open its arms to the Eternal.[48]

It was thus due to the repatriation of black slaves from the United States to West Africa that an imaginary of sovereignty, the nation, and freedom developed there. It was also in Liberia that the first modern critical thinking about the idea of an *African nationality* was sketched—a nationality that would form a political body and would result in the creation of a Christian, modern, and civilized black state. In African thinking of the time, this state was represented as the only place where the former descendants of slaves (a vilified and despised race), scattered throughout the New World, would find peace and repose, and would be able to freely determine their collective destiny. The emergence of an independent black state was a step toward the moral and material regeneration of Africa and its conversion to Christianity. It was thought that this would lead to a renewal of the creative virtues of the black people. For the first time in the modern history of Africa, this people would be faced with the challenge of realizing its values in a place entirely in its charge.

The Liberian politician and diplomat Edward Blyden is the thinker who most contributed to reflection on the new figures of black consciousness made possible by the establishment of Liberia during the second half of the nineteenth century. For Blyden, in the conditions of the period, sovereignty meant above all a "return to self." This return took place through remembering the sufferings endured during the time of captivity and dispersion. According to Blyden, these sufferings were comparable to those endured by the Jews.[49] They were the sufferings of a race struck by total misfortune without limits, in its pure essentiality.[50] Emancipation, on the other hand, meant a surge of singularity, insofar as this singularity could be reconciled with the universal.[51] This experience of emancipation ran up against innumerable problems.[52] Most of these problems stemmed from the bastard nature of the enterprise. The 1847 Declaration of Independence, a charter symbolic of the new nation, proposed no identification with Africa or Africans. The new state was the progeny of the American Society of Colonization, a private philanthropic organization.[53] The return of the exiles to their "homeland" was compared not to a reestablishment of connections with their historical and racial relatives, but to an expatriation. They were severed from "the land that saw their birth . . . in order to form colonial establishments in a barbarian country," West Africa. The God invoked by the new emigrants, the one they called the god of their fathers, was in fact the Christian God, brought back from the United States. Unlike in Haiti, the birth of the new state did not follow from an act of abolition, but rather from a philanthropic gesture and a unilateral recognition. Moreover, the Declaration of Independence compared this birth to a "planned decolonization," rather than to self-liberation. Very quickly, the experiment ran up against questions of race and democracy. The emigrants from America defined themselves in opposition to the "aboriginals," whom they intended to "civilize" and from whom they tried to distinguish themselves by their number, their lifestyle, their color, and a host of other internal and external differences that made the category "Negro" anything but a coherent entity.[54]

Both Haiti and Liberia were republics that emerged directly out of the plantation experience. The process of emancipation of which they became the signs within black consciousness was stricken with an inherent weakness. It had preserved, within itself, the lack of subjectivity that had always characterized existence under the plantation regime. Whence, for example, the pessimism, found even in Blyden, about the possibility of democratic life. These two experiments, Haiti and Liberia, failed because they were haunted, even inhabited, by the spirit of the plantation. This spirit never ceased acting within them like a dead thing, like a bone: reduplication and repetition, but without difference.

CRITIQUE AND INSTITUTIONS

Frantz Fanon is one of the very few thinkers to have risked something that resembles a theory of decolonization—a theory that is at the same time a *hermeneutics* (who the self, the ontological being, or the subject of this process is) and a *pedagogy* (how and through what kind of praxis decolonization is to be achieved and for what aims that could be described as universal). Fanon's theory of decolonization rests almost entirely on a political theory of property and ownership, which is at the same time an ethics of struggle. For Fanon, struggles for ownership are first and foremost about self-ownership. They are struggles to repossess, to take back, if necessary by force, that which is ours unconditionally and, as such, belongs to us.

Racism, in this sense, is fundamentally a technology of dispossession. "To own oneself" is nothing other than a step toward the creation of new forms of life that could genuinely be characterized as fully human. For Fanon, to be was to create—to create time, the first historical Event (with capital *E*) being time itself, the foundation of any subjectivity, that is, of any consciousness of the self as self (see in particular the conclusion of *Black Skin, White Masks*). Being was not only constituted "in" time, but through, by means of, and almost by virtue of time. If there is something we can call a Fanonian theory of decolonization, that is where it lies, in the dialectic of time, life, and creation—which for him is the same as self-appropriation.

It is not difficult to fathom why, for Fanon, decolonization came to be so closely associated with the fundamental concepts of being, time, and self-creation (starting anew, *le recommencement*) and with questions of *constitutive* difference rather than repetition. The reason is that colonization in its essence was a fundamental negation of time. From the colonial point of view, natives were not simply people without a past and without history. They were people radically located *outside of time*. Europe had the monopoly on that essential human quality we call the disposition toward the future, and the capacity for futurity was the monopoly of Europe. This quality had to be brought to the natives from outside, as a magnanimous gift of civilization—a benevolent gift that absolved colonialism of its plunder and crimes.

Furthermore, in the colonial mind, the native was ontologically incapable of change and therefore of creation. The native would always and forever be a native. It was the colonial settler's belief that, were the native to change, the ways in which this change would occur and the forms that this change would take or would bring about would always end in a catastrophe. In other words, repetition was the quintessential native principle.

Fanon understood decolonization as precisely a subversion of the law of repetition. An ontological event, decolonization aimed at radically redefining native being and opening it up to the possibility of becoming a human form of being rather than a thing. It also redefined native time as the permanent possibility of the emergence of the not-yet. To the colonial framework of predetermination, decolonization opposed the framework of possibility—the possibility of a different type of being, a different type of time, a different type of creation, different forms of life, a different humanity, the possibility of reconstituting the human after humanism's complicity with colonial racism. Decolonization, he argued, "is always a violent phenomenon" whose goal is "the replacing of a certain 'species' of men by another 'species' of men."[55] The Latin term *species* derives from a root signifying "to look," "to see." It means "appearance" or "vision." It can also mean "aspect." The same root is found in the term *speculum*, which means "mirror"; in *spectrum*, which means "image"; in *specimen*, which means "sign"; and in *spectaculum*, which refers to "spectacle." A new "species of men" is a class of "men" endowed with a new essence, "men" who are no longer limited or predetermined by their appearance, and whose essence coincides with their image. Their image is no longer something separate from whom they truly are. Nor is it, as in the colonial dispensation, something that does not belong to them. There is no longer a gap between this image and the recognition of oneself as one's own property. Only such "men" can create new forms of life, free from the shocking realization that the image through which they have emerged into visibility is not their essence.

For Fanon, decolonization was first and foremost a *discipline*. It equipped the colonized subject with the knowledge and method necessary for self-understanding and self-interpretation. But it was also a *pedagogy*. It taught the colonized through what kind of praxis he or she could liberate himself or herself. Furthermore, decolonization was a revolutionary process in the service of national liberation. Finally—and even more importantly—decolonization was a practice of violence with the goal of securing state power and using this power as a lever to accomplish planetary social transformations. Violence was crucial to the decolonizing process because of its foundational, constituent functions. It was the means by which a law originally founded on the right of conquest could be overthrown and replaced with a new law founded on the right of self-determination.

The second layer of Fanon's theory of decolonization revolved around the dialectics of self-ownership, destruction, and self-creation. For Fanon, to decolonize consisted in a struggle to own oneself or, to use his own formulation, to become one's "own foundation." He saw self-ownership—which is the other name for disalienation—as a precondition for the *creation of a new species of men and of new forms of life*, that is, forms of life that could genuinely be characterized as fully human.

"Decolonization," he wrote, "was always a violent phenomenon." If indeed colonialism instituted a gap between image and essence, decolonization was *the elimination of this gap and the restitution of the self to its image*. It was about the "restitution" of the essence to the image so that the new self might exist as his or her own law and not in something other than himself or herself, something distorted, clumsy, debased, and unworthy. Indeed what was at stake in the decolonizing act (thought and praxis) was the future of the human as a species. For Fanon, violence was meant to operate at the interface between creation and destruction. Creation was not about tinkering with the margins. It was about turning human beings once again into craftsmen and craftswomen who, in reshaping minds, matter, and forms, did not need to imitate or mimic preexisting models. Thus Fanon's call to "provincialize" Europe, to "turn our backs on Europe," to not take Europe as a model: "The European game has finally ended," he argued, "we must find something different"; "We today can do everything, so long as we do not imitate Europe" (312); "today we are present at the stasis of Europe" (314), that is, the closing of a historical cycle; "It is a question of the Third World starting a new history of Man" (315); "We must . . . try to set afoot a new man" (316).

Critical to his theory of decolonization was the idea that we have to start from a tabula rasa. Underlying every colonial mythology, he thought, was the fiction that natives were not simply people without history. They were people radically located *outside of history*. For Fanon, such a mythology had to be eradicated for decolonization to become an authentic event. As an authentic event, decolonization would radically redefine native being. It would open it up to the possibility of becoming a human form rather than the thing into which it had been made by colonialism. An authentic event was also historical. Following the destruction of colonial mythology, native time would be reinscribed in the horizon of human time, that is, of futurity.

TO SEE OURSELVES CLEARLY

Calls to "decolonize" are not new. In the 1960s, 1970s, and 1980s, they were issued under different names, the most recognizable of which were "Africanization," "indigenization," and "endogeneization." So far—with respect to Africa—the decolonizing injunction has mostly consisted of a critique of the *colonial knowledge chain* (what is taught, produced, and disseminated) and a denunciation of its deleterious effects on African society, culture, and psyche. To be sure, significant resources have been invested in the study of so-called "indigenous knowledge" or "technological systems."[56] Most of these studies can be classified under the rubric of *ethno-knowledges*, so tight are their connections with the politics of identity and ethnicity.[57] Today we still do not have a precise idea of what a "truly decolonized knowledge" might look like. Nor do we have a *theory of knowledge* as such that might compellingly underpin the African injunction to decolonize. Because of the absence of both a theory of knowledge and a *theory of institutions*, the injunction to decolonize may be, at least for the time being, better understood as a *compensatory act* whose function is to heal what amounts to racial shame.

With Ngugi w'a Thiong'o, the decolonization project mostly consisted in a critique of the *colonial knowledge chain* (what is taught, produced, and disseminated) and its effects on the society and on culture at large.

Coming two decades after Fanon, he framed the issue thus in his now canonical *Decolonizing the Mind* (1981):

> What should we do with the inherited colonial education system and the consciousness it necessarily inculcated in the African mind? What directions should an education system take in an Africa wishing to break with neo-colonialism? How does it want the "New Africans" to view themselves and their universe and from what base, Afrocentric or Eurocentric? What then are the materials they should be exposed to, and in what order and perspective? Who should be interpreting that material to them, an African or non-African? If African, what kind of African? One who has internalized the colonial world outlook or one attempting to break free from the inherited slave consciousness?

In Ngugi's terms, decolonization's main aim was "to see ourselves clearly in relationship to ourselves and to other selves in the universe" (87). It was *a project of "re-centering."* It is about rejecting the assumption that the modern West is the central root of Africa's consciousness and cultural heritage, that Africa is merely an extension of the West. "Education," writes Ngugi, "is a means of knowledge about ourselves. . . . After we have examined ourselves, we radiate outwards and discover peoples and worlds around us. With Africa at the centre of things, not existing as an appendix or a satellite of other countries and literatures, things must be seen from the African perspective." Ngugi continues, "All other things are to be considered in their relevance to our situation and their contribution towards understanding ourselves. In suggesting this we are not rejecting other streams, especially the western stream. We are only clearly mapping out the directions and perspectives the study of culture and literature will inevitably take in an African university."

Ngugi drew practical implications from his considerations on culture and literature. Most of these implications had to do with curriculum reform. Crucial in this regard was the need to teach African languages. A decolonized university in Africa, he thought, should put African languages at the center of its teaching and learning project. Ngugi probably assumed that language inevitably shaped knowledge or what it is possible to know; he believed that language inevitably grounds knowledge in a particular culture and influences what we know and how we know it.

As recently as 2008, Paulin Hountondji made a similar argument: "Our scientific activity," he says, "is externally oriented, intended to meet the theoretical needs of our Western counterparts and answer the questions they pose. The exclusive use of European languages as a means of scientific expression reinforces this alienation."[58] In his mind, verticality was to be replaced with horizontalism. The goal was to open the way for "an autonomous, self-reliant process of knowledge production and capitalisation that enables us to answer our own questions and meet both the intellectual and the material needs of African societies." To achieve such an objective required the formulation of original "problematics" grounded in a "solid appropriation of the international intellectual legacy and deeply rooted in the African experience." "Knowing oneself in order to transform" and not simply contributing to the accumulation of knowledge about Africa, a kind of knowledge that is capitalized in and managed by the North—this was the ultimate goal.

Hountondji made a distinction between discourses *on* or *about* Africa that come *from* or are produced or developed *by Africans within Africa* (the study of Africa by Africans in Africa) and those coming *from outside*. And yet, he recognized that in these matters as in many others, there was no unanimity whatsoever within Africa itself about what is "African" and what is not. Rejecting what he called "the unanimist illusion," he extolled the virtues of "pluralism," that is, the internal debates, contradictions, and intellectual tensions conjured up whenever the name "Africa" was convened. He was not opposed to works on what he himself called "universal issues and concepts," including issues in mathematical logic or the foundations of science, the history and sociology of science, the anthropology of knowledge, ethics and political philosophy, the philosophy of language, and the like. Such attempts, he concluded, were "part and parcel of African philosophy."[59]

The end of the twentieth century has coincided with an intensification of the critique of the foundational assumptions and related practices of so-called Western thought. Among some of these assumptions is the belief that language can be transparent and mirror the world for the mind, that accurate language can replicate and represent the world. Another is the belief that there is a real, and then its representation, each operating on different levels of existence, or that nature is fixed and measurable, that material objects act only when acted upon by an external agent, that humans have a separate existence from the world, that they are the masters of the universe.

The problem with these assumptions is that they have enabled a range of binary oppositions such as same/other, human/nonhuman, mind/matter, culture/nature, conscious/unconscious, normal/abnormal, transcendence/immanence, men/women, idealism/materialism. It has been necessary to critique the ontological grounds on which such distinctions have been made and continue to be made. Interestingly enough, some of these critiques come from within so-called Western thought itself. Others emanate from elsewhere in the world.

Such is the case of Latin America, where the critique of the dominant Eurocentric academic model has been gaining ground since the 1980s in particular. This "fight back" has taken at least two major directions. The first has been an assault against what Latin Americans call "epistemic coloniality," that is, the endless production of theories that are based either on European concepts and traditions or on particular procedures of "anthropologizing" Others.[60] This, it is argued, is a process that never fully acknowledges these Others as thinking and knowledge-producing subjects in their own terms. The second has been the rehabilitation of defeated, subaltern, or indigenous knowledges and life-worlds. Worldwide, there is a recognition of the exhaustion of the present academic model with its origins in the universalism of the Enlightenment.

RACE AND THE DECOLONIZATION OF KNOWLEDGE

Race did not operate in the colonies as it did on the plantation. In the case of the French colonial empire, models of racial thought varied over time, in particular beginning in the seventeenth century, when significant nonwhite populations began to live under France's author-ity. Despite some variations, since the Enlightenment these models have all shared three postulates. The first postulate stated that all races belonged to humanity. The second maintained that not all races were equal, even if human differences, far from being immutable, could be overcome. The third postulate emphasized the close relation between the white race, the French nation, and French culture.[61]

The tension between race, nation, and culture has in no way been erased by either the French Revolution or French republicanism. To be sure, the Revolution had affirmed the primacy of equality for all and everyone's shared belonging to the French republican project over all other forms of social or racial distinction. But at the same time, revo-lutionary France never stopped making racial difference a factor in defining citizenship.[62] By the time of colonial expansion, the tension between color-blind universalism and a liberal French republicanism fond of the grossest racial stereotypes had gradually become rooted in French science and popular culture. It was exacerbated within a context where the function of colonial imperialism was to revive the French nation and "character" and to "spread the benefits of our civilization." At the same time, the necessity of spreading "our civilization" was jus-tified only by the national distinction between France and its Others.[63]

During the nineteenth century, models of popular racism in France were in part connected to major social transformations (such as coloni-zation, industrialization, urbanization, and the rise of the bourgeois family), which gave the question of difference in general, and different racial qualities in particular, a kind of urgency. The bourgeois democ-racy's disdain for the nascent working classes corresponded, as if in an echo, to the aristocracy's disdain for the "sans-culottes" of the time of the Revolution. Race was both the result and the reaffirmation of the gen-eral idea of the irreducibility of social differences. All those lacking the nation's racial, social, and cultural characteristics were outside the nation. In the colonies as well, national identity and citizenship were tightly bound with the racial idea of whiteness.[64] For all that one may speak of the citizenship of nonwhite males in Martinique, Guadeloupe, Guiana, Réunion, and the Four Communes of Senegal, in general it applied only to a few million individuals, handpicked out of a vast dominion populated by millions of subjects.[65]

By the end of the nineteenth century, one could observe that assimilation had failed. Until the middle of the twentieth century, the Empire was an empire more of subjects than of citizens. Consequently, natives had to be "civilized" within the context of their specific difference: societies without history or writing, frozen in time. To a large extent, decolonization only reified the failure of assimilation. Decolonization legally sanctioned the idea that nonwhite subjects of the Empire could not become French citizens. Thus, the barrier of race always stood between French citizenship and identity,[66] as I will also discuss in the next chapter. On another level, over the long term, there has always existed a close relationship between a certain expression of French nationalism and a concept of racial difference masked by the universalist, French republican paradigm. And at the same time, there has always existed a kind of French universalism that is itself a product of racial thought. To the extent that France as a nation and French civilization as a culture have been in permanent conflict with those who have been defined as "others," we cannot be surprised to see to what degree the notion of humanity and liberty defended by the Republic is historically based on a racialized opposition between civilized and primitive.[67] Nor should we be surprised that the principal stake of decolonial thought was the disenclosure of the world.

The philosophical aim of decolonization and of the anticolonial movement that made it possible can be summed up in one phrase: the *disenclosure of the world* [*la déclosion du monde*]. According to the French philosopher Jean-Luc Nancy, disenclosure "denotes the opening of an enclosure, the raising of a barrier."[68] The term *disenclosure* is synonymous with opening, a surging up, the advent of something new, a blossoming. To disenclose is thus to lift closures in such a way that what had been closed in can emerge and blossom. The question of the disenclosure of the world—of belonging to the world, inhabitance of the world, creation of the world, or the conditions in which we make a world and constitute ourselves as inheritors of the world—is at the heart of anticolonial thought and the notion of decolonization. One could even say that this question is decolonization's fundamental object. We find it, for example, in Frantz Fanon, for whom it coincides with the project of human autonomy or the self-creation of humanity, as his expression "I am my own foundation" attests.[69] The questioning of human autonomy is an interrogation without end, and it is not new. It was present at the birth of philosophy in ancient Greece. To make a world, to inhabit the world, and to inherit the world mean, as Cornelius Castoriadis and Vincent Descombes remind us, participating in the project of a humanity that posits its own principles of conduct, on its own basis.[70]

Fanon's thinking about the disenclosure of the world is a response to the colonial context of servitude, submission to foreign masters, and racial violence. In such conditions—as under slavery earlier—the concept of the human and the notion of humanity, which are taken for granted by part of Western thought, were not self-evident. In fact, faced with the black slave or colonial subject, Europe never stopped asking itself, "Is this another man? Is this something other than a man? Is he another copy of the same? Or is he something other than the same?" In anticolonial thinking, humanity does not exist a priori. Humanity is to be *made to rise* [*faire surgir*] through the process by which the colonized subject awakens to self-consciousness, subjectively appropriates his or her I, takes down the barrier, and authorizes him- or herself to speak in the first person. This awakening and appropriation aim not only at the realization of the self, but also, more significantly, at an *ascent into humanity*, a new beginning of creation, the disenclosure of the world.

For Fanon, this ascent into humanity can only be the result of a struggle: the struggle for life. The struggle for life—which is the same thing as the struggle to open up the world—consists in forging the capacity to be oneself, to act on one's own, and to stand up by oneself and account for oneself, which Fanon compares to a *rising up* [*surgissement*], rising from the depths of what he calls "an extraordinarily sterile and arid region,"[71] which for him is *race*, the zone of nonbeing. And for Fanon, to emerge from these sterile and arid regions of existence is above all to *emerge from the enclosure of race*—an entrapment in which the gaze and power of the Other seek to enclose the subject. To emerge is thus also to contribute to melting away the space of clear distinctions, separations, borders, and closures, and to make one's way toward the universal that Fanon affirms is "inherent in the human condition."[72] Thus, in the Fanonian conception of the opening of the world, there is a threefold insurrectional, constitutional, and resurrectional aspect, because this opening is akin to a return to life (*anastasis*), to life's escape from the forces of desiccation that were limiting it. For Fanon, the opening of the world is the same as its disenclosure—if, following Jean-Luc Nancy, by disenclosure we understand the taking apart and disassembling of fences, barriers, and enclosures. But, for the disenclosure of the world to happen, it is necessary to detach oneself from oneself, precisely in order to confront what is coming and what, in coming, causes other resources of life to spring up. This is why the Fanonian self is fundamentally opening, distension, and gap: the *Open*. I have mentioned the arid region of existence that is race. In Fanon, the disenclosure of the world presupposes the abolition of race. It can take place only on the condition that the following truths are admitted: "The Negro is not . . . any more than the white man"; "the Negro is a man like the rest"; "a man among other men."[73] In Fanon's eyes, this postulate of a fundamental similarity between men, an *original human citizenship*, constitutes the key to the project of the disenclosure of the world and human autonomy: decolonization.

The theme of the disenclosure of the world occupies a prominent place among other black thinkers. For Léopold Sédar Senghor, decolonization implies the existence of a subject who cultivates care for what belongs to him or her as his or her own. But here again, what belongs to us as our own, what defines us as our own, only has meaning to the extent that it is put in common [*mise en commun*]. Senghor names the project of the *in-common* the "encounter between giving and receiving [*le rendez-vous du donner et du recevoir*]."[74] For him, the renaissance of the world and the advent of a universal *métisse* community that is governed by the principle of sharing differences and sharing what is unique, and that is thus open to the *whole*, depend on this putting in-common. For Senghor as for Fanon, we are inheritors of the whole world. At the same time, the world—this inheritance—has to be created. The world is in the process of being created, and we ourselves are created along with it.

Outside this process of creation, cocreation, and self-creation, the world is mute and ungraspable. It is by contributing to this triple process that one gains the right to inherit the world as a whole. For other black thinkers, like Édouard Glissant, disenclosure consists precisely in going forward to meet the world, and in being able to embrace the inextricable web of affiliations that form our identities and the inter-lacing of networks that make every identity necessarily extend out in relation to the Other—an Other always there, from the outset. The veritable disenclosure of the world is thus the encounter with the world's entirety: what Glissant calls the *Tout-Monde* [*All-World*]. In this, it is above all a *praxis* of putting in relation. This thematic of rela-tion and this question of entirety are also present in the work of British postcolonial writer Paul Gilroy, where they take the shape of a new planetary consciousness.[75] In Gilroy as in Glissant, the project is nei-ther the partition nor the division of the world. To the contrary, the construction of spheres of horizontality must replace the quest for a center. Thus, the project is for a horizontal thinking of the world, one that gives a central place to the ethics of mutuality, or, as Gilroy sug-gests, to conviviality, being-with-others.[76]

In black thought, analysis of decolonization (understood as an emi-nent moment in the project of the disenclosure of the world) cannot be dissociated from the question of Europe. The thought of decolonization is, in this regard, a confrontation with Europe, with what it calls its telos, and, even more precisely, with the question of the conditions in which the process of becoming-European [*le devenir-européen*] could be a pos-itive moment in the world's process of becoming, the "becoming-world" [*le devenir-monde*] in general. In the history of philosophy, Euro-peans have tended to define themselves in three ways. First, they have insisted that "history is not human history from the outset." It only becomes the history of humanity through "the shift from the history of the West to the history of Europe and the enlargement of the latter into planetary history."[77] Second, Europeans have emphasized that the spec-ificity of the history of Europe is to have placed European humanity "at a height that no other form of humanity until then had reached";[78] the fact that "European humanity could have taken itself for humanity in general," and that it could have considered its forms of life to be "generally human," was for them but the mark of a demand for responsibility, even universal captaincy.

According to them, this vocation of captaincy, which is equally a will to power, flows from Europe's various heritages, including Christianity. Jean-Luc Nancy, for example, says that Christianity is inseparable from the West. It is not some accident that befell it (for better or worse), nor is it transcendent to it. It is coextensive with the West qua West, that is, with a certain process of Westernization consisting in a form of self-resorption or self-surpassing.[79]

⚬⚬⚬

As early as the 1930s, Husserl explained that Europe defined itself by reason and by its universality. As for Paul Valéry, he spoke of the Old Continent as a "cape"—a prominent point of land jutting out into the sea—and as that which is at the head or is the head, which leads and dominates, which exercises a sort of captaincy over the rest. He also said that Europe is "the precious part of the terrestrial universe, the pearl of the sphere, the brain of a vast body,"[80] the body of humanity, its final point.

Whether in Husserl or in Valéry, the idea was that in Europe the universal was irreplaceably inscribed, not only as reason but also as the singular. Due to this inscription of the universal in both reason and the singular, Europe became both the advanced point of the mind and a unique testimony to the human essence and to what is "proper to man." Europe's exemplarity resided in the inscription of the universal in the specific body of a singularity, an idiom, a culture, and, in the darkest cases, a race. Since Europe was akin to a philosophical task, its mission was to extend the light of reason in the service of liberty. Among the least obtuse, European belonging was an opening to all of humanity.

Finally, a certain philosophical tradition has privileged a way of thinking about the idea of Europe that starts from what it considered to be the threats, dangers, and perils that the European principle would have to face. The threat was always represented in the form of the Other of Europe. Historically, this Other of Europe has had two faces. As the

French philosopher Marc Crépon reminds us, it first appeared in the shape of "processes by which Europe makes itself the Other of itself, or rather, becomes foreign to itself. Alterity is then the *alteration* of identity, or at least of what is proposed as identity."[81] In Jan Patocka, this threat of alteration always takes the form of a scission. He distinguishes, in particular, three scissions over the course of the past century that have profoundly affected and continue to affect the European principle. The first is the discrepancy within Europe between cultural and political spaces open to this universal vocation, and others tempted to withdraw into singularity. The second scission is the "opposition, within Europe, of two versions of the principle of rationality," including one that is radical: totalitarianism. The third scission is "the perversion of the universal vocation of Europe" into imperial, colonial, or neocolonial domination. The first two forms of scission are within Europe, whereas the third is part of a radical separation between Europe and nonwhite peoples. Here, alterity is understood in the sense of spiritual, geographical, and racial *borders*. The Other is the non-Europeans who oppose us. And the status of this Other serves to pronounce the threat. Thus, for Patocka, the triple danger is the refusal of rationality, the excess of rationality, and the perversion of the principle of universality into universal domination. Closer to my way of thinking, Jacques Derrida has attempted to realize a synthesis between the first and the second directions.

In one of his last texts, Jacques Derrida examines what meaning must be given to the name and concept—and thus also the destiny—of Europe.[82] He calls the Europe he has in mind "another Europe," a Europe "without the slightest Eurocentrism": a Europe that, "without renouncing realism and the indispensable assets of an economic, military, technoscientific superpower, would delve into its memory, from its unique memory, from its most luminous memories (philosophy itself, the Enlightenment, its revolutions, and the open history, still to be theorized, of the rights of man), but also from its darkest memories, the most guilty, the most repentant (genocides, the Holocaust, colonialism, Nazi, fascist, and Stalinian totalitarianism, and so many other oppressive forms of violence . . .), another Europe, the one I dream of, would find in its two memories, the best and the worst, the political strength" not of a politics of the world, but of what he calls an *altermon-dialist politics* [*une politique altermondialiste*].[83] Derrida's quest is for a Europe that would associate goodness and sovereignty: that is, a Europe that would resist the constant temptation to reduce the original community of humans to an animal kingdom, with, at its head, a sort of wolf; a Europe that would set itself against the principle of *Homo homini lupus* (the man who is not a man but a wolf for his fellow man). Derrida is perhaps the only European thinker who implicitly proposes rereading the biography of Europe no longer under the sign of the universal, but on the basis of the thematic of the wolf: that is, the becoming-beast and becoming-animal of a sovereign who only defines himself as sovereign qua animal, and only institutes himself through the possibility of devouring his enemy. Now, this way of writing the biography of Europe can be found in the current of thought known as "postcolonial theory."

THINKING THE WORLD

One may distinguish three central moments in the development of postcolonial thought. The inaugural moment was the moment of the anticolonial struggles. These struggles were preceded and accompanied by colonial subjects' reflections on themselves and on the contradictions that resulted from their double status within the Empire as "indigenes" and as "subjects," by meticulous examination of the forces making it possible to resist colonial domination, and, finally, by debates about the relations between what stems from "class" factors and what from "race" factors. The discourse of the period was articulated around a *politics of autonomy*: that is, to use French philosopher Vincent Descombes's terms, the possibility of "saying *I*," of "acting on one's own" [*agir de soi-même*], of acquiring a civic will [*volonté citoyenne*], and, in so doing, of participating in the creation of the world.

The second moment, generally situated in the 1980s, was the moment of hermeneutics and high theory, the culmination of which was the publication of Edward Said's masterpiece, *Orientalism*,[84] which he later expanded on in *The World, the Text, the Critic*,[85] and then in *Culture and Imperialism*.[86] Indeed, it was Edward Said, a stateless Palestinian, who first laid down the foundations of what was gradually to become "postcolonial theory"—this time understood as an alternative form of knowledge of modernity, and as an academic discipline of its own. One of Said's decisive contributions was to have shown, against the Marxist *doxa* of the time, that the colonial project could not be reduced to a simple military-economic apparatus, but was underlain by a discursive infrastructure, a symbolic economy, an entire apparatus of knowledge whose violence was epistemic as well as physical. Cultural analysis of the colonial discursive infrastructure, or the colonial *imagination*, gradually became the very subject of postcolonial theory, provoking harsh criticism from Marxist and internationalist intellectuals such as Aijaz Ahmed (*In Theory: Classes, Nations, Literatures*),[87] Chandra Talpade Mohanty (*Third World Women and the Politics of Feminism*),[88] and Benita Parry.

It was also during the 1980s that a junction was established between postcolonial thought and various other currents with their own particular genealogies. I will cite only two, whose merit was to offer a historiographical basis to what, until then, had consisted primarily in the analysis of literary texts. First, there was "subaltern studies," a strand of historical reflection born in India, which developed a critique of nationalist and anticolonial historiography while trying to recover the historical voices and capacities of those defeated by decolonization (peasants, women, the caste of untouchables, marginals, subalterns) through a revision and selective rereading of Marxism (see in particular the work of American postcolonial scholar Dipesh Chakrabarty in *Provincializing Europe*).[89] Due to the attention given to the "voiceless" and "powerless," a large part of the initial theoretical inspiration for the school of subaltern studies came from Gramsci. But the "translation" of Marx into non-European contexts and languages aims above all at understanding why, in India, the anticolonial struggle had led not to a radical transformation of society, but to a sort of "passive revolution" characterized by the return of "communalism"—that is, ultimately, to a figure of the antination.

There was, second, an Afro-modern thought that developed around the edges of the Atlantic, a thought that takes this oceanic and transnational formation as the very unit of its analysis (this is the case in particular with Paul Gilroy in *The Black Atlantic*). The current of thought was created by Afro-British, African-Americans, and Afro-Caribbeans. Its central concern is to rewrite the multiple histories of modernity at the juncture of facts of race and factors of class. Within this perspective, Afro-modern thought was interested both in the question of diaspora and in the question of the procedures by which individuals are subjected to defamatory categories that bar their access to any status as subjects in history. This is in particular the case of imprisonment within a race. W. E. B. Du Bois (*The Souls of Black Folk*) is, from this point of view, the African-American thinker who best analyzed the effects of the "somber veil of color" that enclosed people of African origin in the New World.[90] He contended that such a "veil" not only covers the one who is obliged to wear it, but also makes him or her unrecognizable and incomprehensible, prey to a "double consciousness." This is also a current of thought very sensitive to the theme of "freeing minds" and memory within conditions of captivity (notably through religion, music, and the performing arts) and to the problematic of dispersion (diasporas), or what Glissant calls the "poetics of relation." Artistic and aesthetic experience occupied a central place in this current. Speaking of slave songs, "weird old songs in which the soul of the black slave spoke to men," W. E. B. Du Bois wrote, "they that walked in darkness sang songs in the olden days—Sorrow Songs—for they were weary at heart."[91] This musical motif was later taken up by Paul Gilroy, who extended the analysis to jazz and reggae.[92]

On the African side of the Atlantic, the properly postcolonial moment originated in literature. The literary act serves if not as a psychoanalytical moment pure and simple, then at least as a system of symbolization whose primary intention is to cure. The birthplace of this literature is a structure of horror in which Africa appears as that which never came into existence and which, as such, is deprived of all force of representation: because it is the principle par excellence of obstruction and frozenness. Having never really been born, having never come out of the opacity of nothingness, Africa can only enter universal consciousness by breaking and entering—if at all. In other words, it is a *reality without real*. At its origin, the African literary act is a response to this exclusion, which is at once ablation, excision, and pejoration. Within Western discourse, this primitive operation of denegation operates along three axes. First, the denegation appears as an operation of language. Next, it is a kind of repression. Finally, it is a drive to destruction. Africa is an object of pleasure [*jouissance*] and aversion. It is similar to an anal object. The pleasure one takes from it is firstly that of the expulsion of excrement and waste. This anal object lacks neither presence nor image, but it is the presence and image of a hole and of an *originary ruin*. This ruin is what is represented. It is also what literature fictionalizes, arguing that some truth remains beyond the violence, even if this truth has lost its name. And this name is what must be found. Postcolonial African discourse arises out of an "outside-of-the-world"—that somber and opaque zone defined by the nonbeing Hegel discusses in his *Reason in History*. It arises out of obscurity, out of the bottommost reaches of the ship's hold to which Negro humanity had previously been confined in Western discourse. Within the history of African thought, literature, music, and religion have been responses to this debarment, to the disavowal and denegation through which Africa was born into the world. This birth takes place in a nocturnal space. Hence, for example, the response proposed by Senghor in the form of an Orphic hymn: the "song of shadow."[93]

Added to the denial of humanity is an affirmation of the African's irreducible alterity and the inscription of the African sign within a structure of difference presenting psychotic attributes. Anthropology, the sister of psychiatry in the colonies, constitutes the discipline par excellence of this reading of the Other whom one has deprived of reason beforehand. It is a psychotic structure precisely because of the identification of the continent with madness and, in general, with disease in its two forms: organic (like epilepsy) and psychic (like melancholy).[94] This experience of negativity produces fiction. The goal of fiction is to take the subject out of the absence and nothingness in which he or she was confined. From its beginnings, the function of African literature was to counter the lack of reality with which the African sign had been saddled. Unable to kill the "father," it charges him with culpability that calls for repentance.

Another key moment of postcolonial theory is marked by the central fact of our time: globalization, the generalized expansion of the commodity form, and its seizure of the totality of natural resources, of human productions, and, in short, of the entirety of the living being. In these conditions, the literary text on its own can no longer be the sole archive of choice. But critical reflection on contemporary forms of instrumentalization of life can gain in radicalness by considering slavery and colonization, the ancient and recent formations of capitalism. One sees, in fact, how, within colonial capitalism's mode of functioning, there was a constant refusal to institute the sphere of the living being as a limit to economic appropriation. And as for slavery, it was a mode of production, circulation, and distribution of wealth based on a refusal to institutionalize any "nonappropriable" domain whatsoever. From every point of view, the "plantation," the "factory," and the "colony" were the principal laboratories for experiments in the authoritarian destiny [*le devenir autoritaire*] of the world as we observe it today.

As we see, postcolonial theory is an intellectual constellation whose strength and weakness originate in its very fragmentation. Postcolonial theory, which resulted from the circulation of knowledge between various continents and through various anti-imperialist traditions, is like a river with multiple tributaries. It puts its finger on two things. First, it exposes both the violence inherent in a particular idea of reason and the gulf that, within colonial conditions, separated European ethical thought from its practical, political, and symbolic decisions. How, indeed, can the faith proclaimed in man be reconciled with the ease with which the lives of the colonized, their work, and the world of meanings are sacrificed? This, for example, is the question asked by Aimé Césaire in his *Discourse on Colonialism*.[95] Second, this theory insists on *humanity-to-come*, humanity that will be born once colonial figures of the inhuman and racial difference have been abolished. This hope in the advent of a universal and fraternal community comes very close to Jewish thought, at least as it can be read in Ernst Bloch and Walter Benjamin—minus the theological-political dimension.

This theory also strives to deconstruct colonial prose, that is, the mental setup, representations, and symbolic forms that served as the infrastructure of the imperial project. It seeks to unmask the power of falsification—in a word, the stock of lies and functions of fabulations without which colonialism as a historical configuration of power would have failed. It shows that what passed for European humanism always appeared in the colonies in the form of duplicity, double-talk, and, very often, travesty of the real. It is well known that colonization never stopped lying about itself and others. Procedures that racialized the colonized were the motor of this economy of lies and duplicity. Indeed, race constituted the wilderness of European humanism, its Beast. Thus, post-colonial theory tries to dismantle the skeleton of the Beast, and flush out its favored living quarters. More radically, it asks a question: What is it to live under the reign of the Beast? What kind of life does one live, and what kind of death does one die? It shows that, within European humanism, there is something that must be called unconscious hatred of the self. Racism in general and colonial racism in particular constitute the transfer of this self-hate and self-contempt onto the Other. Even more serious was the fact that the figure of Europe that was experienced in the colonies (and, earlier, on the "plantation" under the regime of slavery) and with which they gradually became familiar was far from a figure of liberty, equality, and fraternity. Behind the mask of humanism and universalism, the colonized discovered not only a subject that was very often both deaf and blind. They discovered above all a subject marked by the desire for its own death via the death of others. It was also a subject in whose eyes right had almost nothing to do with justice, but was instead a certain way of causing, conducting, and eternalizing war. It was, finally, a subject for whom wealth was above all a way of exercising the right of life and death over others, as I shall discuss later.

We know now that the rhetoric of humanism and universalism often served in part as a smokescreen for *force*—force that does not know how to listen or transform itself. Once again, it is Fanon who, better than anyone else, grasps this sort of necropolitical force, which by passing through fiction becomes sick of life or, in an act of permanent reversal, takes death for life and life for death. This is why the colonial relation constantly oscillates between the desire to exploit the Other (supposed to be racially inferior) and the temptation to eliminate and exterminate the Other. Another characteristic of postcolonial theory is that it is a thought of *entanglement* and *concatenation*. In this respect, it opposes a certain Western illusion according to which there is no subject except in circular, permanent reference to oneself, to an essential and inexhaustible singularity. Postcolonial theory, to the contrary, insists on the fact that identity originates in multiplicity and dispersion, that reference to oneself is only possible within the *between-two*, at the interstice between *marking and unmarking*, in *coconstitution*. In these conditions, colonization no longer appears as a mechanical and unilateral form of domination forcing the subjected into silence and inaction. To the contrary, the colonized person is a living, speaking, conscious, acting individual whose identity is the result of a triple movement of effraction, erasure, and rewriting of the self.

Having said that, the universalization of imperialism is not explained by violence and coercion alone. In fact, many of the colonized agreed, for more or less valid reasons, to become conscious accomplices to a fable that seduced them in several respects. The identity of the colonized, like that of the colonizers, is formed at the intersection of ellipsis, disengagement, and repetition. This vast field of ambivalence, the aesthetic presuppositions of this entanglement, and its paradoxical effects have all been the objects of many analyses. The critique of European humanism and universalism within postcolonial thought is not an end in itself. It serves to open the way to an investigation of the possibility of a *politics of fellowship* [*une politique du semblable*]. The precondition of this politics of fellowship is recognition of the Other in his or her difference, as will also be discussed in the following chapter. Postcolonial thought's grounding in the future, in the unending quest for new horizons of man through recognition of others as fundamentally human, is all too often forgotten. It is constitutive of Fanon's quest, of Senghor's in his *Oeuvre poétique*,[96] written while he was a prisoner in a German camp (Front Stalag 230), of Edward Said's meditations at the twilight of his life, and, more recently, of Paul Gilroy's thoughts on the possibility of a convivial life in a henceforth multicultural and heterogeneous world (*Postcolonial Melancholia*). The same emphases are found in a large part of African-American thought, which has also been confronted with the difficulties of reappropriating heritages of slavery and racism and using them for resistance without falling into the trap of racialization and the glorification of race.

One may say that postcolonial thought is, in several regards, a world-thought, even if at the beginning it did not use this concept. It shows, first, that there is scarcely any disjunction between the history of the nation and the history of the empire. Napoleon, who reestablished slavery, and the Haitian liberator Toussaint Louverture, the representative of the revolution in human rights, constitute two sides of the same nation and the same colonial empire. Postcolonial thought shows how colonialism itself was a planetary experience and contributed to the universalization of representations, techniques, and institutions (this was the case with the nation-state, and even with commodification in its modern forms). It tells us that, at bottom, this process of universalization, far from having only one meaning, was paradoxical and pregnant with all sorts of ambiguities. Moreover, in the Atlantic, the "colony" was added onto the form of power that was the "plantation," the central unit of an earlier age that could be called the age of protoglobalization. Postcolonial theory shows that our global modernity must be thought to have begun much earlier than the nineteenth century—in the period when the commodification of private property began to operate in concert with the commodification of persons, the moment of the slave trade. The age of Atlantic trade was also the age of great migrations, even if these migrations were forced. It was the age of the forced mixing of populations, of the creative scission through which the creole world of great contemporary urban cultures emerged. It was also the age of great planetary experiences. As Paul Gilroy shows in *The Black Atlantic*, and the historians Peter Linebaugh and Marcus Rediker show in *The Many-Headed Hydra*,[97] it was the moment when men, torn from their land, from blood and country, learned to imagine communities beyond territorial bonds, left the comfort of repetition, and invented new forms of transnational mobilization and solidarity. Before the colonies became the great laboratories of modernity in the nineteenth century, the "plantation" already foreshadowed a new awareness of the world and culture.

In addition to these historical factors, there are other levels of theoretical articulation. This is particularly the case where there was dialogue between postcolonial thought and Afro-modern thought from the United States and the Caribbean in particular. This Afro-modern thought is a thought of the *between-two* and of *entanglement*. It declares that one can only appeal to the world when, by force of circumstance, one has sojourned among others. In these conditions, to "return to oneself" is first to "leave oneself": to leave the night of identity, the lacunae of one's little world. This is a way of reading the world that rests on radical affirmation of the importance of proximity, displacement, and dislocation.[98] In other words, consciousness of the world is born out of the actualization of that which was already possible within me, but through my encounter with and responsibility to the lives of others, to seemingly distant worlds, and, above all, to people with whom I seem to have no connection whatsoever—intruders.

But postcolonial theory is equally the thought of a dream: the dream of a new form of humanism, a critical humanism that would be based above all on sharing what differentiates us, this side of absolutes. This is the dream of a *universal* and *métisse polis*. This is what Senghor, in his *Oeuvre poétique* had hoped for: the "renaissance of the world" of which his poem "Prayer to Masks" speaks. For this universal polis to exist, it is necessary that everyone's universal right to inherit the world in its entirety be recognized. Postcolonial thought is a conception of life and responsibility, but through the prism of that which denies them. It is situated in the tradition of certain aspects of black thought (Fanon, Senghor, Césaire, and others). It is an idea of responsibility: responsibility as the obligation to answer for oneself, to be the guarantor of one's actions. The ethics underlying this idea of responsibility depends on one's coming to remember what one became in someone else's hands, the sufferings endured during the time of captivity, when the law and the subject were divided.

Finally, postcolonial thought is not anti-European. It is, to the contrary, the result of the encounter between Europe and the worlds that were its distant possessions. By showing how the colonial and imperial experience was codified in representations and disciplinary divisions—their methodologies and objects—it invites us to an alternative reading of our modernity. It calls on Europe to responsibly live what it says are its origins, future, and promise. If, as Europe has always claimed, the goal of this promise really is the future of all of humanity, then postcolonial thought calls on Europe to constantly open and restart this future, in a singular manner, responsible for itself, for the Other, and before the Other. That having been said, Europe is no longer the center of the world. Its sovereignty has become ancillary. The contemporary world is decidedly heterogeneous—that is, constituted by a multiplicity of nodes governed by the double logic of entanglement and disconnection. This heterogeneity implies the existence of other forms of life and other modes of thinking, other possibilities of life. Today, the Other is no longer what Europe produces and invents when it takes it upon itself to think about itself under the sign of the universal. It is the Other of both absolute heteronomy and radical proximity and similarity. In this sense, postcolonial theory is right to say that the idea of Europe is both something more and something other than its space and past. What defines Europe no longer belongs to it as its own. Thus, universality is here no more than another name for decentering. The threat then becomes confinement within precircumscribed boundaries: obsession with anchorage to the detriment of concern for the Open.

There is what may be called Europe's autobiography, the way in which it writes and designates itself. At bottom, this autobiography (this self-designation) is nothing other than a polemical field. Today, Europe is no longer the center of the world, except in a fictive mode. The center of the world has moved elsewhere. This is the context within which Europe must relaunch the productivity of the metaphors by which it has tried to speak itself and the world, to make itself an Idea. This Idea must continuously be reinterpreted so that it does not become out of date. We must agree to let this Idea be at stake in readings other than Europe's own. It is on this condition that Europe will enrich itself and become a force of fascination. But the measure of this force of fascination will necessarily be its capacity to contribute to the disenclosure of the world. A Europe that, while proclaiming its universal vocation *urbi et orbi*, reinvents itself under the sign of closure does not interest the world or matter to it.

Thus, Europe must be reimagined as a multiplicity with no outer limit, no outside. It is on this condition that Europe will become the mirror of the world and not a fragment—a significant one of course—of the innumerable archives of the world. Europe must find its definition in an unstable game, always other, always undoing any definition—a counterwriting that breaks all closure and that, far from closing the debate, posits itself in the form of an incomplete, open question. This definition must absolutely allow the wholly-other [*le tout-autre*] to be inscribed in the language of being. If Europe wants to treat its own possibilities differently, it must absolutely give a place to the absolutely other. One of these possibilities is writing its own autobiography starting from the Other, in response to the questions the Other asks it. It is by starting from the Other that all writing of the world truly becomes event. Instead of positing itself as the final point of humanity, Europe should thus be attentive to what is coming. Its vocation—if this term has any meaning—is to advance, as Derrida said, exemplarily toward what is not it, toward what is being sought or promised today. Such a Europe must conceive its borders as not given. It must let the unpredictable event come. It is on this condition that it will contribute to the disenclosure of the world.

BIFURCATIONS

To put it succinctly, "decolonization" in the African context has meant *pêle-mêle*: (1) changing curricula, syllabi, or content (this mostly applies to the humanities); (2) changing the criteria for defining what texts are included in or excluded from the canon; (3) changing student demographics while recruiting more black staff and transforming academic and administrative bodies; (4) recalibrating the activities of teaching and learning in such a way as to institute a different power relation between teachers and learners. In the process, an instrumentalist view of knowledge has generally been privileged, which reduces knowledge to a matter of power (which by the way it is—the famous Foucauldian knowledge/power nexus—but only partly). Curriculum reform is spoken about in terms of the rehabilitation of marginalized or defeated narratives, but hardly in response to current shifts in knowledge landscapes. There is hardly any critique of so-called "indigenous epistemologies," and in more than one instance, the latter are simply conflated with traditional cosmogonies or vernacular *arts de faire*, including crafts, narratives, and proverbs.

In some instances, decolonization is easily reduced to a matter of origins and identity, race and location. What confers authority is where one comes from, the putative community one belongs to, not the truth validity of the claims being made. The concept of Africa invoked in most discourses on "decolonization" is deployed as if there were unanimity within Africa itself about what is "African" and what is not. Most of the time, the "African" is equated with the "indigenous"/"ethnic"/"native," as if there were no other grounds for an African identity than the "indigenous" and the "ethnic."[99]

These observations do not constitute sufficient grounds for an outright repudiation of the decolonizing project. After all, an uncompromising critique of the dominant Eurocentric academic model—the fight against what Latin American critics call "epistemic coloniality," that is, the endless production of theories that are based on European traditions—is still necessary. So is the critique of particular forms of anthropological knowledge (knowing about Others) that never fully acknowledge these Others as thinking and knowledge-producing subjects in their own terms.[100]

Boaventura de Sousa Santos and Enrique Dussel, for instance, have argued that *knowledge can only be thought of as universal if it is by definition pluriversal*.[101] They have made it clear, too, that at the end of the decolonizing process, we will no longer have a university. We will only have what they call a "pluriversity."[102] For them, a pluriversity is not merely "the extension throughout the world of a Eurocentric model presumed to be universal and now being reproduced almost everywhere thanks to commercial internationalism." By pluriversity, they understand a process of knowledge production that is open to "epistemic diversity." The end goal is not to abandon the notion of universal knowledge for humanity, but to embrace such a notion via a *"horizontal strategy of openness to dialogue among different epistemic traditions."* Within such a perspective, to decolonize the university is therefore to reform it with the aim of "creating a less provincial and more open critical cosmopolitan pluriversalism"—a task that involves the radical *re-founding* of our ways of thinking and a "transcendence of our disciplinary divisions."

Properly understood (and in spite of its obvious limitations), the "decolonial"/"decolonization" project (just like postcolonial studies, critical race studies, queer studies, disability studies, and feminist studies) has aimed at expanding our conceptual, methodological, and theoretical imaginary. In most instances, it has resisted unified accounts of the human. Downplaying regimes of knowledge that have constituted the human or even the world as one, or have framed humanity as an undifferentiated whole, it has instead sought to map and interrogate the social, cultural, and historical differences and uneven power relations that divide the Anthropos. In this sense, the "decolonial"/"decolonization" project is premised on the idea that social worlds are multiple, fractured, and contested. Thus the need to embrace multivocality and translation as a way to avoid perpetuating the knowledge/power asymmetries that currently fracture global humanity. In this model, knowledge of the empirical world is thought to be gained through the embrace of multiplicity, of a plurality of narratives from silenced voices and invisible places.

Unfortunately, in the "decolonial"/"decolonization" project (just as in some strands of feminist and postcolonial theories), multiplicity has often been theorized as "difference." Difference itself has often been understood as that which separates and cuts off one cultural or historical entity from another. A decolonial act, in this perspective, is taken to be an act of disconnection and separation (a gesture by which one is cut, or one cuts oneself off from the rest). The challenge has therefore been to understand difference not as a secessionist gesture, but as a particular fold or twist in the undulating fabric of the universe—or in a set of continuous, entangled folds of the whole.

Whatever the case, attempts at "transcending our disciplinary divisions" have in fact been happening partly in response to a set of contestations affecting the disciplines that constitute the foundations of modern knowledge. Some of these contestations are of a political nature. In the case of South Africa, they have to do with profound and still unresolved questions of racial justice. They also have to do with the conditions under which the university can be recognized as a truly common, as *public good*, and as such as a microcosm of a society in which each voice counts, which is built on the idea of radical hospitality, cobelonging, and openness as opposed to separation and closure. Of late, such disputes have crystallized around, among other issues, the problem of student debt and the decommodification of higher education. Other such contestations are of a generational nature. Indeed, massive cultural shifts are underway as we increasingly live our lives in reconfigured environments of intense informational stimuli and as digital technologies become tightly woven into the fabric of our everyday life.

As suggested by N. Katherine Hayles and others, we may suspect that a "technologically enhanced rewiring of the brain" is underway, especially among the younger generations.[103] If indeed, as we are led to believe, dealing with digital and computational media on an everyday basis entails significant neurological changes, then the assumptions we used to entertain about humans and their relations to the world may no longer be entirely valid in relation to the kind of self that is emerging among the younger generations.

Other challenges are of an institutional nature. Not so long ago, institutionalized knowledge used to be all that counted. It was an object to be taught in clearly circumscribed institutions and disciplines. Knowledge produced by the university was bounded and restricted by organizational apparatuses. As a matter of fact, there is no boundary for any knowledge today. Extrainstitutional knowledge is unbounded, uncontainable, and easily searchable. It is no longer so easily restricted by organizational apparatuses. To know nowadays requires the development of a range of new literacies made necessary by, for instance, changes in writing, in reading, in forms of public presentation, in the capacity to interpret images or to work on a screen. Old knowledge platforms now appear dated or, in any case, are falling into obsolescence at a higher rate.[104]

Other contestations are of a pedagogical nature, triggered as they are by new learning methods, devices, and publics. Traditional ways of teaching have been changing thanks to a range of new practices and methods enabled by digital environments. The sense, nowadays, is that everything can be searched and found. This is what Google is for, at least in theory—an efficient way to deliver knowledge to the public. Meanwhile, various open-learning platforms are increasingly created by learners themselves. Such platforms challenge the very notion of disciplinarity—how to think properly, the right questions to ask, the right method to deploy in addressing those questions.

Techno-facilitation of knowledge, with flipped classrooms, innovative project works, and collaborative writing, is increasingly becoming the norm. The epoch is characterized by a massive speeding up (acceleration), which contrasts with the humanistic predisposition to slow down. The role of the teacher in its old form might not exist for much longer. Massive open online courses are no longer a rarity. The old vertical teacher-student relationship is increasingly being replaced by the idea of a *learning community*, one in which the teacher gives away control, and learning encompasses the total social experience of the students. Furthermore, it happens inside and outside the classroom, and it takes seriously the knowledge that students already have.

Yet other challenges are of an epistemological nature. It remains to be seen whether the perennial question of what we can know and how we come to know things will ever be resolved. If anything, old disputes are far from having been settled as standard realist, rationalist, and objectivist understandings of truth and knowledge are undercut by the proliferation of new, *hybrid thought styles* and new *thought collectives.*

NEW COGNITIVE ASSEMBLAGES

As a result of technological innovations and the pressures evoked earlier, epistemic reconfigurations, or shifts, are underway in various disciplines and subdisciplines. They are harnessing new kinds of data and reshaping what constitutes units of analysis. New bodies of thought are involved in rethinking the nature of knowledge itself, the nature of being and matter, and how degrees of agency are distributed across human and nonhuman agents. Contrary to various discourses on the crisis of the humanities, the age is characterized by heightened curiosity and accompanying experimentation.

Some of these shifts are paving the way for *the emergence of entirely new cognitive assemblages*, if not new knowledge formations. I would now like to briefly comment on those transformations that have to do with the changing epistemological landscape. Not so long ago, the sciences—theoretical and applied—could still be systematically ordered and classified. For instance, the life sciences and physics, the organic and the inorganic "could be demarcated and located along methodological axes, along a set of pedagogical practices." Now, within every discipline and every field, the ramifications are so manifold that "they subvert any consistent totality." Each specialization ends up turning into further segmentations, which in turn branch out from their classical roots, in a process that incessantly produces subspecializations within subspecializations.[105]

Against this argument, it can be observed that fragmentation has always been part of the life of the disciplines. In fact, disciplines and fields of studies have never been entirely fixed, neither in form nor in organization. They have always been continuously forming and transforming, sometimes merging but never really progressing toward any general unity or truth. But we are clearly witnessing an acceleration of this process today. It has reached a level where many are now wondering whether disciplines as such have become obsolete. Indeed, established disciplines no longer correspond to or encompass the variety of "fields of inquiry." There is a profound disjuncture between the disciplinary taxonomies and classifications inherited from the nineteenth and twentieth centuries and the proliferation of thematic imaginations, the rhythm of the constitution of diverse subfields.

A corollary of fragmentation is the velocity of so-called "turns." The 1980s were marked by the linguistic turn. Nowadays, many "turns" are happening simultaneously—the affective turn, the new materialism turn, the ontological turn, the neurological turn, the Anthropocene turn. To be sure, some of the turns do not last. Others are not "real" turns since they do not affect deeper questions of epistemology or method. They are part of a vast recycling and rebranding of disciplines that go hand in hand with the creeping commodification of education. Yet, all these "turns" must be taken as "alerts," as searches for different *images of thought*.[106]

A crucial factor in the proliferation of fields and subfields of inquiry is that our sense of *who the subject of cognition is* and *what should count as an object of knowledge* is fast changing. Of particular significance, too, is the fact that *entrenched and historic antagonisms between the sciences and the humanities are breaking down*. They are breaking down as a result of the gradual recognition that we humans are not as special as we once thought. Nor are we as disentangled from other species as we once thought. Actually, "the terrestrial sphere is not only mostly populated by beetles and bacteria in terms of biomass," but the future of our species will thoroughly depend on what we do to other species (principle of entanglement and mutuality).[107]

The humanities have traditionally relied on a distinction between society and nature, or between culture and nature. This was reflected in the division of labor between the social sciences and the natural sciences. The social, in this context, usually referred to the aspects of human life, human activity, and human understanding that required some form or another of symbolization. If nature was understood to encompass both subjects and objects, society and nature nevertheless denoted two realms that could be kept analytically distinct—this was the distinction between the symbolic and the presymbolic.

Many still argue for the uniqueness of human nature, or for the idea "that humans occupy a unique position in the scheme of things."[108] They still believe that humans alone are capable of rational thought; they alone have a capacity to feel emotions such as empathy. The ontological turn (which has given rise to new subfields such as posthumanist ethnography, environmental philosophy and history, Earth System science, and other strands of social science research) has severely strained such beliefs. Common to these subfields are the idea of distributed agency and, to some extent, a rejection of the Cartesian dichotomy between subject and object, society and nature, human and nonhuman, living and nonliving entities. The drive nowadays is to perceive the various nonhuman entities with which we interact as sources of agency.

A renewed dialogue between the social sciences, science and technology studies, the life and biological sciences, and philosophy is in the making. It is not without tensions or contradictions. Issues that have primarily been the subject and object of the life and biological sciences are, in different ways, increasingly becoming the subject of theories and methods within the humanities and vice versa. Emergent fields or subfields that span the life and biological sciences and the humanities are engaged in a search for new terminologies and theoretical apparatuses at points of contact and interface, across disciplinary boundaries and traditions.[109] Humanities-inflected inquiries are being reshaped in ways that make them more open to the biological sciences, just at the time when the life and biological sciences are becoming more receptive to the social sciences.[110]

Of late, this incipient convergence has triggered the development of new research agendas. Such agendas overtly privilege ideas of coconstitution, coevolution, and coimplication. They "emphasize the complex, processual, indeterminate, contingent, non-linear and relational nature of phenomena constantly open to effects from contiguous processes."[111] In other words, they start from the assumption that there are no biological or vital processes that are not "simultaneously technical, cultural, symbolic, material, economic, and immaterial."[112] As for the human, not only is its emergence processual. The human is fundamentally an indeterminate entity. At the heart of this incipient convergence is a deliberate attempt not only at breaking down all kinds of distinctions "between human and other life forms, between binary genders, between the social and the natural, the human and the technical, biology and identity, the mind and the body, self and other, material and immaterial, and many other dichotomous forms of thought and practice,"[113] but also at *relocating the apparent newness of the present conjuncture within longer, deeper histories*. Hence the return of deep history as the best way to elucidate the conditions under which the new emerges.

Of late, two important turns have been the ontological turn and the neurological turn. Both call into question a number of foundational categories that the humanities have relied on for the last centuries—the category of *the human* and the category of *the social*, that of *nature* and that of *culture*. Some of the key categories of the humanities—intention, agency, consciousness, mind, brain and language, autonomy, personhood, beliefs, and feelings such as empathy, sympathy, compassion, suspicion, fear, or love—have also been subjected to renewed inquiry, especially by the life and biological sciences.

In fact, "the webs of human social and cultural life that we had come to understand as our particular object of knowledge seem more and more open to being figured neuroscientifically and experimentally."[114] According to Des Fitzgerald and Felicity Callard, many facets of human life that were, for much of the twentieth century, primarily understood through the abstraction of "culture" or "society" "are increasingly understood as functions of the cerebral architecture of individuals or of groups of individuals." Neuroscientists are now seeking to establish the neural mechanisms that underpin almost every single human activity or emotion. For Nikolas Rose, although brains are constitutively embodied through, saturated by, and dependent upon their constant transactions with inputs from without, mental events can now be read in the tissues of the brain.[115]

The changes sketched earlier are not only affecting the nature of matter and the place of embodied humans within a material world, or how human beings are understood in the present. They are also affecting the very forms of knowing and the subject of knowledge. Not long ago, conscious thought was seen as the defining characteristic of humans. Cognition (knowing) involved an awareness of self and others and it was associated with consciousness, symbolic reasoning, abstract thought, verbal language, mathematics, and so on. The act of knowing also included perception and judgment. Today, thanks to progress in disciplines such as cognitive biology, we have a better and more complex understanding of human cognitive ecology.

As Kathryn Hayles suggests, cognition is no longer "limited to humans or organisms with consciousness; it extends to all life forms, including those lacking central nervous systems such as plants and micro-organisms." Being, as it is, the engagement of all life-forms with their environment, cognition is a much broader capacity that "exists beyond consciousness into other neurological brain processes." In other words, there are nonconscious forms of cognition. Cognition, she argues, is not limited to humans and life-forms. It is also pervasive in complex technical systems. In other words, humans and living organisms are not the only important or relevant cognizers on the planet. Technical systems are also endowed with cognitive capabilities. Furthermore, knowledge does not only reside in the brain. It is also acquired through interactions with the environment. It is partly about processing information, discerning patterns, and drawing inferences. We live in an epoch when the informational streams we rely upon to produce knowledge are so massive, so multifaceted and complex, that they can never be processed exclusively by human brains, she concludes.

Cognitive abilities once resident only in biological organisms have therefore now been exteriorized into the world. "Biological and technical cognitions are now so deeply entwined that it is more accurate to say they interpenetrate one another."[116] All of this is happening amid a return to "big questions," the most important of which are what constitutes human life, how we are to communicate between disciplines, between cultures, between human and nonhuman entities, and whether there is anything we hold dear in our ways of living that we might want to preserve, nurture, and foster, while overcoming the existential paradigm that has set us on a fast track to ecological collapse.[117]

KNOWLEDGE IN A COMPUTATIONAL AGE

It is not only the entire knowledge ecology that is fast changing. It is also what actually counts as knowledge. "Computation has changed the ways in which some of the very basic concepts are framed in all the sciences." The conflation of the mind/brain with the computer is the biggest intellectual event of our times. It is at the basis of current reconfigurations of what counts as knowledge. Knowledge has always been tied to the requirement of "empirical validation." Knowledge is that which has to be validated empirically, that which has undergone a methodical, systematic process of empirical verification. No knowledge is free from these constraints. Whatever is free from it represents at best wisdom, but not knowledge as such.

The epoch is in search of deterministic models of human behavior and decision-making. Knowledge is reduced to an understanding of what lies behind people's decision-making, their responses to marketing: the figures of the citizen, the consumer, and the public, and their behavior. It is a conception of knowledge that claims to possess laws that can be discovered through the use of mathematics. Imitating the natural sciences and mimicking physics have been a crucial trend or feature in the human/social sciences since the nineteenth century—the idea that we will gain privileged insight into humanity generally if we follow or apply the laws of physics to human phenomena.

Whether we have transcended that physics envy (hierarchies of knowledge) remains to be seen. In some instances, it is back with vengeance. Take, for instance, economic theory, where this movement mostly gained steam after the Second World War. If we are to believe historians of science, this was the moment when techniques such as linear programming, statistical optimization, matrix methods, formal logic, information theory, game theory, "and a whole raft of techniques were imported into economics." In the 1960s and 1970s, early developments in both electronic computers and programming were consolidated and an entirely new intellectual epoch was rendered possible by the computer, which "jump-started" what today is known as "econometric empiricism," which ranges from "cybernetics as a theory of certain kinds of human/automaton metaphors, to the incorporation of stochastic models in decision theory, to econometrics and simulation."

With the advent of algorithmic thinking and various forms of automated reasoning, new debates are unfolding concerning the faculties of knowing, desiring, and judging, as well as the meaning of truth. The same goes for intuition, understanding, and imagination.[118] Each of the "turns" evoked earlier has paved the way for the rise of new objects of knowledge and new questions about the ways in which the human world can be reimagined in terms of its relation to the Earth. With the end of the human condition as marked by agency, the times are propitious for a return to "big questions" and "deep history"—"big questions" concerning the relation of human life to planetary life, in a context of geological recasting of historical time. The emerging paradigm is that "human societies and the Earth have now forged a tenuous unity." "Planetarity" is the consciousness of that unity and of the entanglement of nature and society.

The "decolonization challenge" must be taken up in relation to these new global developments. We will not expand our theoretical, methodological, and conceptual imaginary by simply resisting unified accounts of the human. It is nevertheless imperative to situate people and social groups within the rich patterns of cultural and historical diversity that made them into who they are. The task of critical thought, social inquiry, and cultural criticism is not only to document and render visible the marked differences in vulnerability among humans. Nor is it only to map and interrogate the social, cultural, and historical differences and uneven power relations that divide the Anthropos.

To be sure, social worlds are multiple, fractured, and contested. Thus the necessity of embracing multivocality and translation as a way of not perpetuating the knowledge/power asymmetries that currently fracture global humanity. Indeed, knowledge of the empirical world is gained through the embrace of multiplicity, of a plurality of narratives from many voices and many places. But multiplicity cannot only be theorized as *difference* or even as *singularity*. Singularity itself must be understood not as that which separates and cuts off one cultural or historical entity from another, but as a particular fold, or twist, in the undulating fabric of the universe. This is crucial if "decolonial acts" are to be anything more than mere "acts of disconnection or separation," if they are to be more than gestures by which one is cut off, or one cuts oneself off, from the world.

The project of decolonization can have appeal only if it refers to a set of continuous topological *folds of the whole*.[119] For "decolonial acts" to achieve their maximum effect, they must work through connectivity and elasticity, continuous stretching, and even distortion. They must attend to the planetary and the biotechnical infrastructures that are reorganizing the boundaries of life on Earth. Why? Because, as we learn from James Baldwin and Édouard Glissant, a fold is never final. It is never a definitive cut. It always requires further folding and twisting, an unlimited diversity of combinations. This is all the more so now given the ways in which the social and the historical, the political, the technological, the ecological, and the multispecies environments are intertwined with biological life.

3

PROXIMITY WITHOUT RECIPROCITY

Why in this century—said to be the century of the unification of the world through the globalization of financial markets, cultural flux, and the mixing of populations—does France stubbornly refuse to critically think about the *postcolony*, that is, in the final analysis, the history of France's presence in the world and the history of the world's presence within France before, during, and after the Empire? What are the political, intellectual, and cultural consequences of France's anxiety about this issue, and what does it tell us about the limits of the French republican model and its claim to symbolize a kind of universalism? What intellectual conditions could make this old, French-style universalism give way to the constantly repressed alternative: a truly cosmopolitan nation, capable of asking—in entirely new terms and on behalf of the world as a whole—the question of *democracy to come*?[1]

To answer these questions, I am starting from the idea that the problematic of the democracy to come is profoundly linked to the fate of the specific institution of the *border*[2]—by which must be understood both the relation between the constitution of political power and the control of spaces, and the more general question of knowing who *is my neighbor*, how to treat an *enemy*, and what to do with the *foreigner*. The difficulty one experiences in "taking responsibility for" these three figures has mostly been linked to what existing democracies have done with the problem of *race*, as we saw in the previous chapter. By having for so long considered the French republican model to be the perfect vehicle for inclusion and for the emergence of individuality, the Republic has ended up becoming an imaginary institution, and its originary capacity for brutality, discrimination, and exclusion has been underestimated.

The fundamental setting for this brutality and this discrimination was the *plantation* under slavery, and then the *colony* beginning in the nineteenth century. In a very direct way, the problem posed by the regime of the plantation and the colonial regime is the problem of the functionality of race as a principle in the exercise of power and as a rule of sociability. In today's context, to evoke race is to appeal to a reflection on the *dissimilar*, the one with whom one shares nothing, or very little—the one who, while with us, next to, or among us, is not, in the final analysis, one of us. Well before the Empire, the *plantation* and the *colony* constituted an "elsewhere." They partook of the "far-off" and foreignness, beyond the seas. And they almost always appeared in the metropolitan imagination as extreme limits.[3] Today, the *plantation* and the *colony* have moved, and have pitched their tents here, outside the walls of the City (in the *banlieues*). This move complicates the definition of the limits of inside and outside and, in so doing, provokes a calling into question of the criteria of belonging, "once it no longer suffices to be a French citizen to be considered entirely French—and European—and treated as such."[4]

Thus, just as colonization, the world it created, and what came after are entangled, so are near and far entangled. The paradox of this presence is that it remains largely invisible at the very moment when one observes close imbrication of the here and there, the generalization of the foreign, and its dissemination and diffusion in space—the consequence of all of this is the aggravation of the fundamental tension in the French republican model. This is not at all a matter of the opposition between universalism and communalism (as the orthodoxy generally tends to think), but between universalism and cosmopolitanism— the idea of a *common world*, a *common humanity*, a *history*, and a *future that one can offer to share*. And it is reluctance to transform this common past into a shared history that explains France's inability to think about the *postcolony.*

My argument will be developed in two phases. First, I will argue that neither the abolition of slavery nor decolonization resolved the problem posed by those who, though they are with us, among us, or near us, are finally not one of us, in spite of a common past. The extension of citizenship to the descendants of slaves or natives did not bring about a profound transformation in France's political representation of democracy. Nor did it lead to a renewal of the modalities of the imagined institution of the nation. This, by the way, is the aporia at the heart of the logic of integration and assimilation that governs many past and current debates over the presence of foreigners on national territory and the belonging of nonwhite French citizens to the Republic. The form of universalism that underlies the French republican idea indeed seems incapable of thinking the Other (the ex-slave, the ex-colonized) "except in terms of duplication, the doubling ad infinitum of a narcissistic image" to which those who are its target are subjected.[5] Despite a rich philosophical tradition concerning the relations between the Other and the Same, archetypes of the Other within contemporary French thought are still very much dependent on figures of the exotic or on purely essentialist categories.

THE DECLINE OF A FROZEN NATION

Decolonization did not bring an end to the question of what to do with a shared past once this past has been more or less disowned. I evoke decolonization not without awareness of the fact that it is a contested term. Indeed, there are many who wonder whether, with the end of formal colonial domination, everything was really called into question and began again, in such a way that it would be possible to say that the former colonies took up their existences anew and distanced themselves from their former conditions. For some, the answer to this question is negative. Colony, neocolony, postcolony: for them, it is all the same theater, the same mimetic games, with different actors and spectators (and sometimes not even!), but the same convulsions and the same abuses. For example, this is the point of view taken by militant anti-imperialists, in whose eyes French colonization in Africa never really ended. It only changed its face, henceforth wearing a thousand other masks.

To support this argument, one cites, pell-mell, the presence of military bases in several countries that were formerly French-occupied, and a long tradition of direct intervention in the affairs of these states; the emasculation of these states' monetary sovereignty through mechanisms like the Franc Zone and cooperation aid; the networking and patronage of their elites through a panoply of cultural and political institutions (the Institutions de la Francophonie or the African Office of the Elysée); the activism of secret services and various rackets, even criminal networks; and direct participation in politics of violence and even in dynamics of a genocidal nature.[6] In spite of the sometimes polemical character of these statements, it would be naïve to pretend that they are all unfounded. France, like every other power in the world, attends to its ideological, strategic, commercial, and economic interests. The primacy of its interests, both public and private, determines its foreign policy to a large extent. Historically, France has been able to exploit its advantage as a former imperial power in order to cement unequal relations with Francophone ruling classes, marked sometimes by brutality, sometimes by venality.

Alexis de Tocqueville recommended this less costly form of domination over the Arabs as early as 1847:

Experience has already shown a thousand times that, whatever the fanaticism and the national spirit among the Arabs, personal ambition and greed have always animated them even more powerfully and caused them accidentally to make those resolutions that are most opposed to their usual tendencies. The same phenomenon has always occurred among half-civilized men. The heart of the savage is like a perpetually agitated sea, where the wind does not always blow from the same direction.[7]

And de Tocqueville called for a policy that would, either by flattering their ambition or by giving them money, make it so that "the same Arabs who displayed the most furious hatred for Christians could suddenly take up arms for them and turn against their compatriots."[8] In sub-Saharan Africa, this "turning of arms" took various forms. In most cases, it occurred within a simple logic of *mutual corruption*. On the African side, the impetus behind this form of venality was the conjunction of two cultural drives that preceded the colonial moment: on the one hand, unlimited desire to acquire goods and wealth and, on the other hand, long-term reproduction of object-related forms of pleasure. However, in many other cases the relation took the form of a pure panoply of racist attitudes barely hidden under the cloak of well-bred paternalism. And France did not hesitate to use direct force, even assassination, in order to perpetuate its interests.

Racism, mixed with paternalism and contempt, and mutual corruption and the game of the apparent servility of African elites were deeply rooted in historical structures of inequality, which an almost ceremonial civility constantly masked and ratified. But inequality constituted both a form of exchange and a form of gift. Within this game of submission, ceremonies, favors, exchanges, gifts, and countergifts made it possible, on the one hand, to create debts and, on the other, to institute networks of reciprocal dependency that were, at the same time, encouraged by relative interculturality.[9] With that said, it would be erroneous to reduce analysis of the political and cultural dynamics of postcolonial Francophone African societies to the relations between their elites and France. In fact, these relations themselves have never ceased changing. This slow transformation has taken an erratic course due to the financial failure of a number of states and the spread of wars of plunder throughout the continent during the last quarter of the twentieth century in particular. The traditional deal-making networks have not entirely lost their ground, but they can no longer act as if Africa were France's "private hunting grounds." In the name of the maintenance of macroeconomic equilibrium (fiscal discipline, control of public debt and inflation), the liberalization of exchanges, and even the struggle against poverty, the weight of international bureaucrats has increased. In reality, though, the reforms that were supposed to lead to more competitiveness have gotten bogged down. The necessities that came out of rearranging debt, processes of structural adjustment, and privatization made multilateral management of the African crisis—and the wars and humanitarian catastrophes that were, if not its cause, at least its corollary—inevitable. The result was an increase in the influence of international institutions (whether financial, like the World Bank and the International Monetary Fund, or specializing in so-called humanitarian aid) and the emergence of a form of governmentality that I have referred to, elsewhere, as "private indirect government."[10]

As a result, Francophone Africa no longer constitutes France's "reserved domain." Even organizations like the Agence française de développement—in other times, one of the privileged tools of France's economic presence in Africa—must now navigate in the wake of multilateral financing institutions. Faced with the constraints that result from its choice to belong to Europe, France is now obliged to lighten the cumbersome and costly arsenal that for a long time made it a full-fledged "African power." As during the colonial period, the dividends France received from this mode of domination today appear entirely trivial. More fundamentally, France is losing (or, in certain cases, has already lost) a very large part of the cultural influence it used to exercise over African elites. This loss is explained in part by its inability to support movements of democratization, and in part by its immigration policy. Today, there is not a single major African intellectual inclined to celebrate the marriage of "Négritude" and "Frenchness," as Léopold Sédar Senghor did not hesitate to do.[11] The principle beneficiary of this defection is, clearly, the United States, which offers three assets that France does not have. The first is the United States' almost unlimited capacity to receive and recycle global elites. Over the last quarter of the twentieth century, American universities have managed to attract almost all the best African intellectuals (including those who have been educated in France), and even French academics of African origin to whom the doors of French institutions were closed.[12] The second asset is racial. The United States carries an immense symbolic advantage with the presence of a black community whose middle and bourgeois classes are relatively well integrated into national political structures and are very visible on the cultural scene. Of course, this community continues to suffer various forms of discrimination. More than other communities, the African-American community is affected by urban poverty. But one need only look at the number of people of African heritage who have, at one time or another, occupied high positions in the army, the federal government, the Senate, the Congress, the leadership of important cities, and the Supreme Court in order to see the distance that, at this level, separates the United States and France. Nothing illustrates this point more than US president Barack Obama; from 2009 until 2017, the United States was led by a man whose father and extended family hailed from Africa.

In many respects, the cultural globalization spearheaded by the United States in domains as varied as music, fashion, and sport is constantly nourished by the products of the creativity of African diasporas established in this country since the time of the slave trade.[13] The first forced displacements during the centuries of slavery were followed by various other migratory movements from the Caribbean and then, beginning in the 1960s, from Anglophone sub-Saharan Africa. By contrast, with the exception of Haitian immigrants, Francophone migrations are recent. Most are linked to the phenomenon of the circulation of elites, which globalization accelerated. They coincide, at the same time, with the anti-immigrant turn so characteristic of Europe in the last quarter-century—an anti-immigration attitude that in Africa has led to rejection of France and what it represents, even if speaking French and the fact of French colonization are factors that serve to differentiate groups of Africans in America. Other migrations are made up of uneducated people who, thanks to their spirit of enterprise, are changing the faces of certain neighborhoods in major American cities—Little Senegal in Harlem, the presence of Ethiopian and Eritrean restaurants in major metropolises, and so on.

Because of the strong presence of people of African origin in the United States, it has become impossible to imagine American identity without reference to the "black Atlantic": that is, without explicitly recognizing the transnational and disaporic foundations of the American nation and the plurality of its heritages.[14] Thus, two philosophies of the nation and presence in the world are opposed: on the one hand, an imagination of the nation that refers to *land* and is thus conceived in terms of borders and territories and, on the other, an imagination that refers to *flux* and is thus largely deterritorialized. Unlike in France, in the United States, the imperative to equality necessary for making everyone a subject with rights and a full-fledged citizen did not necessarily lead to the form of abstraction represented by *legal consecration* of the individual—one of the cornerstones of the French republican fiction. The policies of affirmative action are certainly contested, but they make it possible to guarantee racial minorities and women a certain visibility in the spheres of public and cultural life.

Finally, powerful philanthropic institutions (foundations, churches, and others)—some of which have headquarters on the continent—play a role. Most of them target academic milieus, civil society organizations, the media, and decision-makers (politicians, businessmen). Through the subventions they distribute, the programs they support, and the ethos they promote, these institutions play a considerable role in the "American acculturation" of activists, businessmen, and elite Africans in general. We may sum all this up in a word: the existence of structures of hospitality. This is not to underestimate the reality of racial violence or the persistence of white supremacist ideology in the United States. Nor is it to occlude the effects of the turn represented by the "war on terror." But, that said, these are structures that are lacking in contemporary France.[15] Their absence explains, in part, France's inability to think the postcolony and, beyond that, the contemporary world. By contrast, these structures are what make the American model so attractive to worldwide elites. A cultural gap is widening between African elites in particular and France, whose model, within a Europe building itself on the model of a fortress, seems more and more outdated to them.[16]

Let us now turn to the question of language as it can be seen in the mirror of the French-speaking world. Here, it is important to distance my position from the principal arguments emphasized in the ideological discourse of pan-African nationalisms. According to that discourse, the European languages spoken in Africa are foreign languages imposed by force on defeated and subjected populations. They represent powerful factors of alienation and division. In addition, according to this discourse, they were only imposed on African consciousness by ousting and marginalizing native languages and all the religious, political, and aesthetic reflections they conveyed. At the purely political level, the colonial language would have had the function of imposing the law of a power without authority on a militarily defeated people. To do this, the colonial language needed not only to kill off the native languages that resisted it or erase all traces of them. It also needed to mask its own violence by inscribing it within a system of apparently neutral fictions (humanism, civilization, universalism). This being the case, there could be no political, economic, or technological liberation without linguistic autonomy. On the other hand, cultural emancipation would not be possible without the total identification of African languages, African nations, and African thought.[17]

The powers of language cannot be denied, especially when language operates in the context of imposed encounter, expropriation, and dispossession, as was the case under colonization. In fact, in these kinds of situations, there is always a linguistic equivalent to the "power of the sword" (raids and destruction, torture, mutilations, purification, and profanation). That said, nationalist/pan-Africanist reasoning rests on a series of errors. The first is that it underestimates the fact that, after centuries of gradual assimilation, appropriation, reappropriation, and trafficking, French has become *a full-fledged African language*. This process was quite different from the "Frenchization" of the various regions of mainland France that Fernand Braudel deals with in his study on the identity of France.[18] The languages, religions, and techniques inherited from colonization went through a process of *vernacularization*—an iconoclastic and no doubt in many aspects destructive process, but one that also brought new resources to imagination, representation, and thought.

Finally, far from seeing their powers of figuration shackled or trapped, native languages took advantage of the vernacularization of French. Out of this entanglement, a creole culture characteristic of major African cities is being born. On the linguistic level, *creolity* here consists in a figurative transformation that inevitably implies a relative loss, dissipation, and even obscuring of the native tongue. This dissipation takes place within an abundance of objects, forms, and things. This is why, at the epistemological and cultural levels, creolity means not mimetic production and alienation, as the African discourse of cultural nationalism tends to make one believe, but verisimilitude, onomatopoeia, and metaphor. Now, it turns out that official French discourse on the French language bears similarities to the discourse of pan-African nationalism. It doesn't matter that today the number of French-speakers outside of France is greater than the number of French living in France, or that these days the French language is spoken more outside of France than on French soil. Many French continue to act and to think as if they have exclusive ownership of the language. They are slow to understand that French is now *a plural language*—that, in being deployed outside of the Hexagon, it became richer, was inflected, and put distance between itself and its origins. Because France has hardly decolonized—despite the end of the colonial empire—it continues to promote a centrifugal conception of the universal, one largely out of step with the real evolutions of the world today.

One of the reasons for this cultural narcissism is that the French language has always been thought of in relation to an imaginary geography, where France was the "center of the world." At the heart of this mythical geography, French was supposed to convey, by nature and by essence, universal values (Enlightenment, reason, the rights of man, a certain aesthetic sensibility). This was its task, but also its power: the power to represent thought, which, distancing itself from itself, reflects on itself and thinks itself. In this luminous flash, a certain process of the mind was to be manifested: an uninterrupted movement leading to the appearance of "man" and the triumph of the European and universal *ratio*.[19] Thus, the Republic was to constitute the dazzling manifestation of this mission and the values that underlie it. The marriage of the Republic and language was such that one could say: the language did not only create the Republic (the State); it created itself via the Republic. In an act of transubstantiation, the Republic delegated its mission to a substitute, the French language, which represents and extends it. As a result, to speak or write French in its purity is not only to speak one's nationality—it is to practice, de facto, a universal language. It is to pierce the enigma of the world, to discourse on the *human genus.*

This metaphysical relation to language is explained by the double contradiction on which the French nation-state rests. On the one hand, the marriage of language and State originated in part with the Terror (1793–1794). The *reflex of monolinguism*—the characteristic idea that, since the French language is one, indivisible, and centered on a single norm, all the rest is nothing but patois—dates from this time. In other words, according to this idea, there is one way—and one way only—to access meaning. On the other hand, this marriage came out of the tension— also inherited, at least in part—in the Revolution of 1789 between cosmopolitanism and universalism. This tension is at the foundation of French identity. Universalism *à la française* is not, in fact, the equivalent of cosmopolitanism. To a large extent, the phraseology of universalism has always acted as a screen for the ideology of nationalism and its centralizing cultural model: Parisianism. For a long time, the language was the wrapping for this phraseology of universalism, and both manifested it and masked its most chauvinist aspects. The triumph of English as the contemporary world's dominant language teaches us that excessive nationalization of language necessarily makes it a local idiom: one that thereby transmits local values.

The other reason for the decline of France's aura in Africa and in the world is skepticism (both in the postcolonial world and in the West), if not doubt, about any abstract universal ideal. The anticolonial struggles radicalized this suspicion on the practical level. On the theoretical level, postcolonial critical theory and critical race theory (two intellectual phenomena that in France continue to be wrongly confused with Third-Worldism) have accentuated the lack of credibility of our ideology. Reflection has for a long time proceeded as if *postcolonial critique* of universalism never took place. By taking these two critiques seriously, one would have quickly learned, on the one hand, that universal languages are those that accept their "multilingual" character and, on the other, how much the fate of great world cultures now depends on their ability to translate the idioms of the far-off into something no longer strange or exotic, but familiar.

Then, there was the triumph, in many spheres of culture, of a cosmopolitan sensibility, encouraged in large part by globalization. As we now know, globalization consists as much in putting worlds into relation as in reinventing differences. Ultimately, one of globalization's successes has been the sentiment it gives to each person of being able not only to live out his or her fantasy of what globalization might be, but also to have the intimate experience of difference within the very act by which one subsumes and sublimates difference. In other words, there is a kind of "we" that henceforth takes form at a global scale and especially in the act by which one *shares differences*. The sublimation and sharing of difference are possible because the distinction between language and commodity has essentially been effaced, so to commune with one is equivalent to participating in the other. Language of commodity, commodity *of* language, commodity *as* language, language *in the form of* commodity, language *as* desire, and desire for language as desire for commodity: ultimately, all this is but a single thing, one single regime of signs.[20]

LIQUIDATING RACIAL UNTHOUGHT

The argument I have been developing here leads logically to the conclusion that the presence of the elsewhere in the here, and of the here in the elsewhere, obliges us to reread the history of France and its Empire. Today in France, the dominant temptation is to rewrite this history as a history of "pacification," of "making vacant, masterless territories valuable," of the "spread of teaching," of the "founding of modern medicine," the "creation of administrative and legal institutions, the establishment of road and rail infrastructure." This argument rests on the old idea that colonization was a humanitarian enterprise, and that it contributed to the modernization of ancient societies—primitive societies on their deathbeds that, abandoned to themselves, would perhaps have finished in suicide. By speaking of colonialism in this way, one allows oneself an intimate sincerity, an initial authenticity, so as to better find alibis—in which no one else believes—for rather immoral behavior. As the philosopher Simone Weil emphasized, colonization nearly always begins by the exercise of force in its purest form, that is, by conquest. A people, overcome through force of arms, suddenly has to submit to the control of foreigners of another color, another language, a completely different culture, convinced of their own superiority. Subsequently, as people have to go on living, and living together, a certain stability is created, based on a compromise between constraint and collaboration.[21]

———— ✦ ————

Thanks to revisionism, today we hear claims that the wars of conquest, the massacres, the deportations, the raids, the forced labor, the institutional racial discrimination, the expropriations, and every kind of destruction were just the "corruption of a grand idea," or, as Alexis de Tocqueville explained, "unfortunate necessities."[22]

Reflecting on the kind of war that one could and must lead against the Arabs, this same de Tocqueville affirmed: "all means of desolating these tribes must be employed." And he recommended, in particular, "the interdiction of commerce" and the ravaging of the country: "I believe that the right of war authorizes us to ravage the country and that we must do it, either by destroying harvests during the harvest season, or year-round by making those rapid incursions called razzias, whose purpose is to seize men or herds." We cannot be surprised, then, when he finishes by exclaiming, "God save France from ever being led by officers from the African army!" The reason for this is that the officer who "has adopted Africa as his theater, will soon contract habits, ways of thinking and acting, that are very dangerous everywhere, but especially in a free country. He will pick up the practices and the tastes of a hard, violent, arbitrary, and coarse government."[23]

This, in fact, is the psychic life of colonial power. Colonization is not a "grand idea," but a well-defined type of racial logic in the sense of the treatment, control, and separation of bodies, even species. In its essence, it consists of a war led not against other human beings, but against different species, which must be exterminated if necessary.[24] This is why authors like Hannah Arendt and Simone Weil, after examining procedures of colonial conquests and occupation in detail, have concluded that there is an analogy between them and Hitlerism.[25] Hitlerism, says Weil, "consists in the application by Germany to the European continent, and more generally to the countries belonging to the white race, colonial methods of conquest and domination."[26] To support her argument, she cites letters written by Huber Lyautey from Madagascar and Tonkin.

It is incontestable that, on the cultural level, the colonial order was marked throughout by its ambiguities and contradictions.[27] The mediocrity of its economic performance is widely accepted today.[28] But it is still necessary to distinguish its different periods. After having long relied on concession companies—whose brutality and methods of predation are no longer denied today—France lived for a long time under the illusion that it could build its empire at a low cost (an "empire-on-the-cheap").[29] The colonized had to finance their own servitude. From 1900 on, France rejected the idea of programs to invest in colonial territories, which would have benefited from metropolitan funds and would have made intensive use of African resources. It wasn't until after 1945 that the idea of "developmental colonialism" emerged—and then it was still a matter of an economy of extraction, fragmented and operating on captive markets, out of more or less disjointed enclaves.[30] This project was quickly abandoned for at least two reasons: first, because of the costs, which were judged to be too high, and, next, because in the end imperial logic was simply untenable. In the long term, indigenous demands for civil rights and racial equality within a single political space had the effect of displacing onto the metropolis the costs that the latter was trying to pass on to the colonial territories themselves. This explains, in essence, the decision to decolonize.

It is in part because of the conviction of having established a "beneficial civilization" in the colonies that there is so much difficulty in trying to decipher the contours of the "new French society." This is the case with what is named—in order better to stigmatize it—"communalism." But does the idea that, for example, this "communalism" groups together all the Muslims of France really make sense? Isn't Oliver Roy right to affirm that there is no more a "Muslim community" in France than there is a "Jewish community"—that, instead, there are dispersed populations that are heterogeneous and, overall, not very interested in uniting or even recognizing themselves as primarily religious communities? Does one really believe that it is possible to refound the social bond by making secularism the police of religion or clothes, or that the problems of immigration and integration are above all security problems? How is it that the figure of the "Muslim" or the "immigrant" that dominates public discourse is never the figure of a full-fledged "moral subject," but is rather always based on devaluating categories that treat "Muslims" and "immigrants" like an indistinct mass, which it is therefore permissible to disqualify summarily?

This way of dividing people also explains why it is so difficult to give flesh to the French republican civic model. The process of political figuration is challenging in a society fragmented into a multitude of voices increasingly separated by new social questions: the racial question and the question of Islam. By mutilating the history of French presence in the world and the presence of the world within France, one makes it seem as if the task of producing and instituting the French nation, far from being an ongoing experiment, was completed long ago, and as if it is the newcomers' duty to integrate into an identity that already exists and that is offered to them like a gift, in return for which they must show recognition, "respect for our own foreignness."[31] A similar violence suggests that the French republican civic model found its canonical forms long ago, and that anything that calls into question its ethnic and racializing foundations comes purely and simply from the much maligned project of a "democracy of communities and minorities," of a way of "ethnicizing" questions that are supposed to be above all "social."

The remarks I have just made only appear curious if one has arrived at the impasse that is created by the prodigious logic of closure (cultural and intellectual) that France experienced in the course of the last quarter of the twentieth century. This nationalist and provincial reflux of thought has profoundly weakened France's abilities to think about the world and to contribute decisively to debates on *the democracy to come*. The reasons for this myopia are all too well known, and there is no need to go over them again here. It is enough to mention two. First, with a few exceptions, France has not been able to properly assess the political significance of the turn represented by the irruption, within different fields of knowledge, philosophy, the arts, and literature, of four intellectual currents: postcolonial theory, critical race theory, reflection on diasporas and on all kinds of cultural fluxes, and, to a lesser extent, feminist thought. The contributions of these currents to democratic theory, to the critique of citizenship, and to the renewal of thinking about difference and alterity are indisputable. In this regard, it is crucial to recognize the fact that, historically, the individual constitutes him- or herself through the mediation of a process of subjectivation. In other words, a citizen is someone who can respond personally to the question "Who am I?" and can, in so doing, speak publicly in the first person. Of course, it is not enough to speak in the first person to exist as a subject. But there is no democracy where this possibility is purely and simply denied. On the other hand, because France has neglected the importance of these theories that came from elsewhere (but that were profoundly inspired by the contributions of French philosophy), it has often found itself incapable of enlarging its reflection on the relations between memory and nation. How is it possible, for example, not to see that the *plantation* and the *colony* are both *sites of memory* and *sites of ordeal*? Here, perhaps more than elsewhere, one experiences what the attempt to become a subject or to care for oneself (self-subjectivation) consists in. How is it possible not to see that the *plantation* and the *colony* radically reject the possibility of belonging to a *common humanity*, that cornerstone of the French republican idea?

In the French form of civic humanism (the Republic), the move from the particular I to the universal I (humans in general) is only possible if one abstracts from individuating differences. Within this logic, the citizen is above all someone who is conscious of being a human being equal to all others and who, in addition, has the capacity to discern what is useful for the public good. Currents of thought concerning the encounter with the wider world show, however, that where attachments to the individuating differences of family, religion, corporation, ethnicity, or race have been denied or obliterated by violence and domination, the ascent toward citizenship is not automatically incompatible with such ties. The sentiment of belonging to the *society of the human genus* (the definition of oneself in universal terms) does not necessarily pass through the abstraction of individuating differences. Abstraction of differences is not a condition sine qua non for consciousness of belonging to a common humanity.

The same currents of thought also show that if we want to "open the future to everyone," it is first necessary to perform a radical critique of the presuppositions that encouraged the reproduction of relations of subjection woven under the Empire between natives and colonizers and, more generally, between the West and the rest of the world. These relations were embodied in military, cultural, and economic institutions. But they were above all visible in mechanisms of symbolic coercion, or in the body of knowledge of which Orientalism, Africanism, and Sinology are the best-known examples. Within this perspective, the *democracy to come* is a democracy that will have taken seriously the task of deconstructing imperial sciences that previously enabled the domination of non-European societies. This task must go hand in hand with a critique of all forms of universalism that, hostile to difference and, by extension, to the figure of the Other, attribute the monopoly on truth, "civilization," and the human to the West.

By performing a radical critique of the totalizing thought of the Same, one could lay down the foundations for a reflection on difference and alterity, a practice of conviviality, an aesthetics of plural singularity—the dispersing multiplicity that thinkers like Édouard Glissant or Paul Gilroy constantly refer to.[32] And in this age of unilateralism and good conscience, we could relaunch the critique of every Sovereign who, seeking to pass for the Universal, always ends up producing an essentialist notion of difference as a hierarchical measure and structure intended to legitimize murder and enmity. Such critique is necessary because it opens the way to the possibility of a truly postracial democracy founded on the obligation of mutual recognition as the condition for a convivial life.[33] To use Jean-Luc Nancy's terms, in this type of democracy, equality does not so much consist in "a commensurability of subjects in relation to some unit of measure" as it does in "the equality of singularities in the incommensurable of freedom."[34] In such contexts, enunciating the plural of singularity becomes one of the most effective ways of negotiating the

Babel of races, cultures, and nations that has become inevitable as a result of the long history of globalization.

If France wants to have any influence in the world to come, this is the direction it must take. But taking this direction implies destroying the wall of narcissism (political, cultural, and intellectual) that it has erected around itself—a narcissism whose unthought comes from a form of racializing ethnonationalism. This desire for provincialism is all the more surprising in that it is flourishing under the protection of a political tradition that, more than any other in the history of modernity, has displayed radical solicitude for "man" and "reason." It so happens that, historically, this solicitude for the fate of "man" and "reason" quickly showed its limits each time it was necessary to recognize the figure of "man" in the face of an Other disfigured by the violence of racism. The dark side of the Republic, the inert depth where its radicalness is bogged down, is still and always *race*.[35] Race is the obscure page where, placed by the force of the Other's gaze, "man" finds it impossible to know the essence of his work and of the law. In France itself, an inviolable tradition of abstract universalism, inherited from the Revolution of 1789 and the Terror, never stopped denying the brutal fact of race, on the pretext that claiming a right to difference—any difference—contradicts the French republican dogma of universal equality. In fact, the force of the republican ideal is constituted, in principle, by its attachment to the project of human autonomy. As Vincent Descombes explains, the project of human autonomy is the project of a "humanity that would posit the principles of its behavior on the basis of itself."[36] But this tradition pretends to forget that "man" always appears in different and singular figures, and that no theory of the subject could be complete if it forgets that the subject is only apprehended in a distancing of the self from the self and cannot be realized except in a positive relation to an elsewhere.

AN ETHICS OF ENCOUNTER

Second conclusion: If the life of democracy participates in an operation—which must constantly be taken up again—of representing the social, then we may affirm that making oneself heard, knowing oneself, making oneself recognized, and speaking of oneself constitute central aspects of every democratic practice. As an expressive enterprise, as the ability to give oneself a voice and a face, democracy is, fundamentally, a practice of representation—a distancing from others in order to imagine oneself, express oneself, and share, within the public space, the imagination and forms that this expression takes. From this point of view, it is difficult to claim that the French ideal of civic humanity has been realized while a portion of its citizens are literally excluded from the public esteem we dispense daily in, as the French historian Pierre Rosanvallon says, "the form of a quota of presence in cultural institutions, educational programs, media entertainment, public parades," and other policies of assistance.[37]

Once again, I am emphasizing that normative individualism largely conceals the unequal and culturally structuring effects of racism. Racism is profoundly inscribed in the ordinary mode of social relations and, above all, in bureaucratic routine. One of the ways of masking it in the ideological field consists precisely in contrasting universalism and differentialism (communalism) or in limiting oneself to abstract reaffirmation of the equality of each individual before the law.[38] For the *democracy to come* to have meaning and form, and in order for this nation that is beginning to be created to emerge in its scattering multiplicity, before our eyes, a new, enlarged economy of representation that takes into account all forms of the production and affirmation of collective identities is necessary. For the moment, too great a mass of citizens, obscure and invisible, is literally akin to foreigners in the public imagination—in an era where the figure of the foreigner is dangerously confused with the figure of the enemy. In these conditions, one can no longer assume that the problem of misrepresentation will be corrected by our capacity to act and speak on behalf of others. What must be dissipated is the opacity that surrounds the presence, in France, of citizens rendered invisible by mechanisms that every day produce forms of exclusion justified by nothing other than race.

Recognition of differences is hardly incompatible with the principle of a democratic society. Such recognition does not mean that society henceforth functions without shared ideas and beliefs. In fact, this recognition constitutes a veritable precondition for these ideas and these beliefs to be truly shared. After all, democracy also signifies the *possibility of identification with the Other*. Without this possibility of identification, the Republic is inoperative. Moreover, the process of becoming a subject—which I have said is fully part of becoming a citizen—passes through, among other things, freely proclaimed particularisms. It is precisely the subjectivation of particularities that globalization makes possible. What, indeed, is it to be oneself in the age of globalization, if not to be able to freely proclaim such and such particularity—the recognition of that which, within the nation common to us, the world common to us, makes me different from others? And, in fact, one may suggest that recognition of this difference by others is precisely the mediation through which I make myself their relation. It thus appears that, at bottom, the *sharing of singularities* is indeed a precondition to a *politics of relation and of the in-common*.

Furthermore, as Jean-Luc Nancy explains, singularity is both what we share and what separates us. To recognize the singularity of the sites of ordeal that served as starting points from which we have historically defined ourselves as a nation does not mean that "differences in being" separate us from one another. This is why Nancy defines "fraternity" as "equality in the sharing of the incommensurable,"[39] but the incommensurable is what is proper to each of us. There is no "we," he says, except in the "'each time, only this time'" of singular voices.[40] And he concludes that *being-in-common* arises fundamentally from *sharing*.[41] Moreover, making up the deficit in representation or breaking the monistic platform of French public culture is not the same as supporting a politics whose foundation would be primarily ethnic, racial, or religious, or the same as supporting cultural practices that are manifestly contrary to human rights. After all, the refusal to validate the biologization, ethnicization, or racialization of the social is legitimate. But this refusal is only possible if one addresses the question of misrepresentation. And only the transition to cosmopolitanism can defeat, on the one hand, a democracy of communities and minorities and, on the other, its masked double: a democracy imbued with its own racial prejudices, but blind to the acts by which it practices racism.

Third conclusion: Just as, since the nineteenth century, the fate of democracy has played out around the figure of the individual endowed with rights independent of qualities such as social status, so the *democracy to come* will depend on the answer we give to the question of knowing *who my relation is, how to treat an enemy,* and *what to do with foreigners.* The "new question of the Other" in all its forms—or, the presence of others among us, the appearance of *the outsider*—is thus placed back at the heart of the contemporary problematic of a human world, of a politics of the world. In these circumstances, the philosophical questions raised by Maurice Merleau-Ponty not so long ago still have all their political topicality: "how can the word 'I' be put into the plural . . . how can I speak of an I other than my own?"[42] Whether we like it or not, things today and in the future are such that the appearance of *the outsider* in the field of our common life and our culture will never again take place in the mode of anonymity. This appearance condemns us to learn to *live exposed to one another.*[43]

France has the means to slow this increase in visibility. But, at bottom, it is inevitable. Thus, it is necessary to symbolize this presence as quickly as possible, in such a way that it enables a circulation of meaning. This meaning will emerge at a distance both from a simple juxtaposition of singularities and from a simplistic ideology of integration. If, as Jean-Luc Nancy maintains, *being-in-common* comes from sharing, then the democracy to come will be founded not only on an ethics of encounter, but also on the sharing of singularities. It will be built on the basis of a clear distinction between the *universal* and the *in-common.* The universal implies a relation of inclusion in some already constituted thing or entity. The essential feature of the *in-common* is communicability and shareability. It presupposes a relation of cobelonging between multiple singularities. It is thanks to this sharing and this communicability that we produce humanity. Humanity does not already exist premade.

A final word: By arguing that what separates is also what goes together, I have rejected both a certain Anglo-Saxon form of multiculturalism (the logic of commingling, of juxtaposition, and of segregation) and a certain kind of French narcissism (the logic of duplication, but duplication that does not prevent discrimination). We must now bring this reflection to an end by emphasizing that if, as Nancy suggests, justice must be done both to the singular absoluteness of the proper and to the common impropriety of all, then democracy must once again find what, at the origin, has always made it an ethical event. Here, it is perhaps necessary to begin by rediscovering the body and face of the other, inasmuch as they represent not only the speaking traces of the other's existence, but also that which makes the other if not my *neighbor* [*prochain*] then at least my *fellow* [*semblable*]. This is perhaps the condition for carrying out the task of the political refiguration of the social, which can no longer be deferred. As for the strength of the French model of universalism, it will come from an ability to invent ever-new forms of human coexistence. This other way of understanding the meaning of the human today constitutes the precondition for any *politics of the world*. This politics of the world rests on our concern for the unicity of every one, expressed by the face of every one. Thus, responsibility for others and for the past will set in motion discourse on justice and democracy and our practices of them.

4

THE LONG FRENCH
IMPERIAL WINTER

I n the rest of the world, the postcolonial turn in the social sciences
and humanities took place almost a quarter of a century ago. Since
then, postcolonial theory has had an influence in numerous political, epistemological, institutional, and disciplinary debates in the United
States, Great Britain, and many regions of the Southern Hemisphere
(South America, Australia, New Zealand, the Indian subcontinent, South
Africa).[1] From its birth, postcolonial theory has been the object of quite
varied interpretations and has, at more or less regular intervals, provoked
waves of polemics and controversies—which continue today—as well as
objections that are totally in contradiction with one another.[2] It has also
given rise to intellectual, political, and aesthetic practices that are just
as abundant and diverse, so much so that one sometimes has reason to
wonder what constitutes its unity.[3] Notwithstanding this fragmentation,
one may say that at its core, the object of postcolonial theory is what may
be called the *entanglement of histories and the concatenation of worlds.*
Slavery and in particular colonization (but also migrations and the circulation of forms, imaginaries, goods, ideas, and people) have played
decisive roles in this process of the collision and entanglement of peoples. Therefore, it is for good reason that postcolonial theory has made
them the privileged objects of its inquiries.

The best postcolonial thought does not consider colonization to be an immobile, ahistoric structure or an abstract entity, but instead a complex process of invention of borders and interspaces, zones of passage and interstitial places, places of transit. At the same time, it emphasizes that as a modern historic force, one of colonization's functions has been the production of subalternity. Various colonial powers instituted, in their respective empires, subordination based on racial and legal statuses that were differentiated, and that always, in the final analysis, produced inferiority. In return, in order to articulate their demands for equality, many colonial subjects had to undertake a critique of the wrongs that the law of race and the race of the law (as well as the law of gender and sexuality) had contributed to creating. Thus, postcolonial thought examines the work performed by race, gender, and sexuality-based differences in colonial imaginaries, and their functions in the very process of producing colonial subjects. It is also interested in analyzing phenomena of resistance scattered throughout colonial history, in various experiences of emancipation and their limits, and in the ways in which oppressed peoples constitute themselves as historic subjects and have their own influence on the constitution of a transnational and diasporic world. Finally, postcolonial theory is concerned with the way in which the traces of the colonial past are, in the present, objects of symbolic and practical work, and with the conditions in which this work gives rise to unprecedented hybrid or cosmopolitan forms in life, politics, culture, and modernity.

DISCORDANCE IN TIME

Thanks to a more or less watertight compartmentalization of disciplines, a more or less accentuated provincialism of knowledge produced and distributed in mainland France (which has for a long time been masked by the exportation of luxury intellectual products such as Sartre, Lacan, Foucault, Deleuze, Derrida, and Bourdieu), and cultural narcissism,

France has long remained at the margins of these new, planetary voyages of thought. Until recently, postcolonial thought has been, if not scorned, little known in this country. Is this cavalier indifference or simple insolence coupled with ignorance? Calculated ostracism or mere accident? It nevertheless remains the case that until the beginning of the millennium, postcolonial theory was not the object of informed critique nor of any debate worthy of the name in France.[4] And, apart from a few texts by Edward Said, almost no works by theoreticians identifying as part of this current of thought or its various tributaries (subaltern studies, for example) were translated.[5]

The fact is that while postcolonial thought is on the rise in Anglo-Saxon academic and artistic milieus, France's politics and culture, advancing in the opposite direction, are entering what one could call a sort of "imperial winter." From the point of view of intellectual history, this winter is characterized by a series of "disconnects," anathemas, and great excommunications, ending in the relative retreat of a truly planetary French thought. From this point of view, we can see the great significance of the break with Marxism and with a conception of the relations between the production of knowledge and activist engagement inherited not from the 1960s, as one often tries to delude us into believing, but from a long history tightly bound up with the history of labor movements, internationalism, and anticolonialism. In fact, because the Empire was deeply inscribed in French identity, especially between the two world wars, its loss (and in particular the loss of Algeria) appears in the national imagination, suddenly deprived of one of its sources of pride, as a veritable amputation. With the end of colonization, France fears having only a provincial place in the world's balance. Imperial history—whose functions included singing the glory of the nation, painting its gallery of heroic portraits with images of conquests, epics, and exotic representations—is relegated to a peripheral and marginal region of national consciousness. Considered by some to have been a great waste, useless death and suffering, and by others a source of shame and guilt, the Empire is now only of concern to the most reactionary sectors of French society who, from the margin, attempt to preserve its memory in nostalgia and melancholy.

In contrast, postcolonial French historiography now tends to treat colonization as no more than "an important but finally belated and 'exogenous' moment in a very long 'indigenous' history."[6] As if it were necessary to get rid of colonization as quickly as possible, no central place is made for it within French thought, where it now plays only an external role, since it is relocated and situated on the other side of the border, as if to mark the disappearance of the Other caused, it is thought, by decolonization. Even more seriously, a certain criticism endeavors to attribute what it calls the "defeat of thought" in France to decolonization. According to this criticism, this defeat is most clearly expressed in the deconstruction of the two signature concepts of Western modernity, reason and the subject, and, during the 1960s in particular, in the various deaths of man, meaning, and history. On the other hand, according to these same critics, this "defeat" is the consequence of the refutation of Western ethnocentrism, legitimized by decolonization. This refutation—which they see as a way of demonizing the West and saddling it with guilt—has, according to them, led to the dissolution of "man," the "'unitary concept of universal significance,'" and the replacement of this concept with the "different man," the cornerstone of cultural diversity without hierarchy.[7] Cultural relativism and the crumbling of the human subject into a series of irreducible singularities in turn, they argue, facilitated the birth of projects for the radical transformation of society, which are incarnated in Third-Worldism and leftism.[8]

At the moment when, leaning on poststructuralism, psychoanalysis, and a tradition of critical Marxism, postcolonial thought is taking off in the Anglo-Saxon world, many thinkers who could have been interested in it—including some who had previously been Communist Party activists or sympathizers, or who had been associated with radical or anti-imperialist organizations—are eager to be done with leftism, Marxism, and their avatars, first among which they place "Third-Worldism."[9] On the left in particular—where struggles and "just causes" had been closely identified with the Communist Party—one is trying to get away from unconditional adherence to Marxist dogma, in order to formulate new critical positions that would make it possible to think Stalinism and the politics of the Soviet Union in terms that do not purely and simply repeat the language of the right, and that do not open the way to a new phase of nationalist exaltation. In this context, Third-Worldism is seen sometimes as expiatory activism, sometimes as self-hate and hatred of the West. This polemical category is arising in France at a moment when the failure of the revolutionary project in the non-European world can no longer be doubted, while in France the ideology of the rights of man is enjoying increasing popularity. Moreover, some intellectuals formerly associated with Marxism oppose a "morality of extreme urgency" (humanitarianism) to the traditional anti-imperialist understanding of international solidarity.[10] This morality emphasizes occasional interventions in places where, in response to the destitution of the world, the project was previously to build socialism. The conviction now is that there will be no nontotalitarian socialism outside the West. In such conditions, it is no use wanting to transfer Western aspirations and revolutionary utopias to non-European countries' movements of struggle.

It is in this context that, with sarcasm heaped on him, Jean-Paul Sartre and, through him, an entire tradition of anticolonial thought have become objects of resounding rejection.[11] Previously, Frantz Fanon, almost condemned to ostracism, was beginning his long purgatory, but his work now only arouses the interest of marginal and quickly stifled voices. Regarding Césaire, the sanctimonious elite wants nothing to do with his *Discourse on Colonialism*, and even less with *The Tragedy of King Christophe* (1963) or *A Season in Congo* (1966).[12] It wants to keep only the image of the man who, turning his back on the sirens of independence, chose to make his island a territorial department of France. Except for in Sartre, de Beauvoir, and few scraps of Derrida, neither of the two great movements to deconstruct race in the twentieth century—the civil rights movement in the United States and the global struggle to end Apartheid— left any salient marks on the leading lights of French thought. Thus, discussing the racial state at the end of the 1970s, Michel Foucault did not have a single word for South Africa, which, at the time, represented the only "really existent" archetype of legal segregation.[13] It is, moreover, in America, and not in Paris, that Maryse Condé, Valentin Mudimbe, and Édouard Glissant—great French or Francophone figures identified with postcolonial thought, even if they do not entirely recognize themselves within it—found refuge and recognition, even accolade.

A part of French colonial humanism consisted in identifying and recognizing the multiple faces of humanity and the countless physiognomies of the Earth in the traits of the peoples France had subjugated. Among colonial reformers in particular, the recognition of differences between human groups did not at all prevent the construction of an asymmetric fraternity. The colonial enterprise itself had been a relatively multiracial affair.[14] From the district commander to the interpreter and the governor, from the colonial infantryman requisitioned during wars of conquest or "pacification" to the deputy at the Palais-Bourbon and the minister of the Republic, the public face of the French Empire was far from being entirely pale.[15] By the beginning of the 1980s, this medley of colors was no more than a distant memory. The project of assimilation—which had been one of the cornerstones of French colonial humanism and which had gained the deep support of many colonial subjects, more so than one often wants to admit—had practically been abandoned in the aftermath of decolonization. Minorities were gradually swept under the carpet, covered with a veil of modesty that hides their visibility in the political and public life of the nation. As for former French possessions in Africa in particular, they are abandoned to their tyrants, to whom the French ruling classes freely give their political and ideological support, by way of corruption and military interventions. Those dissidents who, like the Cameroonian writer Mongo Beti, denounce neocolonial violence from the margins are derided and practically howl in the wilderness.[16] When marginalization is not enough to make them see reason, one does not hesitate to turn to censorship in order to quiet them.[17]

One observes the same process of the recentering of thought on the French mainland in criticism of what is called—in order to stigmatize it—*la pensée 68*. This thought is decried at the very moment when poststructuralism and "French theory" are inflaming the academic imagination in the rest of the world. If Foucault, Derrida, Barthes, Lacan, and others inspire a certain approach to postcolonial thinking, in France these authors are put on "trial" at the very moment when this current of thought is causing their works to be reread in the rest of the world—more proof of the discordance in time. Indeed, they are accused, pell-mell, of being the gravediggers of the Enlightenment and enemies of humanism. They are reproached with having destroyed meaning and transcendence, with having encouraged the advent of action without subject, and with having invented a world and a history that completely elude us.[18] Furthermore, a significant part of the intelligentsia—put off by the unhappy spectacle of the consequences of independence and the authoritarian drift of the new regimes, convinced that it has essentially gone astray, and determined to forget, even deny, its past engagements with the anticolonial cause—constantly admits its guilt and thinks it can find its new road to Damascus in the antitotalitarian crusade.

But, in reality, this great redistribution on the conceptual map, and the decisive transformation of ideological space that resulted from it, began well before decolonization properly speaking. Decolonization served above all to accelerate a dynamic underway in the middle of the 1930s. Already at the time, Christian democrats, certain liberals, and dissidents on the left were questioning the nature of the Soviet Union and the temptations threatening liberal democracy.[19] After the Second World War, with the end of Nazism, a significant part of French thought found itself confronted with the question of Communism in its Stalinist version.[20] But it was over the course of the Cold War period that the passage from antifascism to anti-Communism reached the point of no return. Within the French intelligentsia, the interpretation of international relations henceforth took place within the framework of the antagonism between capitalism and communism on the one hand, and between liberal democracy and totalitarianism on the other.[21] With events like the trials of Kravtchenko and Rousset, the Hungarian Revolution, and the Prague Spring, this dynamic reached its culminating point in the 1950s, and then returned with renewed vigor in the 1970s, when the penitents of the "class struggle" (intellectuals with various trajectories and interests, but who all came out of or were near to Marxism-Leninism) made the shift from philo-Communism and secular faith in socialism to invoking dissidence and the rights of man. Against the background of a crisis in relations between intellectuals and left-wing parties, they seized on the concept of "totalitarianism," which they used for polemical political activism and as a plea for dissidence and human rights within the countries of the Warsaw Pact.[22] The advent of postcolonial thinking during the last quarter of the twentieth century thus coincided with the attempt, in France, to exit from Marxisms (both official and oppositional) and to bring thinking into line with the antitotalitarian project.[23] Contrary to Hannah Arendt's intuitions, most French theories of totalitarianism forget not only Fascism and Nazism, but also colonialism and imperialism. The fact is that the theoretically impoverished concept of "totalitarianism" functions above all—with few exceptions—as a bludgeon. Its elaboration is subordinated to the imperatives of domestic French politics, and it is used above all to prepare the indictment of Marxism.[24]

The factors I have briefly mentioned have slowed the diffusion of postcolonial theory in France and, in addition, have greatly clouded its reception. We must still add what could be called the "epistemic" reasons for this. These reasons have to do with the conditions and modalities of the production of knowledge about extra-European worlds in the social sciences and humanities during colonization and after decolonization. As the French historian Pierre Singaravélou has shown, the years between 1880 and 1910—the culmination of scientism and colonial expansion—correspond to the moment of the institutionalization of knowledge about the colonies and colonized populations.[25] The main object of the "colonial sciences" in France (history, geography, legislation, economy) was the "backward races."[26] The principal function of these sciences was, on the one hand, to contribute to displaying human diversity and, on the other, to elevate this primitive humanity to the level of "evolved peoples" through knowledge.[27] Three postulates lay at the foundation of these sciences: evolutionism, differentialism, and primitivism.[28] If the "colonial sciences" properly speaking gradually disappeared from the scene in the aftermath of decolonization, they were often replaced by the "Cold War sciences." The "great partition" that presided at their birth and that justified a veritable apartheid not only of knowledge but also of institutions persists. Whether it is a matter of historic, geographic, legal, economic, ethnographic, or political disciplines, the valorization of difference and alterity constitutes, from an epistemic point of view, the cornerstone of all cognitive ordering of extra-European worlds.

Difference is the epistemology on which these "sciences" are based. This explains, in large part, the segregation between discourses and knowledge concerning formerly colonized worlds and discourses and knowledge about mainland France. Moreover, because the space conceded to extra-European studies is one of the smallest in the French academic and cultural system, these studies are scarcely integrated into either the "national library of knowledge" or a true world history.[29] To the contrary, a topography of knowledge based on a new division of the world into "cultural areas" (area studies) now dominates. The same logic of discrimination and confinement is found in institutions and publishing houses. Institutions and research centers that deal with extra-European worlds function like ghettos within the university system, while the majority of scientific works or articles concerning postcolonial worlds are, in most disciplines, confined to a separate group of journals and publishing houses.[30]

Intellectually and culturally, France is now looking to places other than the Empire and the vestiges of its resources to nourish patriotism and feed its "imaginary function." Perhaps France is not completely withdrawing into its mainland. But it is by basing itself in the Hexagon, which now serves as a filter, that France is undertaking its reading of itself and the world. Between 1980 and 1995, a generation of academics trained in French institutions and made up in large part of French citizens "of color" and minority nationals from former colonial possessions began to draw the consequences of this cultural and intellectual winter. Having run up against "monocolorism" and the mandarin and bureaucratic system in force in universities and research centers, they are emigrating to the United States, where, whether it is a matter of the linguistic turn, the self-reflexive moment in anthropology, feminist criticism, or critical race studies, a veritable effervescence has seized the humanities and social sciences. These thinkers draw their resources from the encounter of Afro-American and English-speaking Caribbean thoughts, from Sino-Indian and Latin American worlds, and from the new interpretations of French history and literature that are emerging in the American academy.[31]

TREMORS OF PLURAL EXPRESSIONS

The foregoing remarks are not part of a logic of indictment. They aim to contextualize not only the lag in the reception of postcolonial studies in France, but also France's lag in relation to a world that, now that decolonization has been completed, is reconstituting itself on the model of scattered and diasporic fluxes.[32] While France leans on its traditional problematics of "assimilation" and "integration," elsewhere the problematic of "alternative modernities" is privileged.[33] It was at the beginning of the 1990s that France timidly began to shake off its postcolonial languor. As is often the case, this movement began from the margins of society. A tremor was first seen in the artistic and cultural domain. The grafting of elements of African-American popular culture onto the popular culture of the *banlieue* began to produce effects among young minorities. This is notably the case in the spheres of music, sports, fashion, and personal style.[34]

The golden age of African-American presence in the heart of Paris (from 1914 to the 1960s) is certainly over.[35] The very long period of the dominance of jazz, reggae, and rhythm and blues is at its end, and the eruption of hip-hop and the reception of different varieties of rap are hardly lacking in ambiguity. But some of the leading figures of this new form of expression are giving this musical genre an undeniable political tone.[36] This new aesthetic sensibility is also fed, though indirectly, by the gradual domination of soccer (the most popular sport in France) by black and Arab-origin athletes. Moreover, some of these athletes do not hesitate to intervene in debates about racism or citizenship.[37] Like certain black figures in American basketball and in American and Caribbean track and field, they are role models, at least among the *banlieue* youth confronted with contradictory processes of self-identification and burning with a frenetic desire to participate in consumer society, of which global black culture has become a plane-tary index.[38]

The rustling can also be observed in the new forms that minorities' struggles are taking, whether these minorities belong to the category of intruders and complete outsiders (illegal or legal immigrants) to whom the right to have rights is refused, or to the category of the have-nots [sans-parts] of French democracy: those who, though nominally French, consider themselves nevertheless deprived of full and complete enjoy-ment of the symbolic benefits attached to citizenship, beginning with the *right to visibility*. The fact is that since the 1970s, groups of extreme right-wing thinkers have been developing the idea that French national identity is soiled by immigrants. First stirred up by the Front National party, this idea is little by little winning over the French right and is infiltrating a significant part of the left, even the extreme left. Though after the butchery of two world wars France did indeed organize immi-gration in order to respond to the pressing need for manpower in its industries, this immigration was effectively stopped after the oil crisis of 1974. Since then, there has been only limited immigration to France: family reunification, asylum recipients, students, tourists, and illegal immigrants.

However, although immigration is now only marginal, laws continue to grow harsher during this period of freeze, with each minister of the interior making it his or her duty to pass one or more anti-immigration laws, each more draconian than the last. In addition to creating barri-ers at entry, one of the immediate consequences of this cascade of legis-lative measures of repression is to render the lives of foreigners already settled in France more precarious each time. Moreover, the accumula-tion of laws and the surge of regulations have, over the last twenty years, produced a considerable number of undocumented persons whom the state is trying to track in the name of the struggle against illegal immi-gration.[39] France now prides itself on its "deportation quotas."[40] In this context, some no longer hesitate to speak of "state xenophobia."[41]

If the main goal of the first form of mobilization was the right to have rights (beginning with the right of residence in France), the second mobilization (which emerged near the end of the 1990s) is a struggle for visibility and against minoritization and stereotypes. It indirectly attacks a major unspoken premise of the French republican model: the implicit "whiteness" of being French. Indeed, in the name of the French constitutional principle of equality between individuals, differences of origin, race (ethnicity), gender, or religion between individuals and groups cannot be taken into account. The Republic tries to be secular and "color blind." The imperative to equality required "to make each person a subject of right and a full-fledged citizen implies considering people in a relatively abstract manner. All their differences and distinctions must be kept at a distance so that they are only considered in their common and essential quality: as autonomous subjects."[42] As a consequence of this radical indifference to differences, collecting "ethnic statistics" is prohibited by law, and any even vague attempt at affirmative action is decried.[43] The perverse effect of this indifference to differences is a relative indifference to discrimination.

In this respect, until the end of the 1990s, the media in general and television in particular constituted the principal scene of a double symbolic violence: on the one hand, the violence of indifference and minoritization; on the other hand, the violence implied in the production of stereotypes and racial prejudices. At the time, minorities were certainly not invisible on television. But, when they broke onto the screen, it was on music or sports shows. Blacks in particular often only appear onscreen and in the public sphere as actors, singers, or entertainers. When they appear in fiction, it is almost always in American, not French, fiction. The same is true of advertisements and shows about everyday life. Soccer players and other athletes fare no better. They are compared to modern *tirailleurs*, whose bodies and physical strength are entirely dedicated to the flag, but who are constantly suspected of not wanting to sing the national anthem at the top of their voice.

The staging of Arabs obeys a parallel logic. Prejudices about their violent nature and uncontrollable drives constitute enduring elements of historical apparatuses of stigmatization. Due to their supposed propensity to rape, young Arab males of North African descent are a source of fear both within and outside their communities.[44] Islam itself is apprehended less as a religion than as a culture, and, when it is seen as religion, its theology is that of a vehement, angry God, irrational and enamored with blood. The countless controversies over the "Islamic veil" or the *burqa* are saturated with the Orientalist imagery once denounced by Said. These controversies make it possible above all to stage scenes showing the violence that *those* men do to *those* women—violence that does not resemble "*our* violence": circumcision, forced marriage, polygamy, the law of older brothers, the wearing the veil, tests of virginity. One pities the vulnerability of "Muslim women." But, above all, it is feared that French women, threatened in the public space by nonwhite and non-Christian aggressors, might also become the objects of exogenous sexist violence.[45]

As for the production of stereotypes, it aims to refer minorities back to their origins "elsewhere" (as opposed to here) and to attribute to them an irreducible alterity. These stereotypes are then recycled and reinterpreted as constitutive of their essential foreignness.[46] Moreover, if minorities were to be truly integrated into society, this very foreignness would risk contaminating French identity from within. Thus, the French feminist writer Élisabeth Badinter can claim that the full veil symbolizes "absolute refusal to enter into contact with the other, or more precisely the refusal of reciprocity. . . . Within this possibility of being looked at without being seen, and oneself being able to look at the other without the other seeing me, I perceive from my point of view the satisfaction of a triple pleasure over the other in nonreciprocity, exhibitionist pleasure, and voyeuristic pleasure. . . . I think that these are very sick women, and I am speaking very seriously, and I don't think we should define ourselves on the basis of their pathology."[47]

In contrast to people of "French stock," minorities are seen as characterized by the exoticism of their customs, costumes, and cuisines—the tropicality of their places of origin, the fruits and scents to which numerous ads refer, whether ads for tourist destinations or those that display cacao, bananas, vanilla, camels, or sunny beaches. The logic of these representations is to "refer nonwhite French back to the [geographical, climatic, or] cultural causes of their failure to integrate into the nation."[48] The repeated use of the adjective *ethnic* to name them as well as to designate their practices is thus strategic. On the one hand, "ethnic" can only be understood in reference to the assumption that "white French are not 'ethnic.'"[49] On the other hand, the word seeks to emphasize the impossibility of assimilating them. It was against this symbolic apparatus that, in 1998, the Collectif Égalité, made up of black artists and intellectuals, rose up.[50] The starting point of the struggles for visibility and against minoritization is the idea that the French nation does not already exist, fully formed: it is in very large part the sum of the contradictory identifications claimed by its members. These members create the nation concretely, through the way in which these contradictory forms of identification are staged and recited. And, far from constituting an obstacle to the existence of a public space, these contradictory forms are resources for deepening the relation between democracy, reciprocity, and mutuality.

It was also at the beginning of the 1990s that parallel initiatives in the academic field began to take shape. A young generation of historians is beginning to take interest in the exchange of views between (ex-)colonies and (ex-)Metropole, the forms of collision between memory and history, and the permanence and transformation of colonial views in French popular culture. Some focus on studying images and representations, and seek to foreground the central place of colonialism in the development of French modernity.[51] This perspective inevitably leads these historians to examine the constitutive role of colonial ideology in forming the French republican identity. Then, starting from this recognition of the relations between republicanism and Empire, they try to understand the new hybrid forms that came out of French imperial presence in the world, by exploring what they call the "colonial rift." Their approach is thus distinct from a well-established tradition of French colonial historiography on at least three levels. First, by the way in which this generation makes the connection between colonial history and metropolitan history, thus blurring the convenient separation between the study of here and the study of "elsewhere"; next, by the way in which this generation spreads its work throughout the public sphere and contributes, ipso facto, to the creation of a field of research akin to "public history"; and finally, by the way in which it reproblematizes the French national imaginary.[52]

It was only at the beginning of the millennium that, overcoming indifference and many hesitations, a well-founded critique of postcolonialism as such got underway. Thus, in the field of theory in particular, my own book *On the Postcolony*—which is often incorrectly classified under the umbrella of "postcolonial studies"—attacks three golden calves of postcolonial orthodoxy: first, the tendency to reduce the long history of formerly colonized societies to one moment (colonization), whereas it is a matter of thinking in terms of the concatenation of durations; next, the fetishization and conflation of the two notions of "resistance" and "subalternity"; and finally, the limits of the problematics of difference and alterity. Through a historical, literary, political, philosophical, aesthetic, and sculptural exploration of the *qualities* of power after decolonization, I aimed in that work to go against an entire tradition of postcolonial studies and to advance the hypothesis that one of the constitutive—but generally neglected—aspects of the "postcolonial condition" is the inclusion of rulers and their subjects in the same "episteme." At the same time, the work criticizes some postcolonial thought's dependence on hypostasized categories of "difference" and "alterity," and shows how, in the exercise and culture of power after decolonization, the logic of repetition often wins out over the logic of difference. Thus, the work tries to complicate the concept of agency, by showing how the action of subalterns, far from being preordained at the outbreak of revolution, often produces paradoxical situations. These interlocked situations make it necessary, in turn, to distance oneself from false dualism between a victim vision and a hero vision of subalternity, in the interest of a true critique of responsibility.[53]

At the same time, other attempts are appearing, particularly in the field of literary criticism.[54] One observes, moreover, a resurgence of interest in historical-philosophical and sociological studies of race[55] and a rereading of the forms of race's crystallization in slavery and its posthumous consequences,[56] as well as in processes of the contemporary constitution of minorities as distinct political subjects.[57] In *La Matrice de la race*, for example, the scholar Elsa Dorlin studies the sexual and colonial genealogy of the French nation at the intersection of political philosophy, history of medicine, and gender studies. Without necessarily claiming to be affiliated with postcolonial theory, this work echoes studies initiated by it: studies that not only affirm a tight connection between patriarchy and colonialism, but also emphasize the gendered nature of the process of production of race and nation. The cultural theorist Françoise Vergès rethinks the traditional distinction between the French republican nation and the colonial empire, and suggests considering them not as hermetically sealed and separated spheres, but as an interactive unit both under slavery and during and after colonization. At the same time, many works are dedicated to the way in which France treats its immigrants and minorities. Little by little, a critique of alterity as it is produced by French society in its everyday practices is taking form— whether these practices have to do with housing, medical care, the family, the ordinary administration of detention centers for immigrants and asylum-seekers whose applications have been rejected, the everyday life of foreigners in irregular situations, or experiences of racism.[58] Since then, a group of events has allowed for increased visibility of postcolonial thought among the French public. Whether or not this is a trend, several years after the appearance of Edward Said's works in French, important texts of the postcolonial corpus are finally being translated and widely debated.[59] Many young scholars are producing original works presented at countless conferences, in seminars, and in journals.

BYZANTINE QUARRELS

As we have just seen, the irruption of postcolonial thought into the French discursive field and the disputes it provokes stem from anything but contingent circumstances. Recently, postcolonial critical theory has moved from the strictly literary and theoretical field to the social sciences. In the course of this move, it has degenerated into a Byzantine quarrel. This quarrel is led by a group of scorners, whose attacks are full of malicious insinuations and aim above all to take down the authors of works they have not taken the trouble to read well, and they have taken even less trouble to understand. This quarrel neither arises nor unfolds in an ideological vacuum. Especially among the zealots of antipostcolonialism, its stakes are not simply—or even firstly—stakes of knowledge and understanding, as the French historian Catherine Coquery-Vidrovitch convincingly shows in her noteworthy work on colonial history.[60] Moved by a truly Pentecostal fervor, these zealots use postcolonial thought—as others, before them, used "Third-Worldism" and "68 thought"—in order to rile up their readers. This is the case of the fraudulent pamphlet by the Africanist Jean-Loup Amselle, *L'Occident décroché*.[61] In most cases, Amselle literally "fabricates" apodictic statements. He then imputes them to authors whom he describes as "postcolonialist" authorities, whereas these authors do not claim to belong to that current of thought, and in reality have never uttered the arguments that are lent to them and that our crusader attacks. Criticizing an argument that he constructed himself according to modalities that are never made explicit, he can then create an apparently homogenous, but actually imaginary, battlefront and include within it, for polemical needs, texts and authors that have no place there.

Where these intellectual stakes exist, as Jean-François Bayart rightly maintains in a hastily written essay,[62] they cannot be dissociated, as he seems to suggest, from ethical and philosophical stakes.[63] This is because colonization was not only a particular form of *rationality*, with its technologies and mechanisms. It also conceived of itself as a certain *structure of knowledge*, a *structure of belief*, and, as Edward Said emphasized, an *epistemic regime*. Moreover, it claimed a double status as *jurisdiction* and *veridiction*. There is thus indeed a moral singularity of colonization as an ideology and practice of the conquest of the world and as the enslavement of races judged to be inferior—and the critique of historical knowledge must indeed alternate between what Paul Ricoeur called "epistemological concern" (proper to the historiographical operation) and "ethico-cultural concern" (which stems from historical judgment).[64] This is, moreover, what Ricoeur called "critical hermeneutics." It is an approach one may choose to ignore, but it is a legitimate one, just like the nominalist or philosophical critiques of colonization formulated through historical, literary, psychoanalytic, or phenomenological analyses.

In the goal of disqualifying "postcolonial studies" en bloc, its destroyers voluntarily conflate this current of thought with the use certain of its French adherents make of it. In particular, they rail against the way in which postcolonial theory is handled in real life—and notably the fact that, in the hands of its local adherents, it tends to become an instrument of struggle, confrontation, and refusal. In a convenient oversight, they also act as if no tradition of "postcolonial studies" existed—a tradition that, from its origins, has constantly resituated the history of colonization within the perspective of a history of imperialism, or, more precisely, anti-imperialism.[65] Then, arguing from the fact that, in many regions of the world, colonization was brief, they seek to minimize its impact and scope, which they describe as superficial, although it is impossible to know exactly what criteria allow them to establish such an assessment historically. In both cases, the objective is to deny colonization any foundational function in the history of autochthonous societies: to minimize its violence and turn it into a *blank event*, to maintain that there was nothing new about colonial empires, that colonialism was only a particular case of a transhistoric and universal phenomenon (imperialism), and that the imperial world was far from an omnipotent "system," because it was wrought with tensions and internal clashes, impossibilities and discontinuities.[66] Then, there are some who propose turning to "historical sociology"—as if this disciplinary category were entirely clear—in order to explain colonial facts, which they reduce either to a simple problem of transition from empire to nation-state or to a mere comparative inventory of practices of imperial governance.[67]

To this end, they mobilize totemic figures like Max Weber and Michel Foucault, and then try to reactivate the old quarrel between explanation, interpretation, and understanding, which authors like Paul Ricoeur had tried to calm. This was at a time when the social sciences were still feeling the full force of attraction to the quantitative and positivist models in use in the natural sciences.[68] At the same time, as Paul Ricoeur and

Michel de Certeau remind us, interpretation is a feature of the search for truth in history. The same is true of the narrative or literary dimension of all historical discourse. It always contains, a priori, a cognitive dimension.[69] Behind the two presiding figures of Weber and Foucault, and under the cover of a call to reread "imperial history," it is in reality to a marriage between Auguste Comte and structuralism that "historical sociologists" invite us. After all, one hardly needs to doubt the concepts of truth, reality, or knowledge in order to maintain that scientific activity is a social construct. Moreover, to a large extent, facts do not exist except through the language by which they are expressed and the descriptions that produce them. As for the adjective "historical" attached to this "sociology," it often has little to do with the lessons of French theory from the second half of the twentieth century. By insisting on the fact that there is no privileged mode of explanation in history, this theory indirectly maintains that there are a variety of types of explanation.[70] "Historical sociology" is but one type of explanation among others. When it comes to the analysis of colonial situations, it is not necessarily true that small-scale observation is a better tool to think with than large-scale observation, or that details are worth more than the overall picture, or exception more than generalization.[71] It is also not true that "postcolonial studies" only practice textualism, ideology, and activist or "compassionate" denunciation, whereas "historical sociology" does pure and "cynical" "science." To various degrees, both "postcolonial studies" and "historical sociology" work on representations, constantly transmit moral judgments, do not make the distinction between what is true and what is held to be true, manipulate causal series that are by definition contingent, and, at the end of the day, are inheritors of the same discursive genre: the "critical philosophy of history."

It is also claimed that "postcolonial studies" are only concerned with "discourses" and texts, and not with "real practices," as if people's discourses were not part of their "reality" and as if the examination of colonization's imaginary dimensions or psychic or iconographic facts were of no importance in reconstituting the representations and practices of the actors of the time.[72] Thus, one is silent on the fact that one of the favored objects of "postcolonial studies" is precisely the material and symbolic transactions and intersubjective interactions that, in the colonial context, made it possible to create the colonial connection. In reality, many studies belonging to this current of thought dissect not only discourses, texts, and representations, but also the behavior of colonial subjects and their responses to the pressure of colonial norms, the various maneuvers of negotiation, justification, or denunciation that they constantly deployed, most often in contexts of radical uncertainty.[73] These studies show how colonized subjects were caught not only in relations of production, but also in relations of power, meaning, and knowledge—all things that, to follow Weber himself, require combining explanation, understanding, and interpretation from the outset.[74] There is thus room beside "historical sociology" for other (mixed) models of explanation and interpretation of colonial situations and their systems. In the colonial experience, there are no "social practices" (or what the zealots of antipostcolonialism call "concrete realities") separate from "discourses," languages, or representations. In addition to being symbolic and imaginary components in the structuration of the colonial connection and in the constitution of colonized subjects, discourses, languages, and representations are themselves full-fledged sources of action and practices.[75]

If the quarrel begun in France by the adherents of antipostcolonialism is anachronistic from an epistemological point of view, it is very symptomatic from a cultural and political point of view because its stakes now bear on the very identity of France, the limits of its democratic model, and the ambiguities of its republican universalism. For, at bottom, the quarrel over postcolonial thought—like arguments over the regulation of Islam, the "Islamic veil," or the *burqa*, the debates about national identity recently sponsored by the state, the fever of commemorations, and countless projects for monuments, museums, or burial steles—is first and foremost a symptom of a profound chiasmus in the present, and France's malaise in globalization. This chiasmus, another name for what the theorist Ann Stoler calls aphasia, is a direct consequence of the French disease of colonization—in the sense in which one used to speak of diseases of the mind. This disease arises out of the confrontation between two antagonistic desires: on the one hand, the desire—supported by a nebulous neorevisionist movement—for borders and for the control of identities, and, on the other hand, the desire for symbolic recognition and expansion of a *citizenship in abeyance*,[76] defended in particular by minorities and those who support them. One thing unites these otherwise fragmented minorities: what they subjectively perceive as a condition of symbolic dispossession. This dispossession is aggravated by the apparent persistence and reproduction, in France, of practices, patterns of thought, and representations inherited from a past of legal minoritization and racial and cultural stigmatization.

THE DESIRE TO PROVINCIALIZE

The desire for borders—and, thus, for separation and provincialization—brings together quite heterogeneous neorevisionist and provincialist currents, whose unity lies in a quasi-visceral rejection of any non-Western view of the West itself and the world of others. This constellation—in reality, a sum of trajectories with different origins and destinations—groups together ideologues of various outlooks. There are, all mixed together, those for whom the loss of the Empire, and in particular French Algeria, was a catastrophe: dogmatic Marxists, for whom the class struggle is the final word in history; former members of the proletarian left; catechists of secularism and of the French republican model; self-proclaimed defenders of Western values or of the Christian identity of France; critics of materialistic Europe; those nostalgic for the sacred and for classical culture; readers of Maurras and Mao combined; members of the French Academy; adherents of anti-Americanism on the left and on the right; antipostmodernist crusaders and adversaries of "68 thought"; those for whom Auschwitz must remain the axis of the Western world's collective memory and the foundational metaphor for the story of the unification of Europe; various faces of French extremism (from the insurrectional left to aristocratic populism and royalism);

and political-cultural and media intermediaries such as France-Culture, *Le Figaro Magazine*, *Le Point*, *L'Express*, or *Marianne*.[77]

Making free use of racial stereotypes and insinuations, this nebulous group tries to reactivate the myth of Western superiority, while asking the question of national belonging and coherence in strident and skittish terms. But, above all, exploiting the entire arc of popular emotions and passions, it cultivates the phantasm of "man without Other" and a France rid of its immigrants. Against a tradition of philosophical thought that goes from Maurice Merleau-Ponty to Emmanuel Levinas, Jacques Derrida, and Jean-Luc Nancy, the new "Other" is by definition the one with whom one can scarcely identify, whom one wishes would disappear, and whom one must, in any case, prevent from slipping into our forms of life, which would in the end poison them. In what follows, I will examine several political-cultural disagreements around which the neo-revisionist upsurge articulates itself. I will then show how these disputes both feed and exacerbate the desire for borders and separation, how they call for an extremely strict and severe policing of identities, preferably in the form of all sorts of interdictions, and finally, how they negatively influence the reception of postcolonial thought in France.

The first dispute concerns deciphering the time of the world and characterizing the contemporary moment. Neorevisionist currents consider that our epoch is marked by a qualitative transformation of global violence and a new planetary redistribution of hate. This situation, chaotic in several respects, constitutes, according to them, the equivalent of a global civil war, and has a direct impact on the nature of the security risks to France and other Western countries. The very survival of "Western civilization" is at stake. One of the consequences of this ultrapessimistic reading of the contemporary moment is to redefine the foreigner either as an illegal immigrant (the figure par excellence of the intruder and the undesirable) or as an enemy.[78] The polemical status henceforth occupied by the figure of the foreigner in the French imaginary and field of affects, passions, and emotions goes hand in hand with a renewed desire for borders and a reactivation of the technologies of separation and selection associated with this desire: *identity checks* and the logic of expulsions in particular.[79] The foreigner is not only the citizen of another state: he or she is above all someone different from us, whose dangerousness is real, from whom a proven cultural distance separates us, and who, in every form, constitutes a mortal threat to our mode of existence.

Neorevisionist and provincialist currents consider, moreover, that in order to respond to the security aspects of this existential angst, the rule of law in its classical version must be amended. The distinction between the functions of the police (to deal with foreigners on national territory) and the functions of the army (to deal with external enemies) must be tempered. New policies must be put into place in order to defend the territory against illegal immigration and, recently, Islamic terrorism. Thus, we have witnessed the appearance, within the democratic and French republican order, of a specific form of governmentality that could be called the *regime of confinement*. This regime is characterized by, among other things, increasing militarization of civil technologies of government, the expansion of practices and techniques under the seal of state secret, and a formidable expansion and miniaturization of police, judiciary, and penitentiary logics—especially those that have to do with the administration of foreigners and intruders. To manage undesirable populations, countless legal, regulatory, and surveillance measures have been implemented, to facilitate practices of detention, custody, incarceration, confinement to camps, or deportation.[80]

The result has been not only an unprecedented proliferation of lawless zones at the very heart of the rule of law, but also the institution of a radical cleavage between, on the one hand, those citizens whose protection and safety the state tries to ensure and, on the other hand, a mass of people who are literally harassed and, on occasion, deprived of all rights, abandoned to precariousness, and denied not only the possibility of having rights but also any legal existence.[81] A complex of differentiated measures, laws, and formal or informal agreements between France and other states has completed this apparatus. This entire process has culminated in the formation of a "Ministry of National Identity and Immigration."[82] Taken as a whole, the favored targets of this complex are certain categories of individuals and certain social groups

defined in terms of their ethnic, religious, racial, and national characteristics. The ministry aims to restrict their freedom of movement, even
to revoke it outright. Since what is at stake in any policy of border and
identity control is the possibility of controlling the very borders of politics, politics in France is gradually becoming fragmented along biora-
cial lines that power tries, by way of denegation and banalization, to con-
vince common sense to ratify.[83]

The second dispute bears directly on "radical Islam," a phantasmal
object par excellence, which, in contemporary conditions, serves as an
imaginary border to French nationality and identity. In this case, a certain number of Islam's domestic and public practices are called into
question in the name of secularism. Three principles or ideals are supposed to constitute the base of secularism and French republicanism.
First, the ideal of equality, which demands that the same laws be applied
equally to all—the republican law must come before religious rules in
all circumstances. Next, the idea of freedom and autonomy, which presupposes that no one should be subjected to the will of another against
his or her will. And finally the ideal of fraternity, which imposes the duty
to assimilate on everyone—a necessary condition for constituting a community of citizens. In the eyes of the most conservative factions of the
neorevisionist movement, "radical Islam" is defined as the dark side of
the Enlightenment and the inverted figure of modernity. It is thought
to be incompatible with the French republican notion of *laïcité*. After all,
doesn't it aim to apply a "foreign" law in France—the sign of its follow-
ers' refusal to integrate and assimilate? Isn't this law in contradiction
with the principles of liberty, equality, and fraternity that founded the
Republic, since it consecrates the inhuman treatment of women (the
wearing of the *burqa*, the imposed veil, genital mutilations, forced marriages, rape, polygamy, tests of virginity)? In terms of the neorevisionist
consensus, Muslim women suffer under a double yoke: submission to
their husbands or brothers and submission to an inegalitarian religion.
In cases where blacklisted behaviors don't break any laws, it is necessary
to create a law making it possible to forbid and suppress them. It is the
Republic's obligation to emancipate Muslims from this yoke. Eventually, the Republic could force them to be free without asking for their

consent. In a repetition of the process of colonial civilization, it would be possible, in the name of French republican paternalism, to emancipate them through recourse to coercion if necessary.

Behind the controversies over the *hijab* or the *burqa*—or, more generally, the fate of Muslim women—several intertwined processes stand out. The first is the institutionalization of a "state feminism," which uses the question of "Muslim women" to lead a racist fight against an Islamic culture posited as fundamentally sexist.[84] On both the left and the right, French republican feminism is transformed into an incubator of Islamophobia. It is used not only to feed racist representations and practices, but also to make them acceptable, since they are expressed in the mode of euphemisms.[85] The second process consists in a "paradoxical injunction to freedom," which goes along with the culturalization of French republican values.[86] In direct line with the colonial civilizing process, and with a perfectly clear conscience, the project is to emancipate individuals "for their own good," and, if necessary, against their will. This is accomplished using interdiction, ostracism, and the law, whose primary function is no longer to do justice, but to stigmatize and to produce execrated figures.[87]

Within the perspective of neorevisionist and provincialist movements, because French republican ideals are embodied in culture and language, they are realized both within the law of the Republic and in allegiance to a specific culture: French Catholic and secular culture. This culture prescribes private and public behavior and abolishes—or at the very least softens—the separation that had customarily been established between these two spheres of life.[88] No matter if, in so doing, there is confusion between public morality (the values of the Republic) and the cultural prejudices of French society. As the political theorist Cécile Laborde has amply shown, deciphering the meaning of Muslim religious signs is based less on right than on culturalist, stereotyped prejudices. If the secular state was able to make "reasonable accommodations" for Christians and Jews, when it comes to Muslims the state insists that they be the ones to make accommodations, by limiting expression of their public identity.[89] The republicanism advocated by neorevisionist currents tends, moreover, to equate French cultural practices with ideal neutrality. But this strain of thought shows, instead, that the French public sphere is not culturally and religiously neutral. In its eyes, minorities' demands for reasonable accommodations do not constitute demands for justice because these demands are described as "communalism," precisely in order to better disqualify them.[90]

The third process on which neorevisionist and provincialist discourses are fixated has to do with a reenchantment of national mythology at a moment when France is facing an apparent decline and is undergoing a relative downgrade in the international arena. The theme of decline is neither new nor exclusive to this campaign. It resurfaces at regular intervals in French history. Its appearance generally coincides with times of crisis and great fears. It is a discourse of loss and melancholy, and some of its immediate effects are to accentuate tensions in identity, to reawaken nostalgia for grandeur, and to shift both the terrain and content of politics and forms of social antagonism.[91] This was the case during the last quarter of the twentieth century, when the sentiment that the great national narrative had collapsed was shared by many, and not only on the extreme right. According to this view, the collapse was not only caused by transformations of the French economy and the crisis of the French republican model of integration. It was also a consequence of the deconstructionist thought of which May '68 was the avatar. The solid identity and certainties on which this story rested were washed away by waves of ambient relativism and philosophies of the "death of the subject." How, in these conditions, could the national idea be reanimated, if not by reinvesting the past and reappropriating its many symbolic repositories? From this impulse came the attempts at rehabilitating a cultural, sacrificial, and almost theological-political conception of France that began several years ago.

Taking inspiration from turn-of-the-century schoolbooks, this conception of history is turned entirely toward the glories of the past. It situates France at the center of Europe and the world, and makes teaching civics and morality the task of the discipline of history. In addition to being edifying, history must reflect the essence of the nation, which was forged over the course of a series of events. Thus, the homogeneity and unity of the French people were achieved on three dates: the Battle of

Poitiers in 732, which made it possible to stop the Arab invasion; the capture of Jerusalem in 1099, which testified to the extended power of Christian Europe; and the revocation of the Edict of Nantes in 1685, which confirmed the long tendency in France's history to "choose Rome" and demonstrated symbolically that France is above all a Catholic country—but also that its identity has been created on the basis of the exclusion of Arabs, Jews, and Protestants.[92] It is also a glorious history insofar as it accounts for numerous great feats, a succession of "great men," and events supposed to testify to the French genius.

Furthermore, one of the functions of this history is the exaltation of patriotism. It is a history that accords pride of place to the old rhetoric of France bringing its Enlightenment to the colonies and the world. Thus, it is a matter not of hiding colonization as such, but of using it as an ideological template for the education of citizens, as was the case during imperial expansion, when one could scarcely imagine the Republic without its innumerable overseas possessions. It is also a matter of inverting the terms by which the work of colonialism is recognized. For the most zealous, this inversion means attributing heroic characteristics to colonial crimes and tortures. According to them, these crimes demand no repentance, since they are only crimes in the eyes of our contemporaries. Indeed, within the spirit of the epoch, these crimes were instead a mark of French civilization—a civilization capable of asserting itself through both weapons and the mind.[93] For others, even if crimes were perpetrated and injustices committed, the final assessment of colonization is "positive" overall.[94] And France has the right to require gratitude and recognition from its former colonial subjects.

One finds more than just the contours of this sacrificial and cultural conception of history in a series of speeches made by Nicolas Sarkozy during the 2007 French presidential campaign and after his victory. As far as the colonial question is concerned, these speeches are characterized by the same "refusal to repent" and the same urgency of self-absolution and exculpation. These speeches—the Toulon speech on February 7, 2007, as well as the Dakar speech (on July 26, 2007), in which he declared that Africans have not sufficiently entered into history—seek to make official a cultural effort underway for many years in various political and cultural networks, not only on the extreme right, but also on the French republican right and left:[95]

> The European dream needs the Mediterranean dream. This dream shrank when the dream that long ago compelled knights from all over Europe to take the roads to the Orient was shattered, the dream that attracted so many emperors of the Holy Empire and so many kings of France to the south, the dream that was Bonaparte's dream in Egypt, Napoleon III's in Algeria, Lyautey's in Morocco. This dream was not so much a dream of conquest as a dream of civilization. . . . For a long time, the West has sinned by its arrogance and ignorance. Many crimes and injustices were committed. But most of those who left for the south were neither monsters nor exploiters. Many put their energy toward building roads, bridges, schools, and hospitals. Many exhausted themselves cultivating a thankless piece of land that before them no one had cultivated. Many only left in order to heal, to teach. Let us stop blackening the past. . . . One can only disapprove of colonization with our values of today. But we must respect the men and women of good will who thought in good faith that they were working usefully toward an ideal of civilization that they believed in.[96]

The fourth dispute concerns race and racism. Neorevisionist and provincialist movements, purposely forgetting the historical experiences of slavery and colonization, claim that racism never entirely penetrated French society and that, unlike in the United States, racial segregation in France was never legal or institutional.[97] Racism in mainland France was, according to them, always symbolically discredited and never had more than a residual existence. Where discriminations do exist, they are considered negligible and would disappear if, according to some, economic inequalities were greatly reduced or if, according to others, France could "select" its immigrants. Moreover, also according to these currents of thought, the fundamental social problems of the country originate in racism against whites. When the reality of racism against non-whites is admitted, it is treated as a mere cultural difference. Under these conditions, any mention of race either for affirmative action or for the reparation of wrongs done to the idea of equality is stigmatized, for it puts the Republic at risk of "ethnicizing" social relations.

Thus, commenting on the riots that broke out in many French *banlieues* in November 2005, Alain Finkielkraut saw them as a demonstration of the hatred blacks and Arabs harbor toward France. In fact, for him, these riots constitute a snapshot of the war that part of the "Arab-Muslim world" has declared on the West, and its favorite target is the Republic. According to Finkielkraut, those blacks who "hate France as a republic" have the audacity to accord the same exceptionality, the same weight of destiny and sacredness, and the same paradigmatic power to slavery as to the "Shoah": "But if you want to put the Holocaust and slavery on the same plane, then you have to lie. Because [slavery] wasn't a Holocaust. And [the Holocaust] wasn't 'a crime against humanity,' because it wasn't just a crime. It was something ambivalent. The same is true of slavery. It began long before the West. In fact, what sets the West apart when it comes to slavery is that it was the one to eliminate it."[98] Moreover, the Republic has done "nothing but good" for Africans. Wasn't the objective of colonization to "educate" them and, in so doing, to "bring civilization to the savages"?

Therefore, the cause of the riots shouldn't be sought in racism. The riots, for Finkielkraut, are above all proof of supreme ingratitude. And, moreover, "French racism" is a myth fabricated by those who hate France. Of course, there are, here and there, "French racists," "French people who don't like Arabs and blacks." But "how could they like people who don't like them?" "And they'll like them even less now [after the riots], when they know how much they're hated by them."[99] At the same time, blacks and Arabs don't consider themselves French. "Why do they speak French the way they do?" Finkielkraut asks. "It's butchered French—the accent, the words, the syntax." "Their identity is located somewhere else" and since "they're only in France out of personal interest," they treat the French state like "a big insurance company."[100] The fact that today they counter the enormous sacrifices made by the Republic with only hatred and jeers is the manifestation of their radical otherness—the very otherness that means they never have been and never will really be part of us, that they cannot be integrated, and that their presence among us endangers our own existence in the long run. According to Finkielkraut, the real problem is thus *antiracism*, which, he prophesies, "will be for the twenty-first century what communism was for the twentieth century." The primary function of this ideology is to produce guilt out of nothing, as required by "political correctness."[101] Worse yet, antiracism is the new name of anti-Semitism.[102]

COLONIALISM AND POSTHUMOUS DISEASES OF MEMORY

The official politics of memory—whether republican or national—has, in addition to being at the origin of intense passions, confrontations, and divisions, always been marked by enormous ambiguity. Pierre Nora has said that the construction of French republican memory in particular was "simultaneously authoritarian, unified, exclusive, universal, and intensely backward-looking at once." Not only did the Republic owe its coherence to what it excluded; it always defined itself against real or fantasized enemies.[103] How, indeed, to invent a past, occupy space, minds, and time, and bring about a civil religion (with its liturgies, altars, and temples, its statues, frescos, steles, and commemorations), when the new regime that came out of the Revolution was contested on both the left and the right? When it was confronted with dangers from the clergy, a refractory army, and the alliance of the banking and industrial bourgeoisie with the peasant class—all within a country itself historically made up of more or less compartmentalized territories?[104]

The fact that the politics of memory has often constituted an element of national division can be explained, on the one hand, by the capacity of memory to reawaken the wounds of a difficult past, a past about which one wonders how it could be put into the service of the nation's founding narrative. It can be explained, on the other hand, by the close relation that has, since the Revolution, existed in French political culture between death (especially violent death), forgetting, and debt—and, thus, by the relation between death and the idea of justice.[105] This was especially the case when it came to exempting political crimes and acts of violent death from the logic of incrimination.[106] From this point of view, the Revolution set off a sepulchral mechanism that continued under the Restoration (there was an inflation of honors accorded to mortal remains, frantic marking of burial sites, and countless exhumations and reburials). At the time, public mourning constituted a manifestation of political power, and memory itself is likely to be used as an instrument of punitive justice and an expiatory sword. Within state politics, national memory has thus always functioned as a space of atonement, midway between the logic of incrimination and the desire for reparation. Thus, in the presence of commemorative stones or rites, there is what Chateaubriand called a "field of blood." It is this spilled blood that monuments and rites are called upon to expurgate. And this is why their function is to testify to the effort at reconciliation with loss.

The fact that such a close relation has been created between memory and the ordeal of violent death and its internalization can be explained by a conception of the nation that makes the nation a soul and a spiritual principle, and, at the same time, by the social and political virtue that French political culture has always accorded to the cadaver. The constitutive elements of this soul and spiritual principle are the shared possession of a rich legacy of memories (the past) as well as the desire to live together and the will to continue to emphasize this heritage in the present. In addition to these two characteristics, there is also a French republican consciousness that boasts an exorbitant exceptionality, since it claims to make French singularity coincide with the universal tout court. The past itself, made up of sacrifices and devotion, is conceived in heroic, glorious, Promethean terms. The valorization of heritage and shared memories takes place through a kind of *ancestor worship*. The counterpart to ancestor worship is the cult of sacrifice. Because the nation is a moral conscience, it can legitimately demand, as the philosopher Ernest Renan emphasized, the "abdication of the individual," to the benefit of the community.[107] The cult of ancestors with their great deeds, along with the cult of sacrifice, forms a social and symbolic capital all the more decisive for the construction of the national idea since, one generation after the regicide, the country was faced with a crisis of representation and a deficit of sacredness. Love of country and pride in being French were also expressed in public gestures and rituals of civic piety: military parades, museums, memorials, commemorations, steles, statues, the names of boulevards, streets, bridges, squares, and, finally, the Pantheon, France's secular mausoleum for heroes of the nation.

In direct line with the sacrificial and cultural conception of the nation I have just briefly described, on April 4, 1873, for the first time in the history of modern France, a law was passed dealing with the preservation of the tombs of dead soldiers—in this case, those who fell during the war of 1870–1871. This law prescribed in detail "the status of grounds and the type of ossuary tomb to be created."[108] For over a century, the aim of the official politics of memory was above all to commemorate those "who died for France," with civil community originating and symbolically reproducing itself in funeral celebrations and defining itself as a "community of loss," but a loss that is never forgotten. Already at the turn of the nineteenth century, France underwent a funerary revolution. Political passions were expressed through the building of new necropolises, funeral parades and processions crisscrossing the city, the practice of eulogies delivered at tombs, the visible wearing of public mourning (sometimes expiatory, sometimes doleful or in protest), and the cult of profane relics.[109] The cult of the dead is supposed to produce consensus and legitimacy. But everything depends on which dead, for it is also liable to serve as a site of expression of dissent, because the blood of the defeated in particular can be summoned as an instrument not of reconciliation, but rather of communalist vengeance. Beginning in 1830 in particular, a sacrificial republicanism triumphed, and it is in part this paradigm that some are trying to reactualize today.

However, during the 1980s, a shift began. The politics of memory based on a celebration of shared deaths was gradually succeeded by another economy of commemorations, at the center of which are "the deaths caused by France." For a long time, France did not want to recognize its responsibility in the genocide of the Jews. This catastrophe was imputed to the Vichy regime, which alone was to bear the infamy. This attitude began to change, and the first "deaths caused by France" to be recognized were "deaths in deportation." In 1990, the Gayssot law definitively gave these dead the status of "victims" and established the role of the state in the construction of "remembrance of the Holocaust." In 1993, a decree established "a national day of commemoration of the racist and anti-Semitic persecutions committed under the de facto authority of the so-called 'government of the French state,'" followed, in 1994, by the inauguration of the Vél d'Hiv' Memorial in memory of the victims of the Holocaust. The last step in this process was the admission made by Jacques Chirac in 1995 of France's responsibility in the genocide of the Jews. The year 2004 saw the inauguration of the Milles National Memorial, and in 2006 the Shoah Memorial with the Wall of Names (for the seventy-six thousand deported Jews) and the Wall of the Righteous (for those who hid or saved Jews) was opened in Paris. The culminating point of this process was in 2007, when the righteous were inducted into the Pantheon.[110]

If the new politics of memory makes room for deaths caused by France, a distinction nevertheless remains. Whereas the "dead for France" were deaths "endured" by Frenchmen in the name of the nation, and those who died are transfigured into "heroes," the "deaths caused by France" appear on the altar of national memory as "victims." This is notably the case concerning the Holocaust. For other events, it so happens that Frenchmen figure among the deaths caused by France. This is the case of colonization. It not only upsets the distinction that generally separates our dead from the dead of the others, but also divides the political city in its center and at its margins, since, in this event, the city offers itself up as both its own victim and its own torturer.

This is one of the reasons why colonization is the very eye of the memorial storm sweeping through the country. For several years now, the state itself has been stirring up the storm. For reasons mentioned earlier, the state officially wants to "modernize" commemorations. In this inflation of ceremonies, memory, homages, inaugurations of monuments, museums, and public squares, the borders between history, memory, and propaganda are blurred.[111] Thus, in a current project, the war of 1914–1918—which marked a singular retreat of democracy and eventually paved the way for Fascism and Nazism—is dialectically reinterpreted as having been the beginning of the construction of Europe.

The conflict of 1939–1945 is no longer said to have been a "world war," but rather an essentially European war, with significant international extensions. As for the colonial troops requisitioned for combat that, it is now maintained, was foreign to them, one advances that they "died for Liberty and Civilization," thus benefiting from the privilege of having been colonized. In this case as in others, the enterprise of war in general is compared to a crusade, and its dead are martyrs who, in a patriotic swell, voluntarily renounced their lives for a just cause.[112]

The discourse against repentance aims to serenely take on the totality of France's history. Its goal is to rehabilitate the colonial enterprise. It alleges that the real victims of colonization were not the natives, but the colonizers. The former owe the latter gratitude. This logic of exculpation and of self-absolution shines brightest in the case of Algeria, the memory of which is at the epicenter of French diseases of colonization.[113] France was present in Algeria for almost a century and a half. Four or five generations of Europeans made it their homeland between 1830 and 1962. Significant numbers of French army troops (Harkis, draftees, enlistees) fought there. Between 1920 and 1970, there was significant immigration from Algeria. And, to top it all off, the conflict between France and Algeria left hundreds of thousands dead.[114] We still do not grasp to what extent the loss of French Algeria, coming after the defeat at Diên Biên Phu, constituted a veritable trauma for France, of almost the same intensity as the defeat of 1870.[115] This time, however, the defeat was military as well as political and moral, and it revealed, among other things, the generalization of the practice of torture by the French army. It is in particular on the subject of this long-nameless war, surrounded by dirty practices (until recently still known in France by the euphemism "the events in Algeria"), that there has been an organized process of concealment and forgetting.

But, since 2002, there have been more and more testimonies, books, websites, press articles, films (*La Trahison* by Philippe Faucon in 2005, *Mon Colonel* by Laurent Herbiet and *Indigènes* by Rachid Bouchareb in 2006, *L'Ennemi intime* by Florian Emilio Siri in 2007), documentaries and television movies (*Nuit noire, 17 octobre 1961* by Alain Tasma in 2005, *La Bataille d'Alger* by Yves Boisset in 2006).[116] It is in very large part the loss of Algeria that is at the origin of the notorious law of February 23, 2005, whose article 4 speaks of the "benefits of positive colonization"—a law that was perhaps launched by a "stratum of second-rank parliamentarians,"[117] but that was nevertheless adopted by the National Assembly of France. This article was, of course, later repealed by Jacques Chirac in 2006, but the controversy has not died out. This controversy touches on the commemoration of this war, as well as on the question of museums, memorials, walls, and steles in the south of France (Marseille, Perpignan, and Montpelier) and on accounting for the number of French deaths. On the other side of the Mediterranean, in Algeria itself, calls were also heard to account precisely for the number of Algerians that have been killed by the French since 1830, as well as for the number of villages burned, tribes decimated, and wealth stolen. To this must be added the contentiousness surrounding Algeria's call for France to provide maps from this era showing the eleven million mines the French army placed along the Tunisian and Moroccan borders in the goal of preventing ALN (Algerian Army of National Liberation) militants from entering those two territories. According to Algeria, these mines, still in place, have caused great damage, including forty thousand dead and wounded since the end of colonization. In addition to all this there is also the calamitous legacy of nuclear tests in the south of Algeria during the 1960s and the question of medical treatment for the victims of atomic radiation in the Sahara.[118]

Nationals of former imperial possessions and their descendants are not the only victims of colonial trauma in contemporary France. So are the French ex-colonizers of Algeria and their descendants. One must understand these diseases of memory in relation to the crisis of French democracy and to a spirit of the times that accords central importance to the formation and expression of bruised and wounded identities.[119] In order to be taken into account politically, struggles for recognition must more and more be articulated around an exceptional signifier—"my suffering and my wounds." This archetypal and incomparable suffering must necessarily answer to a name deemed more worthy than any other name. Inasmuch as diseases of memory (the chiasmus in the present) often tend to open the way to absolute oppositions between victims of the same torturer, the quarrel is always over what human suffering must be sanctified and what other suffering is, at bottom, no more than an insignificant incident on the scale of the lives and deaths that really count. Consequently, the struggle aims to refuse any equivalence between different human lives and deaths, for, it is thought, certain lives and certain deaths are universal, while others are not at all, and should not even aspire to become universal.[120]

In the spirit of the contemporary world, many believe in the existence of a first Mourning, interminable and constantly called onto the stage of symptoms, but never capable of bridging the gap. In direct line with the spirit of monotheism, this first Mourning cannot be measured against any other mourning. With regard to this first Mourning, all other mourning is nothing but a pagan affair. Only this first Mourning is qualified to appear in the mirror of History. Lacking a double, it fills the surface of the mirror from one edge to the other, in the manner of a One. Thus, all other events, no matter how terrifying, must be forbidden from accessing the field of words and language, because this field is, in any case, already exhausted by the Event. But, by conceiving the first Mourning in this way, one ends up making it into an impossible mourning. And, because of this impossibility and this interminability, one arrives at one of the major paradoxes of contemporary diseases of memory: my mourning consists above all in killing not my executioner, but preferably *a third party*. Our aversion for the suffering of others is demonstrated in the death drive that affects all victim consciousness, in particular when this consciousness only conceives itself in a relation of competition to other consciousnesses of the same name. I must thus silence the Other or, if not, oblige the Other to fall into delirium, in such a way that his or her suffering refers back to a state before language—a state prior to all naming. What in France is called the "war of memories" thus falls within the framework of struggles for transcendence in the context of the victim ideologies that have marked the end of the twentieth century and the beginning of the twenty-first. These struggles are fundamental to *necropolitical* projects. Indeed, inasmuch as one never bases the transcendental on one's own death, the sacred must be instituted on the basis of the sacrificial killing of someone else.

Moreover, our era is far from being one of repentance, and is rather an era of *clear conscience*. Through colonization, the European powers sought to create the world in their image. They believed that they were a "tough, industrious race of machinists and builders of bridges" and statues, and in the end, the colonizers could only complete crude works.[121] But they were armed with a fistful of certainties, which decolonization has scarcely effaced and whose resurgence and mutations in contemporary conditions can be observed.[122] The first certainty was an absolute faith in force. The strongest ordered, organized, arranged, and gave form to the rest of the human herd. The second, entirely Nietzschean certainty was that life itself was, above all, the will to power and the instinct of self-preservation. The third was the conviction that natives represented morbid and degenerate forms of man, obscure bodies waiting for help and demanding aid. As for the passion for commanding, it was nourished by a sentiment of superiority over those who had to obey. To this was added the intimate certainty that colonization was an act of charity and kindness, for which the colonized had to display gratitude, attachment, and submission.

The foundations of European clear conscience are located in this triple complex. This clear conscience has always been a mix of laissez-faire, indifference, the will not to know, and a quickness to unburden oneself of one's responsibilities. It has always consisted in wanting to be responsible for nothing, guilty of nothing. This obstinate refusal of any sentiment of culpability rests on the conviction that instincts of hate, envy, covetousness, and the lust to rule, "fundamentally and essentially, must be present in the general economy of life."[123] Further, there could not possibly be one morality valid *for all*, strongest and weakest alike. And, since there is a hierarchy among men, there should be a hierarchy among moralities. Hence the cynicism with which questions concerning the memory of colonization are treated. In the eyes of many, reminders of this past serve only to debilitate European virility and render its will listless. Hence, also, the refusal to see the "horned beast" that Nietzsche said had always held the greatest attraction for Europe.[124] Half a century later, this beast has not stopped tempting it.

5

THE HOUSE WITHOUT KEYS

I t is one thing to make a normative and outside judgment on African objects without taking into account their history, their heterogeneity, or the enigma of which they are the expression.[1] It is another to seek to grasp, through their distinctive properties, their substance and their functions, the ways of being and seeing of Africans, or again, taking them as an intermediary, to want to learn about the metaphysical kernel on the basis of the world authored by Africans made sense to them.[2]

Indeed, whether or not they were linked to the exercise of particular cults or rituals, whether or not they were taken as works of art, these objects, often viewed as disconcerting, have always aroused on the part of the West all sorts of sensations, ambiguous feelings, visceral and even contradictory reactions—obsessive fear, fascination and wonder, horror, frustration and repulsion, or even execration. Everywhere that they made their appearance, they tended to give rise to effects of blindness. Considered from the start as dirty, ugly, and monstrous objects, as signatures of the shadow resisting all translation, they shook up existing ocular frameworks and put back on the agenda the old question of understanding what an image is and how it differs from a simple silhouette, about what art or aesthetic experience in general is, and how it manifests itself in its pure truth.

ANIMISM, PAGANISM, AND IDOLATRY

Of all the gazes brought to bear on these manifestations of the cultural creativity of our peoples, three in particular merit our attention.

Let us start with the missionary gaze, in whose eyes these artifacts were essentially the effects of a satanic imagination. This theological-pastoral gaze began to take shape during the first evangelization, which occurred in the kingdoms of the Congo between 1495 and 1506, and again between the seventeenth and eighteenth centuries, then in the kingdom of Dahomey in the seventeenth century.[3] Evidently, the diabolization of African objects from the fifteenth century proceeded from an unconsidered heritage that, with few exceptions, numerous missionary figures carried along.[4] Indeed, the devil long constituted the nocturnal part of Christian culture in the West.[5]

Between the twelfth and thirteenth centuries, the diverse demons that had populated old imaginations were reduced to a single one, Satan, absolute master of Hell and God's rival on Earth. Little by little, the figure of Satan invaded several domains of social and imaginary life.[6] Satan symbolized the war of worlds and the confrontation between good and evil, reason and madness. At the same time, he attested to the split character of the human figure that he surrounded and within which he hollowed out an almost insuperable void.[7] Between 1480 and 1520, and again between 1560 and 1650, demonic obsessive fear reached its culminating point—as is attested by the interminable trials, the great witch hunts, and the many witches burned at the stake—when a connection was established between the figure of Satan on the one hand and the body and the sexuality of women on the other.[8]

The first phase of missionary expansion into Africa bore in it the traces of this essential tension. As the "mission" came to be, the "devil's place" would thus move to Africa, a region of the world deeply ruled, it was thought at the time, by chaos, by a life requiring order to be put into it and in need of a salvation that could only come from outside.[9] Quite unsurprisingly, the first missionaries interpreted African objects through the paradigm of "diabolical witchcraft" that had prevailed in the West for many centuries. These objects were put on trial similar to the proceedings carried out, under Christianity, against dolls pierced with needles, against the curses cast about here and there, against the potions one concocted, against the contact one sought with the dead, against the witches' sabbaths, against broomsticks and black masses, against host desecrations, bestial copulations, and all sorts of gory sacrifices, all of which were only made possible, it was argued, by belief in Satan and in his powers. Presented as material symbols of Africans' proclivity for engaging in idolatry, worship of the dead, and the practice of gory sacrifices, cultural objects in particular were subject to the reprobation of missionaries.[10] For the most part, the missionaries saw in them only a marker—yet another—of the essential difference between the savage mentality and that of civilized humanity.[11]

The same gaze was assumed in the context of the second evangelization, which began in 1822 (the year the Society for the Propagation of the Faith was founded). Complex and in many respects ambiguous, the goal of missionary acts was to convert Africans to the only valid monotheism, that of the truth, which "recognized only one God and for which no other gods existed."[12] In theory, it was not a matter of importing to Africa the social habits of European nations, but rather of announcing the Gospel to backward peoples, whose ideas and mores had to be rectified and elevated, and whom it was necessary to deliver from the weight of superstitions and to lead along the path to salvation. In reality, missionary campaigns were founded on two pillars: refutation of the metaphysical foundations of natives' worship and, wherever necessary, religious repression with the aim of conversion.

In the logic of Christianity, the convert must recognize that the path that he has been on leads straight to his ruin. Renouncing his life and his previous ways, he has to repent and undertake an internal reversal, at the end of which a new subjectivity is to be acquired, as well as new ways of inhabiting the world and relating to the body and objects. In missionary theology, submission to the devil—and therefore to the principle of spiritual death and corruption of the soul—wittingly or otherwise often had its fulcrum in objects and the relationships that the primitives entertained with them. Moreover, in its opacity, the pagan mode of existence was characterized by human subordination to all sorts of fetishes, which these humans ceaselessly envied, feared, constantly sought to acquire or to destroy, and to which they transferred the force, power, and truth due exclusively to God. In practice, conversion led to the invention of mixed cultures, made up of borrowings of all kinds, games of mixtures, risky reappropriations, and hybrid aesthetic practices.[13] Conversion led to manifold misunderstandings, multiple paradoxes, and a complex process of redefinition of each of the protagonists in the encounter.[14]

This is the context in which the missionary *antipagan discourse* developed. This discourse influenced, more than has been recognized, the West's conceptions of African objects, their substance, their status, and their functions. It rested on the postulate according to which blacks lived in the night of the inmost animal. As for the African world, it was a priori bereft of the idea of a sovereign God that would be the norm of every norm and the cause of every cause. There was, at least, no clear awareness of any such principle. In contrast, this world was peopled with a multitude of beings, multiple divinities, ancestors, soothsayers, intercessors, all sorts of genies who ceaselessly vied for preeminence. Primitive societies entertained relations of immediacy and immanence with these forces and entities.[15] One could hardly call this heap of beliefs any sort of religion, for it was nearly impossible to sort out what pertained to ritual murders, what was spirit worship, and what participated in mere worship of matter.

Alongside these figures, a panoply of forces (maleficent for the most part) structured the universe and presided over each person's life. Some of these forces could assume a human appearance. Others could become embodied in all sorts of elements, including natural, organic, vegetal, and atmospheric elements, to which worship and sacrifices were offered.[16] Ceremonies of worship could take place in circumscribed places, just like temples. But at bottom, it was the entire universe—organic, vegetal, and mineral (whirlpools in rivers, sacred woods, water, earth, air, lightning)—that one could summon and that served as a receptacle for powers that one adored, often in obscurity, through all kinds of fetish-objects, which the missionaries likened to idols.[17] These idols, in their roughness and their excessive features, constituted the objectal manifestation of the state of corruption in which the black race was plunged.[18] Through such objects, did primitive peoples not seek to constrain and control powers? Did these objects not simultaneously manifest the fear and dependency that such peoples experienced in their regard? Such dependency nevertheless had no divine aim. It implied nothing less than nothingness, the mere nothing of man in the face of an absolute supremacy, the sheer presence of the horrifying.[19]

Accordingly, many of these objects were destroyed during major religious feasts, while many others—due to practices of collection, theft, pillage, confiscation, and gift-giving—came to be found in museums of the West.[20] "Do not forget to send us, at the earliest opportunity, a collection of things from your new country," Father Augustin Planque hastened to write in 1861 to the missionaries sent to Africa. "We would like to have in our museum all your gods for a start, weapons, tools, household utensils; in a word, nothing should be left out."[21]

Christianity indeed presented itself as the religion of truth and of Salvation. Religion of the radical rupture, it sought to abolish ancient forms of worship. Thus, vast campaigns were organized to extirpate idolatry.[22] Accordingly, temples were ransacked or literally desecrated. Manifold fetishes—figurines made of diverse materials (hair endings, fingernails, metal nails), shells of various forms and colors, dried insects, collections of roots, pots and pitchers filled with vegetal preparations and ointments—were offended. In their place, crosses were planted. Amulets were confiscated and rosaries were handed out, as were effigies of saints. Demons and sorcerers were prosecuted through public punishments and punitive spectacles.[23] An attempt was made to end all feasts and rites, to aggress musical instruments and prohibit certain dances as well as the supposed worship of the dead and practices of contacting the invisible.

DIFFERENCE AND APOCALYPSE

A second type of gaze emerged in the nineteenth century against the backdrop of the theories of "universal history" and of differences between human races that were in vogue at the time. The language of race and blood was on people's tongues. On the one hand, the idea that God revealed himself in the Christian religion, the only true religion, endured. On the other, the notion that the history of the world was fundamentally the history of progress toward the consciousness of freedom took hold.[24] This universal history, it was maintained, presented itself to us in the form of a rational process that ought to lead to the triumph of reason or, in any case, to the reconciliation between the rational and the real.[25] But it was only held to have become concrete where reason was able to insert itself into the great human passions (including need, forces, and instincts), and even wherever it left passions to act in its stead. In other terms, universal history could only be envisaged on the condition that reason and truth consciously took on the form and structure of myth.[26]

As it happens, the great myth of the nineteenth century was that of race.[27] It was through race, it was thought, that the "Absolute Idea" would be accomplished. Hegel, for example, considered that in each era of history, there is one and only one nation, one and only one people that is the real representation of the world spirit and that "has the right to rule all the others."[28] Faced with this nation, people, or race, "other nations are absolutely without rights." They "no longer count in universal history."[29] In this system in which a given race grants itself the title of "sole bearer of the world-spirit," and where reason turns to myth, race was no longer the name of a supposed community substance. It was a structuring force, a fiction in possession of its own reality and able to produce reality.[30] The racial was a biological determination, of the order of blood and hereditary transmission as well as of the order of the body, the body of a people endowed with a will to power. But it was also an available affective disposition that could be mobilized if necessary; it was the phantasmagorical representation of ontological difference.

The black race in particular was deemed an inferior variety of the human race. The things of which it was the author were, by principle, bereft of life. Its objects were not the manifestation of any sort of sovereign will, or of its own proper energy, whose ultimate aim would be freedom. In them, the very idea of the symbol met its end, yielding only to a hideous ugliness—the field in which a fundamental arbitrary force circulates. Because they were not created by moral subjects, the objects made by blacks could only arouse scorn, terror, and disgust. Before these objects, one experienced either a sort of impotent horror or a vertiginous feeling of danger. This is because, in the profane world of things and bodies, man, as a living animal, had only ever been an always already alienated thing, ready to be cut up, cooked, and consumed during gory sacrifices.

During these feasts of matter, when violence exerted its ravages within, the body itself, similar to the object that was supposed to represent it, was no longer the substrate of any spirit.[31] The maker and user of an object controlled the object the same way that this object controlled its maker. At bottom, a relationship of strict similarity connected the two. Neither one nor the other existed for its own end, but instead for an end that was foreign to them. If there was bedazzlement, it could only be blind. And creation was not put in the service of any durable order. One created precisely with the aim of making the operation of sacrifice and destruction possible. And that is what these objects signified—the impossibility of escaping the limits of the thing, of returning from animal slumber, of rising up toward humanity.[32]

In these works, the exorbitant and the banal came together. They attested in any case to the tragic character of an arbitrary existence, destined for nothing. If, in fact, they fulfilled practical functions, they nevertheless had no substance. As the receptacles of the obscure passions of human existence, they above all fulfilled desires that were either turned away from reality or else nonsublimated. Moreover, they were linked to repugnant bodies. The feeling of shame and the strange measure of scorn with which these bodies were beset was displaced onto these artifacts, as objectal metaphors of substanceless function.

Lastly, in their excessive crudeness, their sensual coarseness, and their barely veiled erotic stain, the objects of blacks were above all sexual objects. They testified to an uninhibited thrust toward the outside, to a nonsublimated life of organs typical of primitive sexuality. In keeping with the missionary gaze, the art of the pagans was considered to be driven by an unintegratable violence. This is because this art, in its very origins, was seized by torment of the sexual. Here, bodily functions and genital functions were demetaphorized. If, in some way, art is the enactment of the unconscious, the latter was, among primitives, dominated by archaic images of penetration, of savage and epileptic coitus, and of primordial bisexuality. The individual was in truth neither a man nor a woman, but each time also animal and object, or all three at once, only one more than the other, as Freud might say.[33]

As a result, these objects expressed above all the predispositions of the primitives' drives. When they concerned the body and the sexual, or when they presented them to be seen, it was hardly to open the way up to representation, less still to sublimation, but instead to sensation. They were therefore not about representation. They were about excitation. The drives that they triggered in those who saw them did not aim to throw any ray of light into the darkness. They aimed to reawaken and to reactivate a sort of link to originary destructiveness that shocked as much as it attracted, that fascinated, but also deranged, ultimately generating a deep anxiety of castration. The affective intensity that they freed up was not of the order of rapture. They were capable of shocking the person who might encounter them; they fit the appearances of the real yet were cut loose from them; they gave free rein to fundamental passions of existence that the West had wanted to keep under its yoke, as condition for passing from the world of the indistinct to that of culture.

At the start of the twentieth century, a third type of gaze—at times ethnographic, at times conceptual—emerged.[34] The conceptual gaze asserted the plastic and purely formal qualities of "black objects," the sensation of depth evoked in African sculpture or its way of engendering space, that is, its power of affective intensification of the image. These objects, it was deemed, liberate sculpture not only from all perspective but also from every pictorial aspect. The ethnographic gaze sought to anchor these objects in context of their birth in order to disclose their social meanings. In the process, these objects were conferred the status of works of art, even if, once again, they were not really deciphered in their own terms.[35]

For Carl Einstein, for example, the art of blacks is above all shaped by religion. Sculpted works are venerated, as they were by all the peoples of Antiquity. The executant fashions his work as if it was divinity. Further still, the artist creates a god and his work is "independent, transcendent and free of all ties." This work is not commissioned to imitate nature, as in the European tradition. "The African work of art does not mean anything. It is not a symbol. It is the god." It brings to the point of collapse every distinction between signifier and signified. For others, the strength of African works can be explained by their capacity to manipulate the world by way of magic.[36] This is seen as interesting because they are held to be a platform on which one can rest in the hope of going beyond the limits of Western civilization.

Europe, it was argued, had forgotten something fundamental, something that a return to the African sign might enable it to rediscover, something stemming from the memory of pure forms, freed from every origin, and, in this respect, able to open the path to an ecstatic state—that ultimate degree of expressive intensity and the sublime point of sensation. This freeing from all origin was at the same time a freeing from all perspective. In black art, so the claim went, the psychic distance between spectator and image was reduced. Suddenly, the invisible aspects inherent in the image appeared. What thus took shape was the possibility of absolute perception. The object was no longer contemplated only by consciousness, but also by the *psyche*.

If this is so, it is because black art suggests other ways of representing space, ways that are both symbolic and optic. What it gives to be seen is the mental equivalent of the image rather than the image itself. It therefore gives rise to another modality of seeing. The eye does not require immobilization in order to see. On the contrary, the point is to liberate the eye, to render it active and mobile, to set it in relation to manifold other psychic and physiological processes. Only on this condition can seeing actively reconstruct reality. The eye, in these conditions, is not a dead organ. Going on what it sees and what it recognizes, its work is to explore what is missing: that is, to reconstruct, on the basis of multiple traces and indications, the object staged in the image—in short, to give rise to its appearing, to its coming alive.[37]

The Europe that rediscovered African objects at the start of the twentieth century was haunted by two tales: (re)commencement and ending.

As the commencement is the point of departure of a mutation toward something else, it poses the question of whether art can effectively serve as a point of departure toward a future that would not merely be a simple repetition of the past. As for the end, it may be inflected either in the mode of accomplishment (the spirited experience of meanings that would be unconditionally valid) or in that of catastrophe. There are ends that render any recommencement impossible. And there are conflagrations that prevent the advent of the end, or that portray it only in the mode of catastrophe.

At the start of the twentieth century, African objects contributed to rekindling this debate at the heart of a Europe searching for other ideas of time, the image, and truth. This Europe was one of conquest, whose world domination was relatively established, but that was simultaneously beset with doubt, for, in the last instance, its dominion over the rest of the world—and colonialism in particular—rested, as Aimé Césaire would later suggest, on an apocalyptic structure.[38] This Europe wondered whether its dominion over the world was ultimately purely spectral, and whether it was possible to elaborate an idea of time, image, and truth that would not be a simple idea of nothingness, but a veritable *thought of being and of relation.*

African objects have thus had an irreplaceable role in the historical trajectory of Europe. They have not merely served as tokens of its chimerical (and often disastrous) quest for the unveiling and manifestation of truth in the world, or of its desperate search for a compromise between spirit, the sensible, and matter. In almost spectral fashion, they have also served to remind Europe of the extent to which the appearance of spirit in matter (which is the proper question of art) always requires a language, another language, the language of the other, the other's arrival in language.

Today, nearly everywhere in the West, the question being asked is whether or not to restitute these objects to those entitled to them. Very few people, however, care to understand what originally justified their presence in Europe or to know what they signified in European consciousness. In such conditions, it is important to return to the essential issues. What precisely does one want to divest oneself of? What is one seeking to repatriate and why? Is the work that these objects were sup-posed to accomplish in the history of European consciousness finished? What will this work have produced in the end, and who ought to bear the consequences of it? After so many years with these objects present in its institutions, has Europe finally learned to come to terms with those who come from outside, and even from extremely remote places? Is Europe finally ready to embark on the path toward destinations that are still to come, or is it no longer anything other than the pure event of a fissure, a thing split in pure loss, without depth or perspective?

MILLSTONE OF DEBTS

Legalism and paternalism comprise the two sorts of response generally mobilized by those who oppose the project of restitution. On the one hand, some are wont to claim that, in the last instance, the law (as it hap-pens, various strands of European property law) by no means autho-rizes the return or transfer of these artifacts to those rightfully entitled to them. Care is taken not to call into question the external origin of these artifacts and their creators. Nevertheless, the response given to the question of to whom they belong is presented as if it is absolutely inde-pendent of the—supposedly prejudicial—question of where they come from and who their authors are.

In other words, a caesura is introduced between the law of property and use on the one hand and the act of creating and the creating subject on the other. It is asserted, notably, that having made something does not automatically make one the owner of that thing. To make an object is one thing. Having the right to use, enjoy, and dispose of that thing, exclusively and absolutely, is something else altogether. And just as mak-ing is not the equivalent of possessing, a work's origin is not a sufficient condition to lay claim to its possession or to a right of possession.

One also acts as if, in truth, the conditions under which these objects were acquired were entirely unproblematic, as if, from start to finish, this involved transactions between equals on a free market, on which the value of these objects was determined by an objective pricing mechanism. The conclusion drawn is that, having endured the market test, these objects are no longer "vacant and without masters." They are alleged henceforth to be "inalienable": the exclusive property either of a public authority (which manages them through its museums) or of private individuals who, having bought them, are qualified, in the eyes of the law, to enjoy them fully, unhindered. From a legal viewpoint, the debate over the restitution of African objects is thus declared unfounded, on the grounds that their presence in Western museums and other private institutions has nothing to do with confiscation and, in this respect, requires no moral or political judgment.

Some others—sometimes the same individuals—claim that Africa does not have the necessary institutions, infrastructures, technical or financial resources, or qualified staff or know-how to ensure that the objects in question will be protected and conserved. Returning these collections to such environments would put them at serious risk of destruction, deterioration, vandalism, or despoliation. Keeping them in Western museums is thus deemed the best way to safeguard them, even if this requires loaning them out to Africans from time to time. Others, lastly, certainly want to restitute the objects, even in the absence of any claim from the allegedly despoiled African communities, but they maintain that there can be no question of recognizing a debt of any sort to anyone whomsoever.

Posing the problem of restitution in this way—insofar as it entails recognition neither of debt nor of any other substantial obligation—is neither innocent nor neutral. It is one of the strategies of obfuscation used by those who are convinced that in war, whether declared or not, the victor is always right and plunder is its compensation. The defeated party is always wrong; it has no choice other than to thank its executioner should the latter spare its life, and there is no automatic right to justice for the defeated. In other words, might is right and the law has no might that does not depend on the power of the victors.

How can we prevent such a cynical conception of law from masking the real nature of the disagreement thus obfuscated, that is, from reducing a cause as eminently political and moral as this one to a simple fight between lawyers and accountants, other than by turning our backs to it? To claim, as a pretext, that law and right are autonomous and need no supplement indeed amounts to detaching the law from every obligation to justice. The law's function is then no longer to serve justice, but to sanctify existing relations of force.

We need, instead, to leave behind an exclusively quantitative approach to restitution, since such an approach considers restitution from the sole viewpoint of the institution of property and the law that ratifies it. So that the restitution of African objects does not become an occasion for Europe to buy itself a good conscience at a cheap price, the debate must be recentered around the historical, philosophical, anthropological, and political stakes of the act of restitution. One then sees that every authentic politics of restitution is inseparable from a *capacity for truth*, such that honoring truth and acts of repairing the world become, by the same token, the essential foundation of a new connection and a new relationship.

Of all the regions of the Earth, ours—though this is certainly not the entirety of its history—is no doubt distinguished from others by the nature, the volume, and the density of that of which it was dispossessed, forcibly or otherwise. Is it because the continent never ruled over an undisputed empire from over the seas? Or, as the poet Aimé Césaire recalled in other circles, because it invented neither gunpowder nor the compass?[39] Or because its name was never known and feared in faraway lands, except perhaps for the harshness of its climate—and, according to Hegel, the ferociousness of its potentates and its cannibal festivities, the alpha and omega of all racist phantasmagoria?

It is still the case that if so many treasures are to be found abroad, it is because there is a brutal part of Africa's history made up of depredations and ransacking, lacerations, continued removals, and successive seizures—hence Africa's extraordinary difficulty in keeping its people at home and holding on to the finest of its endeavors for itself. In fact, from the fifteenth century on, Europeans intruded on the African coastlines. For close to four centuries, and with the active complicity of local chiefs, warriors, and merchants, they maintained a lucrative and armed trade in human meat, seizing possession, in the process, of the bodies of millions of men and women of working age. Then came the nineteenth century. In the course of many and various expeditions and other incursions, Europeans would confiscate, bit by bit and despite multiple forms of resistance, everything that they were capable of laying their hands on, including territories.

Anything they were unable to carry off, the Europeans ransacked and often burned down. Predation upon bodies was not enough. During the colonial occupation properly speaking, they held countless inhabitants as ransom or destroyed what the latter held to be precious.

With the granaries run dry, the livestock wiped out, and the harvests burnt, many lands were depopulated, subjected as they were to illness and malnutrition, to forced labor, to the extracting of rubber, and to other forms of *corvée*, not to mention the ecological disturbances brought about by colonization.[40]

Practically no domain was spared—not even ancestors or the gods. Europeans even went so far as to desecrate burial places. In the whirlwind, they carried off just about everything—objects of finery; others related to the basic necessities of life; delicate fabrics; sumptuous necklaces; rings; artistically made jewelry inlaid with gold, copper, or bronze; belts; diverse gold-broached objects, including swords; shields used by warriors; doors; ornamental openwork seats and thrones with figures of men, women, and animals and elements of flora and fauna; magnificent fibulas, bracelets, and other spangles; and thousands and thousands of "medicaments" that they would equate to so many "fetishes." What to say of the sculpted wood pieces with their finely carved curved lines and knotwork? Or of the braiding and weaving of all sorts, the countless reliefs and bas-reliefs, the bronze or wooden human figures, combined with heads of quadrupeds, images of birds, snakes, or plants, like the marvelous landscapes of popular tales, sounds, and multicolored fabrics? How can we forget, in addition, the thousands of skulls and human bones, most of which were stacked high in university basements, hospital laboratories, and the storage rooms of Western museums? When all is said and done, is there a single Western museum that does not rely, in its concept, on African bones?[41]

As several observers have noted, a good number of ethnographic missions began to resemble such predatory activities as abductions and pillages, hunts and raids.⁴² Indeed, the adjacency of natural objects, diverse artifacts, and stuffed wild animals in many Western (ethnographic and military) museums of the nineteenth century attests to these amalgams. The collection of material objects belonging to these "peoples of nature" often went hand in hand with that of hunting trophies, and therefore with the killing and dismembering of animals.⁴³ A museological process then ordered these items, transforming the totality of the spoils (animals included) into cultural products.⁴⁴ Practices of collection were therefore not limited to objects or to the dismemberment of human bodies.⁴⁵ The capture of wild animals was also part of it, including everything from "the smallest insects to the largest mammals."⁴⁶ Such was also the case with manifold zoological and entomological specimens. Little wonder, then, that during the collecting of masks, the heads of masks were, in a dramatic gesture of decapitation, separated from their costumes. As Julien Bondaz suggests, "The vocabulary used to designate the practices of collection well accounts for such overlaps." If we must recognize that not all these objects became items of collection through exclusively violent means, the modes of their acquisition were nonetheless often in keeping with practices of predation.

LOSS OF WORLD

All these objects were part of a *generative economy*. Products of an open system of mutualization of knowledge, they expressed the marriage between the individual and singular genius [*génie*] and the common genius, as part of participatory ecosystems in which the world was not an object to be conquered, but a reserve of potentials, and in which there was no pure and absolute power but that which was the source of life and of fecundity.

Concerning restitution, it is therefore necessary to come back to the essential issues. To explain the permanence of the removals we have suffered by an absence of scientific and technological prowess and of firepower is only a veil that hides what is most at stake. For starters, the history of African technical systems and their operating frameworks remains to be written. Further, sight has probably been lost of the fact that science and technology do not exhaust the relationship that the human genus entertains with the world, matter, and all living beings. Science and modern technology are only some mediations, among many others, of the human presence in nature and in existence. Science and religion are not necessarily opposed to magic, the profane is not the antithesis of the sacred, and the magical mode of existence is not necessarily pretechnological. There exists no single evolutive scale, extending along a linear trajectory, that would serve to provide an authoritative measure and judgment over all modes of existence.

That Africa did not invent thermobaric bombs does not mean that it created neither technical objects nor works of art, or that it was closed to borrowings or to innovation. It privileged other modes of existence, within which technology in the strict sense constituted neither a force of rupture and diffraction, nor a force of divergence and separation, but rather a force of splitting and multiplication. At the heart of this dynamic, each concrete and distinct reality was always and by definition a symbol of something else, of another figure and structure.

In this system of permanent reflections, mutual relationships of correspondence, and multiple schemes of mediation, each object ceaselessly enveloped, masked, disclosed, and exposed another object, extending its world and inserting into it. Being was not opposed to nonbeing. Within a tension as intense as it was interminable, the one would strive each time to incorporate the other. Becoming acted as identity, a reality that emerges only after the event—not qua that which completes and consecrates but that which always begins, announces, and prefigures, that which authorizes metamorphosis and transition (to other places, to other figures, to other moments). For this plastic humanity, it was more important to insert oneself into the world with the aim of participating in it and extending it than it was to mathematize, dominate, and subjugate it.

As we see in the Amerindian cultures described by Carlo Severi, it was not only human beings that were endowed with speech, with movement, and indeed with a sex. Many artifacts were as well, or could be. The same applied to animals and other living creatures. If all was begotten, all was equally subject to demise.[47] Everything had its emblem. Further still, all that exists, so it was believed, was in a movement of constant transformation and, at precise moments, could take on the emblems and powers of another being, or even of several beings at once. Different modes of existence could characterize any individual at all "whatever its nature, animal, vegetal, human or artifact," observes Severi.[48] Nothing expresses better this idea of the potential and ceaseless transformation of all beings than what Carl Einstein called "the drama of metamorphosis," by which we must understand the constant renewal of forms by their "displacement and their plural recomposition."[49]

This principle of relation expressed not by a dead identity but by "continual circulation" of vital energy and by constant passages from one form to another did not only apply to human beings. Animals, birds, and plants could take on the form of humans and vice versa.[50] This did not necessarily mean that, between the person or the existing being and its outside double, there was a total lack of distinction, or that the singularity of each was reduced to nothingness. The same goes for the wearing of a mask. Wearing a mask did not turn one into a god. The masked initiate celebrated the epiphany of a *multiple* and plastic being, one constituted of multiple other beings of the world, with their own specific characteristics, the whole being reunited in a single body. The capacity to perceive oneself as an object or as a medium did not necessarily lead to a complete fusion of subject and object.

As a result, the concept of ontological limit never had the authority that it acquired in the trajectories taken by other regions in the world. The important thing was not to be oneself, to have been oneself, or to repeat oneself in fidelity to a primitive unity. Neither was denying oneself or repeating oneself when necessary a matter of censure. *Becoming other*, crossing the limits, being able to be reborn, at another time, in other places, and in a multitude of different figures, in an infinity of others, and summoned in principle to engender other flows of life— such was the fundamental demand existing within a structure of the

166 THE HOUSE WITHOUT KEYS

world that was, strictly speaking, neither vertical, nor horizontal, nor oblique, but *reticular*.

If not all works of art were ritual objects, they were nonetheless made to come alive by way of ritual acts. For that matter, no object existed except in relation to a subject, as part of a reciprocal definition. The attribution of subjectivity to any inanimate object took place through rituals, ceremonies, and these relations of reciprocity. Such is the world that we lost, that African objects bore, and whose epiphany they celebrated through the plurality of their forms. This world is one that no one will ever be able to restitute to us.

These objects were vehicles of energy and movement. As living matter, they cooperated in life. Even when mere utensils and devices in themselves, they had a share in life: that is, in physical, psychic, and energetic life; in the sort of life whose primary quality was circulation. Perhaps this is why, being powers of engendering, subversion, and masquerade, as much as privileged markers of paganism and animism, they were subject to such diabolization. Today, how can one intend to restitute them to us without dediabolizing them beforehand—without oneself having "renounced the devil"?

We have therefore been, over a relatively long period, the warehouse of the world, at once its vital source of supplies and the abject subject of their extraction. Africa will have paid the world a heavy tribute, and it is far from being over. There is something colossal, uncountable, and almost priceless that has been lost for good, and that is attested by the life of all our objects in captivity, just as that of all those of ours inside the carceral landscape of yesterday and of today.

In certain circumstances, some of these objects played a properly philosophical role. They also served as mediators between humans and vital powers. For humans, they served as a means to think their own shared existence. Indeed, behind the technical gestures that went into making them, a particular horizon was hidden—the mutualization of resources that generated ways not prone to endangering the whole of the ecosystem; the unconditional refusal to turn everything into commodities; the duty to open the door and speech to the dynamics of partner relationships and the uninterrupted creation of commons. Losing them thus led to a real impoverishment of the symbolic world.

Behind each one of these objects lies some métier, and behind each métier lies a font of knowledge and understandings that were incessantly acquired and transmitted, as well as technical and aesthetic modes of thinking, figurative sorts of information, a certain spark of magic, in short human effort to tame the very matter of life, the assortment of its substances. One of their functions included putting forms and forces in relation while symbolizing them: that is, activating powers making it possible to move the world.[51]

All that is gone—and this is the heavy tribute that Africa will have paid Europe, that region of the world to which we are tied by an intrinsic relationship of extraction and removal. This is perhaps one of the reasons that many Africans attach to the memory of Europe a note at once of fascination and of infamy. There is a perverse fascination with the brute force and power exerted, a power of deliberate untruth and of the practically permanent denial of responsibility. And infamy, because many Africans are convinced that Europe wants nothing as far as they are concerned; that what it wants is an essentially obedient and docile Africa; that it wants an Africa akin to a corpse stripped of its shroud, which, although basically lifeless, ceaselessly revives itself and rises up in its coffin; that the sort of African that Europe tolerates and accepts is the African whose energies it continually captures and hijacks, one who obeys with the docile fidelity of an animal able to recognize its master once and for all.

THE CAPACITY FOR TRUTH

The West long refused to acknowledge that it owed us any debt at all. It refused to acknowledge the millstone of debts that—accumulated over the course of its world conquest—it has dragged along ever since. Today, most of the West's defenders claim, instead, that we are indebted to it.

As they put it, we owe it a debt of "civilization," insofar as some of us have, they point out, benefited from the wrongs that, sometimes with our own complicity, were done to us. Today, the West does not simply want to rid itself of the strangers that we are. It also wants us to take back our objects. Without giving any account of itself, it finally wants to be able to declare: "Not having done you any wrong, I owe you all strictly nothing."

By inviting us to take back our objects and to liberate the spaces that they occupied in its museums, what, then, does it seek? To weave new relationships? Or, in this era of closure, does it seek to reiterate something it has always suspected, namely that we were person-objects, disposable by definition? Will we facilitate its task by renouncing every right to remembrance? Will we dare to go further and decline the offer of repatriation? By thus transforming these objects into eternal proof of the infamy that it committed, but that it wants to take no responsibility for, will we ask it to live forever with what it has taken and assume its Cain-like figure to the very end?

But suppose that we yield to the offer, and that instead of a veritable act of *restitution*, we satisfy ourselves with a simple *recuperation of artifacts henceforth without substance*? How are we to sort out objects and their use-value, on the one hand, from works of art, on the other? Or objects of ritual and worship from ordinary objects, when very few people are sure of what each of these objects is in itself, of how they were made and how they "functioned," of what energies they served as repositories for and were able to release, of the circumstances in which they did so, and of their effects on matter as well as on humans and the living in general? When it comes down to it, all this knowledge was lost.

As Pol Pierre Gossiaux explains, African art corresponded to an aesthetics that may be qualified as cumulative. Its objects resulted "from the assembling and accumulation of disparate elements" whose "sense and function came from the formal and semantic relations thus created by their accumulation." The object assembled in this way was qualified as "beautiful" only to the extent that it fully assumed its ritual functions. Such accumulations, Gossiaux makes clear, did not come about by chance. They demanded lengthy apprenticeships and initiations into the handling of secular knowledges that have been lost.[52] Beyond the objects as such, who will restitute the acts of thought that were associated with them, the types of cognition at stake in them, the forms of memory and imagination that they mobilized and of which they were, in turn, the product?

In addition, between that which left and that which returns, the gap is great. Most of these objects have been deformed and become unrecognizable. The objects present in collections and museums were not only cut off from the cultural contexts in which they had been summoned to take part.[53] Some have endured numerous wounds and amputations, including physical, and now bear considerable scars.[54] Let us take, as an example, the masks and other objects previously used in dance ceremonies. Most arrived in Europe coiffed, adorned with all sorts of finery (feathers of owls, eagles, vultures, quails, or roosters, or porcupine quills, and even dresses made from the inner bark of pigmented papyrus). These distinctive styles and bits of finery, as well as the context in which they were invited to make their appearance, made them receptacles of meaning. And they were as important as the morphological qualities of the objects or, as Gossiaux points out, "the articulation of their geometry in space." Nevertheless, Europeans systematically stripped them "of everything that seemed to conceal their apparent structures."[55]

Even if among most of the peoples that produced these objects the opposition between myth and technology, and between technology and ritual, was by definition weak, how are we to identify, among the masks, statues and reliquary-statuettes, flyswatters, vegetal debris, human bones and amulets, animal skins, kaolin, seashells and padouk powder, assegais, drums, and other objects consecrated to rites of passages or initiation, all the various customs, that is, to distinguish those that were intended to honor the dead or to chase away evil spirits from others that were required for therapeutic or divinatory practices?

Who can honestly deny that what was taken were not only objects, but along with them enormous symbolic deposits, enormous *reserves of potential*? Who does not see that the large-scale monopolizing of African treasures constituted a colossal and practically incalculable loss, and, consequently, cannot be remedied by purely financial compensation, since what it led to was the *devitalization* of our capacities to bring about worlds, to give rise to other figures of our common humanity?

The issue, therefore, cannot simply be the restitution of materials, styles, decors, and functions, for how is the meaning to be restituted? Is it lost for good? Who will recompense the fact of having to live with this loss forever? Is it no more than compensable? A certain Europe does not want to trouble itself with these questions. For it, restitution is not an obligation. Faithful to a variant of legalism inherited from its long history, it considers that an obligation can arise only when a legal constraint exists. In its eyes, all restitution, whatever one says, is one modality of payment among others. There is nothing to be paid without the prior existence of a debt. All restitution consequently entails the existence, avowed or disavowed, of a debt.

Now, Europe deems that it is not our debtors and that we are not its creditors. So no debt needs honoring. Were there any debt, we would be unable to oblige its payment. It is not obligable. Europe considers that, in the current state of affairs, there are no legal means of obliging it to restitute our objects. What characterizes obligation, properly speaking, is the possibility of sanctioning noncompliance. And if, despite all this, Europe does end up returning these objects, it will be done voluntarily, in an act of generosity and liberality and not as an obligation to anyone. In this case, as in others, the issue is one not of justice, but rather of an act of gratuitousness and benevolence. The act of restitution does not stem from gratuitousness and kindness. The act of restitution stems from an obligation. And there are obligations from which one cannot be discharged in keeping with existing legal constraints. They continue to be obligations for all that. Indeed, other obligations arise, from which one can discharge oneself voluntarily through a duty of conscience. But we have long since stopped believing in the use of appealing to one's conscience.

Any restitution, if it is to be authentic, must be enacted on the basis of a corresponding recognition of the seriousness of the harm suffered and the wrongs inflicted. There is strictly nothing to be restituted (or to be returned), whenever one considers that one has caused no wrong, that one has taken nothing that required permission of any sort. In this way, the act of restitution is inseparable from the act of making reparation. "To reestablish" or "to restore" (other words for restitution) is not the same as "to repent." For that matter, one is not the condition of the other. Similarly, restitution without compensation (or restoration) is by definition partial. But there are irreparable losses that no compensation can ever undo—which does not mean it is not necessary to compensate. To have given compensation does not mean that one has erased the wrong. It does not result in any absolution. To compensate, as Kwame Anthony Appiah underlines, is about offering to repair the relationship.[56] Further still, restitution is an obligation whenever a conscious, malicious, and deliberate act of destruction has been undertaken against another's life. In precolonial systems of thought, the most damaging wrongs were considered those that caused harm to what Tempels called "vital force."

In contexts where life was fragile, or was liable to being diminished, every attack on the integrity of being and on the intensity of life, however slight, merited restoration. In its plenary meaning, restoration (or restitution) implied that the damages suffered could be valued. The calculation of damages could be expressed in economic terms. But, in the last instance, damages were established according to a measure of the value of life. It was ultimately the measure of violation of life suffered that served as a basis for the valuation of damages or restitution.[57] Wholly in keeping with this philosophy, veritable restitution is therefore one that participates in the restoration of life. The law subtending it is more oriented toward persons than to goods or property. There is no restitution without reparation. Wherever material damages and interests come into play, the only sense they have is to perform that restoration of life.

Neither is there any real restitution in the absence of what we must indeed call *the capacity for truth*. From this viewpoint, "to render" pertains to an unconditional duty—the duty to the infinitely irrecusable thing that is life, all life, that form of debt unable to be discharged as a matter of principle. For Europe, restitution of our objects means that it ceases to approach us with the attitude of someone who considers that only their own reality counts and is necessary. Europe cannot purport to return our objects to us while remaining convinced that being a subject depends on insisting on one's own distinction, rather than on the sort of mutuality demanded by the reticular world that became ours. Each singular life counts. History is not a matter of force; it is also a matter of truth. Authority and dignity are not merely a donation coming from strength and power. One is therefore called upon to honor truth, and not only strength and power.

The truth is that Europe took things from us that it will never be able to restitute. We will learn to live with this loss. Europe, for its part, will have to take responsibility for its acts, for that shady part of our shared history of which it has sought to relieve itself. The risk is that if it fails to give an account of itself while restituting our objects, it will conclude that, with the restitution complete, our right to remind it of the truth is removed. But for new ties to be woven, it must honor the truth, as truth is the teacher of responsibility. This debt of truth cannot be erased as a matter of principle. It will haunt us until the end of time. Honoring it goes by way of a commitment to repairing the fabric and the visage of the world.

Honoring truth also comes with the commitment to learn and remember together. As Édouard Glissant never ceased to reiterate, "each of us needs the memory of the other."[58] This is not a matter of charity or compassion. It is a condition for the survival of our world. If we want to share "the world's beauty," he added, we ought to learn to be united with all its suffering. We will have to learn to remember together, and, in so doing, to repair together the world's fabric and its visage.

This is not about withdrawing into oneself, about allowing oneself to be inhabited by obsession with one's own place, about being among one's own kind, about a transcendental in itself, but rather about contributing to the rise of a new planet where we will all be welcome, where we will all be able to enter unconditionally, where we will all be able to embrace, eyes wide open, the inextricability of the world, its entangled nature and its composite character, in memory of this Earth that we share and in memory of all its inhabitants, humans and nonhumans.

6

AFROPOLITANISM

P ostcolonial Africa is made up of forms, signs, and languages nested within one another. These forms, signs, and languages are expressions of the effort of a world seeking to exist by itself. It has not been sufficiently repeated that this effort unfolds along several lines—sometimes oblique, sometimes parallel, sometimes curved. Frenetic lines that constantly break and continually change direction, opening the way for a whirlwind movement: accident rather than event, spasms, pulling from the bottom, movement in the same place, and, in every instance, paradoxes, complexity, and ambiguity. We must now describe not the movement of contraction, but other structural changes that operate according to other logics: collision, saturation, open-endedness. It is this production of intervals and other forms of composing life that the present chapter will examine.

SOCIAL RECOMPOSITIONS

At the center of these transformations is a redefinition of the terms of African states' sovereignty. This first factor of change is in part the result of multilateralization, most visibly carried out by international financial institutions over the last twenty years and, in even more caricatural manner, by the actions of innumerable agents whose status exceeds by far the classical distinctions between public and private (nongovernmental organizations, private actors, and so on). At the same time, a labyrinth of international networks has emerged at the local level. All claim to belong to "civil society," but in reality most of them arise out of the overlap of networks inside the state and others that constitute an informal extension of the state. Others are either umbrellas for political parties or urban elites, or local branches of international organizations. The heterogeneity of the logics that these different actors put into motion explains, in very large part, the fragmented nature of the forms of composing life that now prevail, at least in urban settings. The old world is crumbling without its customs necessarily becoming outdated.

Forms of social stratification have also become varied. Near the bottom, precariousness and exclusion touch larger and larger segments of the population. In cities in particular, mass poverty has become a structural factor in dynamics of reproduction. Near the top, a smaller and smaller class of owners is being formed, thanks to its ability to capture rents and its reliance on international networks. Between the two, a middle class is attempting to survive by combining the resources of both the formal economy and parallel markets. With increasing economic vulnerability vis-à-vis the rest of the world, African private and state actors have been obliged to look elsewhere for new sources of revenue, even as competition for control of state apparatuses has intensified. At the same time, the transnationalization of economies within the context of globalization has opened up a large space of autonomy to private entrepreneurs, who do not hesitate to occupy it. One form of exercising this relative autonomy is, paradoxically, by waging war.

War, the second factor at the root of the social recompositions of the last quarter of the twentieth century, is everywhere the consequence of an intertwining of several processes. Some are political. Many wars are in fact the result of constitutional disagreements to the extent that they bear, ultimately, on the political community's raison d'être and on the morality of its systems of distributing responsibilities, powers, resources, status, and privileges. These disagreements have to do with the conditions of exercising citizenship within a context of decreased benefits distributed by the state and increased possibilities for openly claiming these benefits (democratization), and even for seizing them by force. These disagreements henceforth crystallize around the triptych of identity, property, and citizenship. At stake in them is the refounding of the nation-state.

At the same time, the arguments that, following independence, served to legitimate the project of a nation-state are the objects of sometimes bloody contestations. Postcolonial authoritarian regimes had indeed raised the double construction of the state and the nation to a categorical imperative. In parallel, they had developed a conception of the nation based on the affirmation of collective rights, which rulers purposely opposed to individual rights.[1] Development, as a central metaphor of power and as the utopia of social transformation, represented the site where these rights, as well as collective well-being, were to be realized.[2] It was thought that development would be easily achieved if Western forms of democracy were curtailed and native traditions of communalism promoted.

Postcolonial communalism—whether it saw itself as inspired by socialism (for example, the *ujama* in Tanzania) or by capitalism (Ivory Coast, Cameroon, or Kenya), whether it was based in civil government or military regimes—emphasized, even if only in words, the quest for consensus, regional and ethnic equilibrium, reciprocal assimilation of different segments of the elite, and the construction of a shared world by means of social control and coercion, as needed. The goal of these tactics and mechanisms was to prevent dissent as well as ethnic strife. By foregrounding notions of individual rights and reigniting debates over the legitimacy of property and inequality, multipartyism and the market economy model have ruined this ideological construction of consensus. However, they have not led to automatic transition to the liberal democracy model either, and even less have they led to local reappropriation and translation of its main philosophical tenets (political recognition of the individual as a rational citizen, capable of making independent choices on his or her own, and affirmation of individual freedom and the rights attached to it). Thus, one of the ambiguities of democratization

in the specific circumstances of the atomized capitalism that Africa
has experienced is the relaunching of disputes over the morality of
exclusion, at an unprecedented scale.

New imaginaries of the state and the nation have emerged out of these
disputes. Two in particular merit attention. The first attempts to resolve
the apparent contradiction between citizenship and identity by advocat-
ing a constitutional recognition of ethnic identities, cultures, and traditions. This tradition of thought denies the existence of individuals in
Africa: only communities exist. According to this tradition, communi-
tarianism is the manifestation par excellence of African political culture.
In this context, refounding the state and the nation would consist in a
subtle art of organizing each group's or community's access—if necessary, by rotation—to the advantages and privileges that come from controlling the state apparatus. Access to these advantages would be based
on differential affirmation of the identity, culture, and traditions of each
ethnic community, rather than on the equal dignity of all human beings
as citizens endowed with practical reason.

Under these conditions, the state's legitimacy would rest on how well
it takes these differences into account in order to give particular treatment to each group and community, proportionate to the despoliations
it considers itself to have suffered. Several versions of such treatment are
at work already in parts of Africa. In South Africa, for example, where
the Apartheid regime left a legacy of some of the most inegalitarian
structures of revenue redistribution in the world, preferential or affirmative action policies have been put into place for historically disad-
vantaged groups. However, these policies go hand in hand with the recognition of individual rights, prescribed by one of the most liberal
constitutions in the world.[3] By contrast, in the most perverse configurations, attempts at reconstructing the state and nation on the basis of
the principle of difference and the recognition of particular identities
serve to exclude, marginalize, and eliminate certain components of the
nation.[4] This is notably the case in countries where distinctions between
natives and nonnatives are used in political struggles. In other countries,
groups that feel that their rights have been violated and that they are
marginalized in national politics use the discourse of difference to claim

collective rights, including the right to greater access to the resources extracted from beneath their land.[5]

The second imaginary of the state and nation currently being constituted is based in phenomena of transnationalization. At least two versions of cosmopolitanism have emerged over the last quarter of the twentieth century. The first is a practical cosmopolitanism, of the vernacular type, which, while resting on the obligation to belong to a distinct cultural or religious entity, leaves room for intense commerce with the world.[6] Out of this commerce, hybrid cultural formations on the path to accelerated creolization are emerging. This is the case, in particular, in Muslim Sudanese-Sahelian Africa, where migrations and long-distance trade go along with the peddling [*colportage*] of identities and the skilled use of modern technologies.[7] This is also the case in Pentecostal religious movements in Christian countries.[8] For many Africans, a relationship to divine sovereignty now serves as the principal purveyor of meanings. Almost everywhere, religious life is becoming the site from which new kinship structures are formed. These structures are not necessarily biological. Often, they transcend old affiliations, whether these are based on lineage or on ethnicity.[9] The development of new divine sects rests on the exploitation of four ideological-symbolic formations whose influence on contemporary conceptions of the self is obvious: the notion of charisma (which authorizes the practices of oracles, prophecies, and healing); the theme of miracles and wealth (that is, the belief that everything is possible); the theme of war against demons; and, finally, the categories of sacrifice and death. It is to these discursive figures that one turns in order to think about discord and death. They constitute the mental frameworks by which memory of the recent past is reinterpreted and the ordeal of the present is rendered meaningful.[10] These figures also serve to institute relations of the imagination with the world of material goods.[11]

This brand of cosmopolitanism, that of lower-class migrants, has led to the proliferation of fragmented spheres. We see this in the creation of veritable "holy" cities.[12] We also see it in the fluid practices adopted by undocumented immigrants in their destination countries and the xenophobia that, at the same time, contributes to keeping them even more in the shadows.[13] Within these spheres of illegality, communal frameworks are shattered, and new bonds are formed. In extreme cases, lawless zones appear and create significant rifts in the urban fabric. A criminal economy emerges at the intersection of local and international environments. Social actors are forced to create resources within conditions of permanent instability and near-absolute uncertainty and on an extremely short temporal horizon.

At the level of elites, one finds a second form of cosmopolitanism, which endeavors to reconstruct African identity and public space in accordance with the universal demands of reason. This reconstruction goes in two directions. The first consists in an effort to reenchant tradition and custom. The second proceeds by abstracting from tradition, since its main concern is the emergence of a modern and deterritorialized self. In this version, the emphasis is on the theme of civil government, which must encourage the creation of institutions favoring egalitarian participation in the exercise of sovereignty and representation. On the philosophical level, this version of cosmopolitanism foregrounds the ways in which Africans are identical to other humans.[14] The problematic of property and individual rights takes precedence over racial, cultural, or religious individualities and philosophies of irreducibility.[15]

This second form of cosmopolitanism is inseparable from the difficult emergence of a private sphere of life. The push toward the constitution of a private sphere is the result of several factors. The first is connected to the possibilities for migration enjoyed by the elite. Elites can escape from the demands of their immediate families and free themselves from the social control of the community. The second factor is connected to the new possibilities of becoming rich without encroachment by the state—possibilities that ideologies of privatization have only legitimized. Thus, the enjoyment of individual rights, notably in connection with property, becomes a critical element in new ways of imagining the self.

A third phenomenon is the tension between the transnationalization of African cultural production and forms of production of locality and indigenousness. Over the last quarter of the twentieth century, this tension has been found in three areas in particular: the transfer of powers from the central state to new territorial collectivities (decentralization), the metropolization of the continent around major regional and cosmopolitan urban centers, and the appearance of new, modern lifestyles.[16] On the one hand, the movement toward decentralization has gone along with significant territorial redivisions that have multiple social and political stakes. Indeed, such rezoning has generally translated into allocations of services and jobs. Even more important is the fact that within the context of the transnationalization of African societies, control over local resources has proven to be a powerful factor in accessing international resources.[17] In several countries, the re-zoning of territories has allowed local elites to strengthen their positions as intermediaries between towns, the state, and international networks. Because the mobilization of local resources is indispensable for negotiation with the international world, it has become clear that, far from opposing each other, logics of locality and logics of globalization mutually reinforce each other.

Moreover, because control over local resources is mostly in the hands of local bureaucrats, politicians, chiefs, and religious leaders, many social actors have sought to mobilize traditional solidarities in order to win the newly opened-up competition. This is one of the reasons why processes of decentralization and democratization have so clearly contributed to the resurgence of conflicts over autochthony and the worsening of tensions between natives on the one hand and migrants and nonnatives on the other.[18] Everywhere, solidarities based on kinship and territory are reactivated, and rivalries and disagreements within local societies are rekindled. The production of locality and the production of nativeness constitute two sides of a single movement, carried out by various actors: traditional chiefs, public figures, marabouts, professional elites, subprefects, bureaucrats, networks for mutual aid and solidarity, urban elites.[19] All these actors shape local arenas by way of procedures both formal and informal.

This process, at once cultural, political, and economic, is driven not only by the market.[20] It is also fostered by the state, international financial organizations, and nongovernmental organizations involved in the struggle to protect the environment and the rights of indigenous peoples. In several countries, the devolution of power over renewable resources from the state to rural communities has given rise not only to the creation of new communes and regions—most of which are established along kinship and ethnic lines—but also to the promulgation of new legislation and, sometimes, to a de facto recognition of traditional rights and so-called biocultural heritage.[21] Land tenure is one of the domains in which the recognition of traditional right took place. This was notably the case when it came to drawing the borders of reservations and natural parks, or to defining the conditions of exploiting forests or protected areas.[22] The confiscation of so-called traditional lands and the attribution of these domains to individuals who are supposed to develop them are no longer the only means of intervention. The state is no longer necessarily trying to counterweigh the influence of tradition or weaken the authorities responsible for ensuring it.[23] The result is an inextricable entanglement between the laws of the state and local traditions.[24] This legal and normative pluralism determines the behavior and strategies of private actors and communities in conflicts over the appropriation of lands and the management of key resources.[25]

However, new regulatory measures are not enough to produce social consensus, and disputes within populations have multiplied. In the case of former settlement colonies, where the commercialization of lands took place at the expense of natives, land struggles have taken a more radical turn (as in the case of Zimbabwe). This is also the case in regions where the consequences of the commercialization of land and resources have not been controlled, and where conflicts are fed by unequal relations of force between multinational enterprises and local communities that feel they have been harmed.[26] Elsewhere, the persistence of traditional rules of inheritance and the weight of kinship are at the origin of the heightening of tensions between natives and nonnatives.[27]

THE FAR-OFF AND LONG DISTANCE

Let us now turn to a key feature of African life during the last quarter of the twentieth century, the tightening of monetary policy and its revivifying effects on imaginaries of the far-off and practices of long distance. This tightening was in part due to the shift in Africa's place in the international economy, just ten years after independences. This shift, which began in the early 1970s, spread over almost a quarter century. It is far from over. The structural adjustment programs of the 1980s and 1990s constituted some of the most impactful turning points of this shift, even if, on their own, they did not play the role generally accorded to them by their critics. These programs hardly permitted modification of the structure of African countries' international economic specialization in these countries' favor. But they greatly contributed to putting into place new economic configurations that can no longer be described either by the old structuralist "center-periphery" scheme, or by theories of dependence, or by theories of "marginalization."

Indeed, between the years 1980 and 2000, an atomized capitalism, unaccompanied by any agglomeration or enormous centers of growth, developed on the ruins of a revenue economy dominated by state companies, controlled by the clientelist systems in power and by monopolies dating back to the colonial era of captive markets. The dichotomy between urban economy and rural economy and between formal economy and informal economy that characterized the moment immediately following the end of colonization exploded. These dichotomies were replaced by a patchwork, a mosaic of spheres—in short, a diffracted economy, comprising various, more or less intertwined, sometimes parallel, regional nodes that maintained changing and extremely volatile relations with international economic networks. A multiplicity of economic territories, often within the same country, sometimes nested within one another and often disjointed, is emerging out of this extreme fragmentation.

Let us note that this new economic geography is not unlike the geography that prevailed in the nineteenth century, just prior to colonial conquest and partition. At the time, each economic space was part of a vast, more or less coherent regional and multinational ensemble, within which power and commerce often went together. Such regional and multiethnic ensembles were not characterized by stable and precise borders, or by clear figures of sovereignty, but rather by a complex series of vertical corridors, lateral axes, and networks that were often mutually imbricated according to the *principle of intertwining and multiplicity*. At the time, every economy was underpinned by a double dynamic of spatial order and demographic order. Let us take the example of the Chad Basin. Before colonization, this region was tightly connected to three poles of power and influence: Cyrenaica (at the far edge of the Ottoman Empire), the Egyptian Sudan, and the Sokoto Caliphate and Haoussa cities (Sokoto, Katsina, Kano). Within this triangle—whose base lay along the Equator, whose eastern and western sides extended toward the Sahara and the Nile, and whose tip was the Mediterranean—roads ran from Kanem and Wadai, through Murzuq on one side and Koufra on the other, leading directly to Tripoli and Benghazi after crossing many oases. This north-south axis was complemented by an enormous corridor connecting the region to the Sultanate of Darfur, Kurdufan, and Bahr el-Ghazal.

A second, properly institutional dynamic was added to this two-dimensional (vertical and horizontal) organization. Until the beginning of the nineteenth century, the two dominant institutions responsible for the socialization of elites, as well as for the mobilization of resources and ideas, were the *zawiya* (religious schools) and the *zariba* (enclosed villages). The functions of these two highly original institutions included, among other things, regulating transnational caravan commerce; cementing commercial, political, and religious alliances; negotiating proximity with neighbors (the Bideyat and the Toubou, for example) and conflicts between various factions; and, finally, when necessary, conducting war through a series of fortified sites—there was thus nomadism and citadelization. A third dynamic combined war, mobility, and commerce. Here, war and commerce went hand in hand with the practice of Islam. There was no commerce without the capacity to create transversal alliances and to extend and invest nodal points in a constantly moving space. In the same way, war itself was always a war of movement—never local, always transnational. The institutions in charge of regulating war and commerce were, moreover, run by the Senussi religious order. Caravans covered enormous distances and contributed to various commercial cycles (the cycle of grains and dates, livestock, ivory, slaves, and, today, the cycle of petrol and so on). Though most of the commercial establishments of Tripoli and Benghazi were in the hands of Italian Jewish and Maltese merchants, the intermediaries were Mejabra and Zuwaya Arabs.

Here, the drama of colonization was not so much the arbitrary division of previously united entities—the Balkanization that the Afronationalist vulgate is always invoking. It was, rather, the attempt to shape pseudostates on the basis of what fundamentally was a *federation of networks* and a *multinational space* made up not of "peoples" or "nations" as such, but rather of *networks*. It was an attempt to set rigid borders in what was structurally a *space of circulation* and negotiation—flexible and with a changeable geography.

Historically, the real wellsprings of power in this region have always structured themselves through a double cycle: the cycle of commerce and the cycle of predation. Commerce and predation have always been underpinned by the possibility of war, most often in the form of raids. Struggles for power and conflicts over the capture, control, and distribution of resources always unfolded along lines that were by definition translocal. No matter whether these lines referred to religious orders, clans, or lineages, their formation always obeyed what could be called the *logic of moving sands*. Unable to transform these logics, colonization attempted to use them for its own profit—with the catastrophic results with which we are familiar. It is not new for power to become structured and disorganized as a result of predatory cycles. This was the case in the desert economy, dominated by commerce in fruits and grains, control of oases, the technique of raids, and the building of storehouses. Nor is the system of circulation, with moving borders that constantly shift as a function of opportunities for exploitation, new.

Prior to colonization, warriors, merchants, and marabouts could easily cross the Tibesti massif from Koufra and occupy Abéché, the capital of the Ouaddi Empire. There were many Arabized Nubians from the Dongola region as well as *jallaba* traders along the axis of Darfur, Kordofan, and Bahr el-Ghazal. It was the *jallaba* who, profiting from Turkish-Egyptian expeditions in the 1840s, opened up the economic border of south Darfur, the Nuba Mountains, from the Blue Nile to the border regions of Ethiopia. More significantly, they extended their tentacles toward the Equator and forced their presence onto the great plains that extend west and south from the Nile, toward Congo and present-day Central African Republic, where they excelled in the commerce of slaves and ivory. There, they established fortifications (*zariba*) in the midst of Nile peoples such as the Dinka, the Nuer, the Azande (present-day Sudan), the Banda (present-day Central African Republic), and the Bongo and the Sara (present-day Republic of Chad). These *jallaba* are found further to the east as well, in Darfur, in Kanem and Burnu.

Today, the new border—at least in this region—is defined by oil. Elsewhere, it is other resources: wood, diamonds, cobalt. Exploitation of these resources has given rise to new cycles of extraction and predation. A large part of the draining of natural resources is carried out by means of war or endless, low-intensity conflicts. It is the extreme fluidity and volatility of this new border created by draining, extraction, and predation that give African conflicts their international significance. It is in this context that mining, oil, and fishing enclaves have taken on decisive importance. Whether they are maritime or land-based, enclave economies are extractive in nature. They either are disconnected from the rest of the national territory or are only connected to it by tenuous networks. This is notably the case with offshore oil operations. On the other hand, these economies are directly connected to networks of international commerce. When enclaves do not feed the logic of war, they themselves tend to be disputed spaces. Sometimes controlled by multinational corporations to whom the central state subcontracts—or practically delegates—its sovereignty, sometimes in collusion with armed dissident movements, enclaves present an economy that symbolizes the osmosis between activities of extraction, predation, war, and commerce.

Another aspect of the transnationalization of African economies in the last quarter of the twentieth century is the emergence of "free" or "gray" zones or corridors, one of whose characteristics is to protect intensive exploitation of rich territories and to encourage the circulation and flow of resources produced in contexts of latent militarization. These "gray" or "free" zones operate in the manner of capitations or concessions. They are made up of abandoned territories, or parks and natural preserves—veritable extraterritories administered by various indirect regimes and exploited by private companies that often have their own military forces. Of all the consequences of this atomization of the market economy, two in particular have played leading roles in creating imaginaries of politics as a bellicose relation, a game of chance, and confrontation with death. Two forms of violence are henceforth combined and prolong each other. The first is the violence of the market. It is set off by struggles for control and privatization of the new borders of extraction, predation, and draining. The second is social violence, rendered uncontrollable by the state's loss of monopoly over it. An example of the violence of the market is the tightening of monetary policy and the widespread drying up of liquid assets, followed by their gradual concentration along a few channels, which have become more and more difficult to access. This has caused a brutal reduction in the number of individuals capable of making loans to others. The nature of debt itself is changing, with "debts of protection" (which include the duty to nourish) becoming the ultimate signifier of kinship relations (whether real or fictive) or social relations tout court. More than before, money has become a force of separation between individuals and the object of intense conflicts. A new economy of persons has appeared, based on the commodification of relations that had hitherto escaped—at least in part—commodification. Connections through objects and goods have solidified, as has the idea that everything can be bought and sold.

Faced with the constraints resulting from a drastic reduction in monetary circulation, a central fact of recent decades has been the emergence of practices consisting in traveling to far-off places in order to earn money. New dynamics for securing income, caused by the scarcity of money, have led to an unprecedented revivification of imaginations of the far-off and long-distance travel. This revivification has led to an unprecedented increase in private agents' mobility, but also to violent attempts to immobilize entire categories of populations in space, and even to the organization of mass deaths. Management of the mobility of persons and even of groups is sometimes overseen by extrastate jurisdictions or armed groups. This management is itself inseparable from mastery over the bodies subjected to work in concessions that blend·

mercantilism and militarism, bodies that are appropriated for labor power in numerous military markets, that are pushed to mass exodus or are immobilized in spaces of exception, such as camps and other "security zones," that are physically incapacitated through various mutilations or are destroyed en masse in massacres. A more tragic choice is now replacing the choice between obedience and disobedience, characteristic of the model of colonial *commandement* and postcolonial potentate, which, during the authoritarian period, used techniques of police and discipline to control individuals: the choice between decline, survival, and slow or deferred death.

Henceforth what is at stake in the exercise of a power more fragmented and capillary than ever is, in large part, the possibility of producing and reproducing life at all. This new form of power, based on the multiplication of situations of extreme vulnerability, attacks bodies and life only in order to better control the flux of resources. But because, more so than in the past, life has become a colony of immediate powers, the terms of this power are not only economic. It is thus important to consider the meaning of this work of destruction, an important part of which consists in the expenditure of countless human lives. Georges Bataille observed in his time that this form of expenditure calls into question the classical principle of utility. Basing himself in particular on Aztec sacrifices and wars, he focused on what he called the "price of life" and its relation to "consumption." He thereby established the existence of a formation of power in which the goal of sacrificing and immolating as many lives as possible constitutes, in itself, a form of "production." In the case of the Aztecs, human sacrifices were explained by the belief that the sun needed to eat the hearts and blood of the greatest number of people—and in particular prisoners—in order to continue to shine. This being the case, war was necessary to ensure the reproduction of the solar cycle. It was not primarily linked to any will to conquer. Its central meaning was to make the act of consumption possible. Through this act, the risk of the sun darkening—and, thus, of life being extinguished—was reduced. As for human sacrifices, they made it possible to restore to the sacred world what servile usage had denigrated and made profane. For Bataille, this form of destruction—or violent and profitless

consumption—constituted the best way of negating the utilitarian relation between men and things.

In the case that interests us here, massacres and the destruction of
human life partake in a more or less similar principle of negation. It is,
however, not certain that such bloody wastefulness contributes to producing sacred things—the function Bataille assigns to sacrifice in general. To the contrary, at the origin of this wastefulness is the idea of an
enemy, a foreign body that must be excreted or eradicated. Insofar as the
relation to an enemy—antikin par excellence—presents itself as a struggle between different species, it is possible to maintain that such a logic
of enmity is a form of "total politics." Here, the complex of war (which
includes draining, extraction, and predation) includes the group of activities that Bataille describes as "expenditure." These are all the so-called
"nonproductive" forms, which, as such, do not always serve production
in either the short or the long term: luxury, mourning, worship, spectacles, perverted sexual activities, pain and cruelty, partial torments,
orgiastic dances, lewd scenes, fleeting pleasures, the violent satisfaction
of coitus—in short, the fit of exaltation that encourages excretion. The
enemy, as a foreign body or "poison," is thus subjected to the excremen-
tal drive: the enemy must be excreted, like an abject thing with which it
is necessary to break abruptly. In these conditions, violence is likely to
take on aspects of defecation. But the logic of defecation does not exclude
other dynamics, such as another form of violence that aims to swallow
and incorporate a slain enemy or parts of his body. The goal of this logic
of eating is to capture the victim's virility and power of germination.
Both the logic of defecation and the logic of eating require the violation
of prohibitions and taboos—a kind of profanation.

Because the new dynamics of securing income are based in large part
on values of itinerancy rather than sedentariness, they have contributed
to a profound change in figures of belonging. Social violence tends to
crystallize around the now crucial questions of identities, modalities of
citizenship, the management of the mobility of persons, and the circulation and control of flowing resources. In these new forms of social and
political struggle, three themes are privileged: community of origin (territory and indigenousness), race, and religion. At least two conceptions

of citizenship have emerged, which sometimes contradict and sometime complement each other. On the one hand, there is the official idea that a citizen of a country is someone whom the state recognizes as a citizen. On the other hand, another conception also dominates: the conception that the principle of citizenship comes mainly from blood ties (real or supposed), from birth and genealogy. Indeed, blood ties make it possible to ground the distinction between "natives" and "nonnatives," between "native-borns" and "foreigners." This production of identities has allowed the reestablishment of old kingdoms and chiefdoms and the birth of new ethnic groups, either by separation from old groups or by amalgamation. It has also given rise to violent conflicts, which have led to numerous population displacements. It has, finally, strengthened irredentism, notably in countries where minorities felt excluded from the material benefits of power.

Thus, two *poleis* and two types of civic spaces, with complex forms of entanglement, have appeared: on the one hand, the *intra-muros* city (the site of origins and custom, whose signs one carries if one travels far from it), and, on the other hand, the *extra-muros* city (which is made possible by dispersion and diving into the world). From the fact that each polis now has its double or its "elsewhere" comes the emblematic role now played by migrants and diasporas. As for the rest, the double process of the transnationalization of African societies along with a retreat to origins, combined with the increased commodification of work as a result of increased capacities for extensive mobility, has had the effect of rekindling conflicts around community, belonging, and property. The dispersion and scattering that go along with the necessity of making money in distant places have of course not abolished old characterizations of community. In many cases, the community has remained a territory of origin, concrete and geographically situated, which one appropriates, defends, and seeks to protect against intruders and those who are not part of it. It is also a fiction in whose name one is ready to kill and to be killed as needed. Considerable inflections have nevertheless appeared in the relation between what belongs to more than one, to some, or to all (what is shareable because of the debt of giving that arises from belonging to the same community of origin) and what is strictly private, limited to strictly individual enjoyment.

Due to the fact that mastering the consequences of transnationalism implies not only control and domination of distances, but also the art of multiplying ties of belonging, the status of intermediaries—those who weave connections with the outside world, brokers and specialists in the negotiation of objects, stories, and identities—is now overvalued. This overvaluation has benefited from the growing gap between official borders and actual borders. The result has increased not only the speed of migrations, but also the constitution of connections and networks that, exceeding the territorial frameworks of postcolonial states, have specialized in the long-distance mobilization of resources. On another level, the possession of money (or the impossibility of possessing it) has profoundly displaced frameworks for the formation of individuality and regimes of subjectivity. On the one hand, where scarcity predominates, the intensity of needs and the impossibility of satisfying them have been such that there has been a break in how social subjects experience desire, want, and satiation. The perception now prevails that money as well as power and life are governed by the law of chance. Immense fortunes are built from one day to the next, and the factors contributing to them are not apparent at all. Other fortunes disappear at the same rhythm, without visible cause. Because nothing is certain and everything is possible, one takes risks with money as one does with the body, power, and life. Time and life as well as death are reduced to an immense game of chance. On the other hand, among those belonging to social groups capable of easily amassing fortunes, the relations between desire and its objects have changed, and a sensualist and hedonist preoccupation with consumption, idolatrous possession, and ostentatious enjoyment of material goods is now the site for staging new styles of life.

In cases of both scarcity and wealth, however, the cultural contents of the process of differentiation have been the same: that is, on one hand, a keen awareness of the volatility as well as the frivolity of money and fortune and, on the other hand, a conception of time and value based on the instantaneous—the short term of life. Although the strategies pursued by individual agents have varied from one situation to another, the conception of time and value as contained and exhausted in the instant and the conception of money as volatile and frivolous have greatly contributed to transforming imaginaries of wealth, destitution, and power. Power and fortune, enjoyment, misery, and death were first experienced according to materialist criteria. Whence the emergence of subjectivities at whose center is the need for tangibility, palpability, and tactility. At the same time, one finds these characteristics in forms of expression of both violence and enjoyment, and in the general usage of pleasures.

RIDING THE PHALLUS

Within the context of strong economic fluctuation and intense volatility characteristic of the last quarter of the twentieth century, social fragmentation has affected household structures in particular. This has been the case notably in major metropolises.[28] In this area, the principal social mutations are linked to conditions of youth access to employment, the transformation of women's position in economic activity due to crises, and changes in forms of union and marriage.[29] The relative weakening of the social and economic status of young men and the reorientation of their timescapes to the short-term time of survival represent, in this regard, an unprecedented phenomenon.[30] Unemployment has increased considerably among this social group. The passage from adolescence to adulthood is no longer automatic, and in many instances, the average age of heads of households is higher now than it was several years ago. Age at first marriage no longer corresponds to age at entry into economic or professional activity. The distance between social juniors and seniors is widening, while the redistribution of roles and resources among generations is becoming more complex. Many young men are now kept in forms of prolonged dependence, which they can only escape by migrating or enlisting as soldiers in armed organizations.

Relations between men and women and parental roles are also in the process of redefinition.[31] As for the makeup of households, it has changed profoundly. Married couples without children, polygamous families without collaterals, and single-parent families all testify to the diversity of family forms being composed. Almost everywhere, the mobility of men is profoundly changing control of households. In part due to the fact that mothers and fathers may not be living together, many households now have women at their head.[32] With job insecurity and increasing social exclusion, masculine and feminine roles within marriage are also changing, and a leveling of the status of women and young men is underway.[33] All this is creating a proliferation of microstrategies on the part of social actors. Polygamy, for example, makes possible new strategies for both men and women to gain resources within the domestic structure, in a context where women's activities are contributing more and more to family income.[34] Systems of solidarity based on kinship or traditional practices now coexist with often-brutal market relations.

Another major recomposition that has arisen over the last quarter of the twentieth century is the gradual appearance of a sphere of private life drawing its symbols from global culture. No space is more characteristic of this transnationalization than the domains of clothing, music, sport, cinema, fashion, and care for the body in general.[35] New imaginaries of the self are connected to all this, as well as to sexuality.[36] In several cities, divorce is more common among women than singlehood.[37] New conjugal models, living arrangements, and household structures are emerging, about which little is known.[38] Thanks to access to modern means of communication, the sexuality of young people outside of marriage is also being transformed. There are many who now live at the margin of what only recently was considered the norm. This is the case with homosexuality.

Three arguments are generally put forward by Africans who consider homosexuality to be a symptom of absolute depravity. First, in their eyes, the homosexual act exemplifies "demonic power" and behavior that goes against nature—the application of genitals to a vessel other than the natural vessel. Second, for them homosexuality constitutes a perverse and transgressive structure of sexuality. It effaces all distinctions between humans and animals: the homosexual act, vile and filthy, is nothing but a bestial coupling that goes counter to the perpetuation of human life and the human species. For the most devout, it is also a source of lechery and a sign of the *immoderata carnis petulantia*, the immoderate wantonness of the flesh. Finally, there is the argument of inauthenticity: the claim that homosexuality was unknown in precolonial Africa and was only introduced to the continent through European expansion.[39]

There are three central presuppositions at the base of such affirmations. First, there is the very phallocentric idea—shared by both men and women—that the male organ is the natural symbol of the genesis of all life and all power. This being the case, there is no legitimate sexuality that does not always make good use of seminal capital. This capital, entirely directed toward reproduction, could not possibly degrade itself in pleasures of pure loss. Next, there is the widespread belief that licit coitus only occurs *within* the female organ, and that ejaculation outside of the vagina is the very mark of filth and impurity, even witchcraft. The principal function of the vulva is thus to relieve the phallus of its semen and preserve it carefully. Finally, there is the dominant sentiment that any other practice of coitus—notably, practices that, instead of putting genital organs into immediate contact, associate them instead with orifices and other channels of excretion, swallowing, and sucking—is a profanation of the flesh and an abominable abuse.[40]

Such points of view, which accord an eminent place to the phallus in symbolizing life, power, and pleasure, generally remain the norm. By giving so much weight to the work of the phallus, they neglect female homosexual practices, which are, however, becoming more and more visible.[41] Furthermore, they rest on a very contestable reading of the history of sexuality in Africa and its political meanings. In fact, before, during, and after colonization, power in Africa has always sought to wear the visage of virility. Power has always operated in the mode of an infinite erection. The political community has always seen itself above all as the equivalent of a society of men or, more precisely, old men. Its effigy has always been the erect penis. We may also say that the entirety of its psychic life has always been organized around the event of the swelling of the male organ. This is what the postcolonial African novel has expressed so well. In the work of Sony Labou Tansi, for example, the process of turgescence is part of the major rituals of the postcolonial potentate. It is indeed experienced as the moment when the potentate doubles in size and projects himself beyond his limits. At the time of this push toward extremes, he multiplies himself and produces a double phantasm, whose function is to erase the distinction between real power and fictive power. From this moment on, the phallus is endowed with spectral qualities. But, by seeking to go beyond its own contours, the phallus of power necessarily exposes its nakedness and limits and, in exposing them, exposes the potentate himself and proclaims, paradoxically, his vulnerability in the very act by which he claims to manifest his omnipotence.[42]

The potentate is thus by definition sexual. The *sexual potentate* rests on a praxis of jouissance. Postcolonial power in particular literally imagines itself as a jouissance machine. Here, to be a sovereign is to be able to achieve *absolute* jouissance without restraint or hindrance. The range of pleasures is expanded: for example, there is a connection that links the pleasure of eating (the politics of the stomach) to the pleasure procured by fellatio and to the act of torturing one's real or alleged enemies.[43] Whence the tragicomic and theatrical dimensions of the sexual act and metaphors of copulation in the imaginary and practices of *commandement*.[44] The sexuality of the autocrat functions according to the principle of devouring and swallowing women, beginning with the virgins he gleefully deflowers. Bankers, bureaucrats, soldiers, policemen, schoolmasters, and even bishops, priests, pastors, and marabouts go about emptying, depleting, and sowing wherever the wind blows. Coarse language and copulation are in fact the favorite caprices of elites and powerful people, just as others give themselves over to hunting or the pleasures of alcohol.[45]

The phallus is thus at work. It is the phallus that speaks, orders, and acts. This is why here, the political struggle almost always takes on the aspects of a sexual struggle, with every sexual struggle ipso facto taking on the character of a political struggle. It is thus always necessary to go back to the penis of the potentate if one wishes to understand the psychic life of power and the mechanisms of subordination in the post-colony. The penis of the potentate, adept in gluttonous rape and brutal affirmation of the desire for power, is a furious, nervous organ, easily excitable and prone to bulimia. This is in particular the case when the potentate hounds the wives of his collaborators and subjects, or all sorts of boys (including his subordinates)—along the way blurring any distinction between homo- and heterosexuality. Indeed, for the potentate, fellatio, venality, and corruption are supposed to open up the floodgates of life. In the forest countries that have converted to Christianity as well as in Muslim regions, the autocrat, clinging to his subjects, reigns over people ready to give in to his violence. Pressed by the logic of survival, they must thus flatter power in order to augment its engorgement and relief. By pushing his phallus to the bottom of his subjects' throats, the postcolonial potentate always nearly strangles them.

Moreover, the patriarchal traditions of power in Africa are based on an original repression of the homosexual relation. Although in practice this relation took various forms, practices of repression target the relation through the anus. Indeed, in the symbolic universe of many precolonial African societies, the anus was—contrary to the buttocks, whose beauty, eminence, and curves were praised—considered an object of aversion and associated with filth. It represented the very principle of the anarchy of the body and the zenith of intimacy and secret. The symbol of defecation and excrement par excellence, the anus was, of all the organs, the "wholly other" par excellence. We know, moreover, that in the symbolic economy of these societies, the "wholly other," especially when blended with the "wholly intimate," also represented a figure of occult power. Homosexuality was often the privilege of the powerful. It could function as a ritual of subordination to those stronger than oneself. It was also present in certain sacred rituals. Today, the proclaimed refusal of homosexual submission to another man does not at all signify the absence of men's and women's desire to acquire and appropriate the ideal and idealized penis. In fact, degradation of and disgust with the anus in public discourse go along with the anus' recurrent appearance at the level of symptom, in the form of various phantasms. In this respect, one need only look to the functions the anus plays in phantasms of permutation of masculine and feminine roles, or in the desire—experienced by most men and common in political techniques of subjection—to use other men like so many women subjected to coupling and to live out their domination as the consumption of coitus. Let us add to the preceding the existence of double-sex creatures in tales and myths, as well as the practice, within social and political struggles, of stripping the enemy of everything that constitutes the emblems of virility and consuming them, and the obsession with regenerating declining virility by using all sorts of concoctions. Homosexuality is thus inscribed in the very deep stratification of African societies' sexual unconscious.

Finally, if the sexual map of the continent appears blurry today, this is in very large part because the last quarter of the twentieth century has been marked by a silent revolution, which unfortunately has hardly been documented. We are only now realizing that this revolution has radically and definitively transformed the way in which many Africans imagine their relation to desire, the body, and pleasure. This "silent sexual revolution" has taken place in a context characterized by the unprecedented opening of African societies to the world. Today, there is not a single African city where pornographic videos are not in circulation. The phallus, as the central signifier of power and the privilege of masculine domination, has also undergone profound questioning. In certain societies, the contestation of phallic power has taken the form of relatively chronic marital instability and the circulation of women. In other societies, it is expressed by worsening conflicts between men and women. Everywhere, the poorest men have the impression they have been demasculinized. As we have seen, the role of "head of family," generally held by men, has undergone a loss of status among the most impoverished categories of the population, notably where the power to nourish can no longer be fully exercised due to a lack of means. Here and there, we have witnessed urban panics at whose center was the fear of castration. Within the cultural cartography of the end of the twentieth century in Africa, we are thus confronted with a phallic dynamic that, more than previously, is a field of multiple mobilities.

The successive crises of the last thirty-five years have, in certain cases, contributed to widening already existing inequalities between the sexes.

In other cases, they have led to profound modifications in the general terms in which both masculine domination and femininity are expressed. The result has been a worsening of conflicts between the sexes and increased brutality in the relations between men and women. In parallel, previously repressed forms of sexuality are little by little emerging in the public sphere.[46] The repertory of sexual pleasures has significantly expanded. Practices of fellatio now proliferate. The language of sexuality has also been greatly enriched. Among the young, thousands of new expressions have appeared, each more prosaic than the last. A large part of social discourse focuses on the theme of declining phallic force. Among old men there is more and more recourse to plants and roots, which, it is claimed, tone the man's penis and allow the multiplication and frenzy of coitus. All sorts of additives are now integrated into liturgies of coupling—incense, fresh onions, the testes of wild animals, or pulverized bark and roots. Finally, homosexual practices are generally more widespread than many in Africa want to admit. Though in certain countries regimes in power are leading a war against homosexuals and consider them to be human rubbish and waste, in South Africa the constitution guarantees homosexuals rights, including the right to marry. Contemporary homophobia is also used by the lower classes as a way of disqualifying the ruling classes. These transformations are taking place as the AIDS epidemic is affecting increasing percentages of the population. Through AIDS, sex and death are now entangled.[47]

THE HORN OF PLENTY

We will not rehearse here what many feminist critics have already taught us about the intersection of gender and nation—that the concept of "woman" has been made to play a paradoxical role in national liberation and nation building; that the institutionalization of unjust gender systems and their reproduction in the law are a constitutive dimension of the masculinist state; or that the social scripts of patriarchy give us different valuations not only of sons and daughters, but more radically of any life built around female connections in a world of men.[48]

What is needed is a genealogical analysis of the symbolic systems that in Africa have historically tied the social worlds of sexuality and of power to the phantasmal configurations of pleasure [*jouissance*] on the one hand, and to structures of subjection on the other. There is no doubt that, historically, sex and gender norms were central to the fabric of power and economic life. But so were cultural and symbolic categories in the definition of what stood for womanhood and for manhood. But our knowledge of how power operated through the medium of actual gendered bodies is, at the very least, lacunal.[49] To account for the paradoxes of ongoing sexual struggles, it might be useful to first highlight the kinds of imaginaries of body, sex, and gender relationships that contribute, in a decisive way, to the constitution of that figure of brutality I have called the postcolony as well as to its psychic life.

In a study of Vodun sculptural representations of the body and the dynamics of Vodun artistic expression, Suzanne Preston Blier shows how cultural definitions of the body and anatomy are at the same time discourses on being as well as figural imagings of the psyche.[50] To be sure, sexuality and gender are not first and foremost about anatomy or genitality. But neither are they completely divorced from questions of how, what, and why particular part-objects (Melanie Klein), or organs, express and reveal and how they are set apart in the mind and psychically and politically valorized. Sexuality and gender are both social imaginaries (norms, rules, languages, values) materialized through different forms and a whole complex of sociohistorical institutions and practices. This being the case, it can be said that, in ancient Africa, sexuality and gender were first and foremost about the exercise of specific sets of capabilities. There was no imagination of sexuality and gender that did not revolve around the question "What can a body do?" In turn, a body's structure was fundamentally the sum of its relations.

For instance, Preston Blier shows how, in Vodun sculptural representations, the stomach was imagined as the seat of human emotions (especially the two sensations of appetite and satisfaction) and how, as such, it was frequently referred to in the context of divination and geomancy. Kidneys, for their part, were the site of concentration of all sensations that penetrate the body by way of the eyes, the ears, and the senses. The penis emerged in this imaginary under the sign of the gap and of negation. It was a force of disruption associated with Legba, a deity of trickery and deception. "Erect phalluses distinguish[ed] this latter deity's shrines and ritual objects." Preston Blier observes that sculptures varied considerably with respect to the amount of attention (and proportional size) given to the genital area. The meanings attached to an erect penis were always polysemic. Paradoxically, an enlarged penis might well allude to "fears concerning infertility, sexual inadequacy, and impotence." On the other hand, adds Blier, erect or enlarged genitals may refer to power and trickery, deception and danger.[51]

The vagina, by virtue of the manner with which it was supposed to be hollowed out by the penile erection, came to be construed at times as a container, at times as an envelope or a sheath whose function was not only to enfold, but also to discipline the excess and immoderation of the penis. As in the Islamic contexts described by Hachem Foda, the function of the vagina was to "border, contain, mold, and delimit that which owed its existence to its erectile status."[52] Other qualities were attributed to the vagina: a voracious and insatiable appetite (the abyss); a guarantee of life (through its reproductive functions); the quintessential threat (the hole in the other, the original wound notably symbolized by menstrual blood). These symbolic significations were almost always contradictory. In the masculine imaginaries, the vagina was an object of both attraction and repulsion,[53] and was seen as both the source of an obscure fear of engulfment (the ostensible castrating power of woman) and the seat of life (the maternal function).[54] According to Preston Blier, the term designating the vagina could be used as an insult. But ancillary terms describing the woman's genitals could also refer to inertia, tomb, and glutton. Like its counterpart, the penis, the word employed in reference to the vagina, *minona*, was the name of a powerful deity of both witchcraft and motherhood.[55]

These examples point to the fact that body and sexuality were fraught with ambivalence, uncertainty, and danger. That this was the case

testified to the very precariousness of everyday life and of gender assig-
nations as well as to the potential porosity of gender borders. The forces
mobilized for sexual and bodily performance were not transparent. Vulnerability was a mode through which power and sex were mutually
constituted and circulated. In combining opacity, obscurity, and vulnerability, sexual power was fundamentally precarious, a potential zone
of betrayal. Through its ethos of a flesh devoted to penance and self-
wounding, colonial Christianity added to the circle of anxiety that
already surrounded sex.[56] In reinforcing the dramaturgy already attached
to precolonial understandings of sex and the body, it fostered the internalization of sexual repression and firmly inscribed sex within the realm
of sin and death. Islam, by contrast, glorified a celestial sexuality whose
earthly counterpart constituted a kind of foretaste.[57]

Among the many stereotypes of gender roles generated during the
confrontation between Africa and the West is the womb-focused cliché
of the African woman. In her study of the complex historical negotiations of gender and other social hierarchies in late imperial China, Francesca Bray argues that women were seen neither purely as biological
reproducers nor purely as victims of patriarchal control and oppression.
The same can be said of many precolonial African societies. To be sure,
the pursuit of maternal status and natural fertility were decisive criteria
by which womanhood was judged. But just as in late imperial China, so
was social motherhood. In a number of African precolonial kingdoms
and under certain circumstances, it could even be more important than
giving birth. Even more crucial, it could not be confused with the role
of wife per se. Since most hierarchical societies functioned according to
the principle of a double public sphere, one that was visible and, beneath
it, or parallel to it, one that was contiguous, social motherhood fundamentally determined, to a large extent, women's ideas about themselves
and one another. It was also a crucial factor in the way they were treated
by men and how they treated one another. Whatever the case, Bray
observes, "bearing a child did not necessarily make one a mother, nor
did infertility necessarily make one not a mother."[58]

To this should be added the existence of autonomous, exclusively feminine spheres beyond the world at home, including in societies in which

the practice of women's seclusion was the norm. All these factors contributed to the development of traditions that established a more or less clear distinction between, on the one hand, orgiastic and libertine sexuality and, on the other, sex for reproductive purposes. The latter was all the more critical because the political economy of the centuries of slave trade and colonialism was based on the ability to reproduce dependents of all sorts (wives, sons, strangers, slaves, and so on). Although the reproduction of dependents did not entirely depend on the practice of sex, it is quite clear that sex as such became a pivotal institution in a political economy of use-value. But libertine sexuality was just as important as sex for reproductive purposes. Should it be written one day, the history of libertine sexuality in precolonial Africa would probably be read from within a general anthropology of bodily appetites and pleasures, including appetite for food.[59] Indeed nurturing sex with an array of herbal substances and decoctions was, for men and women, part of an ethos of jouissance and good life. Sexual inversion was more common than generally assumed.[60]

Although no amount of guilt seemed to be attached to the carnal act as such, an array of interdictions surrounded copulation. A complex of taboos clearly delimited the extent to which male power could be deployed. But even though male power was not a boundless field, ancestral and colonial traditions all shared the idea according to which the phallus was the veritable horn of plenty. The phallus was at the same time the privileged organ of power and, in a word, the signifier of signifiers. Monotheistic religions (Christianity and Islam) both regarded masculine sovereignty as endowed with both theological and juridical properties. Indigenous imaginations espoused, without contention, the idea that the difference between virility and femininity rested on the material difference between two specific organs.

The entanglement of Christian and indigenous imaginaries was a decisive aspect of the process by which gendered reality has been experienced at least since the nineteenth century. Such representations helped to legitimize gestures, rules, and ritualized enactments of sexual subjection and autonomy. But gender symbolism and the male/female antinomy were always contested categories.[61] To be sure, social actors did incorporate a masculinist habitus that exaggerated the formal and symbolic opposition between male and female domains, objects and moral qualities. But if anything, the tension between the production of gender boundaries and processes that constantly undermined them was a common occurrence. As the cultural anthropologist Mariane C. Ferme argues in a detailed study of gendered practices in Sierra Leone, zones of ambiguity and transgression abounded, and in fact, boundaries were almost always, if not overcome, at least unmade in what she calls "the context of practice."

Ferme pays particular attention to the performance of gendered differences and what she terms the logic of exaggerated display of gender exclusiveness. The latter, she shows, could easily mask both hierarchical distinctions among women and instances of appropriation by women of ordinarily male domains. She suggests that any account of the sexual politics of the postcolony should consider the coexistence of multiple public spheres, some "open spaces" and others "concealed sites." It would appear that the tension between the "overt" and the "concealed," or between visible and esoteric orders of power, is the source of (1) the production of a vast array of significations around the understanding of a gendered social world, (2) the nature of female power and the constitution of sites identified entirely or partially as female domains, and finally (3) the strategic uses of polysemy and covert associations that can be appropriated by either men or women, depending on the context.[62]

A dramatic figure of this strategic use of polysemy (and the logic of display and concealment/dissimulation that underpins it) is the figure of the *mabole*. The *mabole* epitomizes the absence of transparent gender distinctions. A "middle-sex" character, the *mabole* is supposed to combine elements of both sexes in an ongoing and unresolved dialectical tension. According to Ferme, she is "both man and woman." As a "ritually male-identified woman," she participates in the social roles typically associated with both genders. But because she has to manage "a regime of ambiguity without resolving it dialectically into a stable order of meaning," she is "always on the brink of exclusion."[63]

All of this does not invalidate the centrality of the male organ in the social imagination. Such a centrality consecrated, in fact, the law of the father and of the elders [aînés]. And, as Lacan argues, "it is with this penis that one will make a signifier of the loss that appears at the level of *jou-issance* by virtue of the function of the law."[64] This explains the prolif-eration of rituals of phallus worship in different precolonial and contem-porary African traditions. Indeed, in many traditions, the sexual act is assimilated to a totemic feast governed by the dialectic of ingestion and excretion, or radical expenditure.[65]

THE ANAL AND THE NOCTURNAL

The postcolony's patriarchal traditions of power are founded upon an originary repression. The central figure of this repression is the anus. In effect, in the symbolic universe of many precolonial African societies, the anus—unlike the buttocks, whose beauty, eminence, and curves are gladly sung by poets and musicians—was considered an object of aver-sion. Owing in part to their prominent gourdlike shapes (and name), the buttocks in particular are identified with capability and capacity. They constitute, according to Preston Blier, a critical part of an individual's physical attractiveness. They are also identified with body movement. Large buttocks serve as signifiers of plenty. "Thus a well-off woman, one who has acquired economic autonomy, often is called *gogonu*, or 'mother of buttocks,'" Preston Blier reports.[66]

In contrast to the buttocks, the anus is the accursed organ and the sign par excellence of abjection. Its potency derives from its supposed dangerousness and esoteric nature. In most instances, the anal is akin to the nocturnal. It represents not only a potential zone of entrapment, but also the principle of opacity and bodily anarchy—a horrifying anom-aly. As a universal symbol of defecation and excrement, it is, of all the human organs (male or female), the quintessential "wholly other," shady, ugly, and comical, imprisoned in a kind of stupid obstinacy. Now, in indigenous imaginaries, the "wholly other" equally represents one of the figures of occult power and, above all, of that "other of desire," uncon-querable envy—the power to devour.[67]

The repression of the anal is explicable only by way of the heightened presence [*sur-présence*] of masculine homosexuality particularly—if not in ordinary sexual practices, then at least in the sacred rituals and the sexual unconscious of society.[68] The proclaimed denial of the existence of homosexuality in precolonial African societies hardly signifies the absence of homosexual or same-sex desire and practices. To be sure, homosexuality—or for that matter same-sex practices—is not reducible to anality. But the degradation and disgust with which anality is made the object of public discourse go hand in hand with the recurrent appearance of the anus on the scene of the symptom, in a variety of phantasmatic shapes.

One only has to consider the function anality plays in various male sexual fantasies. Such is the case of fantasies of the permutation of masculine and feminine roles, or masculine fantasies of appropriating women via sodomistic acts. Such is also the case of the desire— experienced by men of power—to subject those they dominate to various forms of copulation, including anal penetration or, in other contexts, the fetishization of the ruler's anus. To the preceding should be added the existence, in various myths and legends, of hermaphroditic creatures, or the practice, in political and social struggles, that consists in stripping the enemy of everything that constitutes the emblems of his virility and consuming them (the principle of the *manducation* of power), or the obsession with regenerating a dwindling virility by means of potions and all sorts of pelts.[69] Homosexuality and same-sex practices thus belong to a very deep stratification of the sexual unconscious of African societies.

If indeed the semiotics of power in the postcolony takes place in the form of an infinite erection, can we therefore say that the postcolony is, as Judith Butler argues, "an impossible sign"? Yes, if we consider that the psychic life of power originates from, and rests on, power's desire for an infinite erection. The project of an infinite erection itself corresponds to a longing for absolute sovereignty—empty infinity. This form of sovereignty originates from two polarized impulses Georges Bataille wrote about not long ago: excretion and appropriation.[70] This is, indeed, an insatiable desire. It is explicable only in power's awareness of being surrounded at once by the threat of vulnerability and feminization for which the vulva is the primordial emblem, and by the possibility of emasculation that anality—indeed, the seat of shame, but equally the symbol of the other of omnipotence—represents. Only by turning itself into an even more powerful excrement can the thing fend off the challenge of anality.

Political struggles in the postcolony are nearly always fought in the guise of sexual struggles, and vice versa. For those holding power as much as for common men and women, it is always a question of maximizing on each occasion their virile or feminine assets, as the case may be. It is as if one's virility or femininity had to constantly undergo multiple rites of verification. In this context, the object of power is to secure for whomever possesses it a surplus pleasure [plus-de-jouir]. In the masculine anatomy of the postcolony, the manhood constitutes the privileged symbolic signifier of this surplus pleasure.

Among men, this surplus pleasure operates via the fantasy of "consuming" as many women as possible. Sexual consumption can occur only because the female body is each time treated as a foreign body. Akin to gluttony or drunkenness, sexual consumption has as its main goal the increase of masculine *mana*. Now, since it is impossible to possess the female body once and for all, *jouissance* is possible only in repetition. The act of consumption must ceaselessly begin anew. Because of this neurotic compulsion to repeat, the male-female relationship is fundamentally a frustrating relationship. In the exchanges between the sexes, the female subject might seek, if not to disempower the penis (*mettre hors-jeu l'instrument*)[71] in obtaining, by every means, its flaccidity and failure, then at least to frustrate virility and to despoil masculine pleasure in such a manner that, the vain hope of total satisfaction being ceaselessly deferred, male power is deflated by the penis being trapped by, and enslaved to, the vulva.[72]

Sexual commerce and the commerce of power consequently acquire a purely repetitive character, in the midst of an always-open totality. Men and women then take to treating each other as objects within a sexual economy dominated by men's constant attempts to control the flow of life-giving via various forms of violence.[73] Hence the apparent destructive character of desire. This seems to be particularly the case in racialized social formations that have historically experienced brutal forms of degradation of life. In such social formations, the assertion of manhood has, at times, taken the form of the capitalization of women's bodies as man's property.

BLACK MANHOOD IN THE SHADOW OF THE RACIST STATE

Since the everyday structures of gender domination that have emerged in the process (as well as in the aftermath) of racial domination tend to replicate the routine of colonial and racial brutality toward black men, it is important to understand how the black body came to be constituted in and through this economy of violence in the first place.

In this regard, many studies have shown that what determined the fate of manhood in a racist state was closely linked to an ongoing war of races. As Michel Foucault has argued, racism does make the relationship of war function in unexpected ways. On the one hand,

> Racism makes it possible to establish a relationship between my life and the death of the other that is not a military or warlike relationship of confrontation, but a biological-type relationship. . . . The fact that the other dies does not mean simply that I live in the sense that his death guarantees my safety; the death of the bad race, of the inferior race (or the degenerate, or the abnormal) is something that will make life in general healthier: healthier and purer.

On the other hand, "the enemies who have to be done away with are not adversaries in the political sense of the term; they are threats, either external or internal, to the population and for the population." In such a context, "killing or the imperative to kill is acceptable only if it results . . . in the elimination of the biological threat to and the improvement of the species or race."[74]

Indeed, whether in South Africa or in the United States (two late-modern racist states), the war between races was constructed as a war between men, but a war in which the main assets were women's bodies. Women's bodies were themselves imagined as territories to be invaded, to be protected against the enemy, or, when lost to the enemy, to be won back. At stake in these racist states was the body as a territory of male power. The body was what gave substance to the signifier (race) and what marked the limits of territorialization. Reflecting particularly on reproduction in bondage, Dorothy Roberts has shown how the control of black procreation not only helped to sustain slavery, but was a central aspect of whites' subjugation of African people in America. Critical to the dehumanization of slaves was the capitalization of black women's wombs as vessels.

Two forms of sexual violation were particularly strategic in the process by which black female slaves were disowned of their personhood. The first was rape by the white master—a weapon of terror that reinforced whites' domination over their human property. As a matter of fact, sexual terror under slavery was a means to subjugate both black men and black women. Significant, in this regard, was the fact that in addition to the rape of black women, the ownership of the body of the white female by white masters became the terrain on which to lynch the black male.[75] As shown by Roberts, white sexual violence not only attacked black men's masculinity by challenging their ability to protect black women; it also invaded black women's dominion over their own bodies.

The second form of sexual violation was the practice of breeding that consisted of compelling slaves considered "prime stock" to mate in the hope of producing children especially suited for labor or for sale.[76] Edward Covey purchased a twenty-year-old slave named Caroline as a "breeder," writes Frederick Douglass. Covey mated Caroline with a hired man and was pleased when a pair of twins resulted.[77] Men of exceptional physical strength could be rented to serve as studs: "The master was might careful about raisin' healthy nigger families and used us strong, healthy young bucs to stand the healthy nigger gals," recalls Jephta Choice, once a "stockman" or "breedin' nigger." "When I was young they took care not to strain me and I was as handsome as a speckled pup and was in demand for breedin',” he adds.[78]

As evidenced by the practice of lynching, the paradox of the black male body and black sexuality was that the black male body was seen as a threat, while black sexuality was a site of envy and fear. As a way of internalizing white supremacy, the black male body had to be isolated from a sense of anything but its own vulnerability and abjection.[79] It had to be trapped in occupied and outlawed spaces (the township, the reserve, the compound) and other peculiar institutions. But the fact of its being trapped in occupied zones and subjected to trials of humiliation had to do with an even darker ritual: the becoming-animal of a scapegoat, as dramatized by the ceremony of lynching—the ultimate form of castration and a cruel form of negative breeding.

Deleuze and Guattari use the notion of the becoming-animal of a scapegoat to refer to the torturing of the body that occurs in the confrontation with the face or the body of the despot (the sovereign). In their mind, the scapegoat represents a form of increasing entropy in the system of signs. From their argument, we can infer that in the logic of the late-modern racist states, body, sexuality, and territory are brought together in a system in which every sign not only refers to another sign but also is brought back to race—the supreme signifier. In this system, the black body is condemned as that which constantly eludes or exceeds the supreme signifier's power of territorialization. At the same time, the same body is assigned a negative value. It is charged with everything that is under a curse. It is dread as everything that resists meaning. As everything that exceeds the excess of the supreme signifier, its face has to be effaced.[80]

Such was the logic of the calculated destruction of black manhood under early- and late-modern regimes of racialized sovereignty. This is one of the reasons that in most narratives of black emancipation, the “birthing of the nation” is almost akin to the “birthing of manhood.” If love is involved in this process at all, it always takes the form of an angry love itself linked to the memory of a male body on the cross—the political crucifixion and physical pain experienced over so many years in the hands of an enemy state. As Robert Carr shows in his brilliant study of black nationalism in the New World, in that context the attempt to step outside the white man's law and the project of becoming a law unto oneself (self-determination) almost seem to entail, first and foremost, a confrontation with one's own body.[81]

But because nationalism conceptualizes power as a masculinist prerogative and firmly inscribes resistance in the framework of a war between men, to wrestle one's body from the property of the racist state or to confront it as an irretrievably physical and corporeal phenomenon is often reduced to a mere recapturing of one's lost manhood. It is obvious that in such a calculus of manhood, women's bodies are still assigned to the status of territories as well as superfluous and interchangeable assets. Power relations, in other words, are still naked, as evidenced by the fact of rape.

These arguments equally apply to the postcolony. Here, the speech that articulates sexuation ultimately assigns to each sex a place supposedly founded on a physical natural law that is at the same time a law of destiny. This law is ultimately settled by anatomy. It is equally a speech that thrives on the trivialization of sex. Sex as such is constantly granted a ludic character.[82] A dominant part of sexuality is lived according to the masculine model of discharge. In local imaginaries of sexual commerce, this valorization of the excretory functions can be opposed to the involution that the woman is supposed to experience. As Sony Labou Tansi's novels indicate, the female's body conserves the memory of the potentate and the signs of his labor. In the phallic logic of postcolonial power, woman is conceived as much as the subject in the hollow as the originary compartment [habitacle] of the penile guest. In return, the masculine potentate constantly runs the risk of being transformed into a fallen and deposed object—a defective power. As Judith Butler has pointed out, the masculine drains itself in eliminating the overload of semen that it has accumulated. The primordial terror that power ceaselessly endures is that of aspects of its virility being stolen from it (the terror of ablation).

But to say of the phallus that it is made the object of petrification in the postcolony—or to affirm that radical political struggles here consist

first of all in a manner of confrontation with the statue (the phallic)—
does not mean that the vulva is not the subject of a privileged deci-
pherment. In fact, the vulva appears not only as a fragment of the body,
but, basically, as a fragment of that which, "within the corporeal itself,
announces itself as the promise of another body and of another life, a
life reassembled around this corporeal reserve."[83] Without making
these reproductive capacities the only idiom of female power, it is this
strategic control over the living [*le vivant*] that is contested by men.
Woman, in reality, is therefore never reduced to the position of the
object, either entirely or only once. Resultantly, the penis and the vulva
constitute emblems of two types of well-differentiated powers and
capacities.

AFROPOLITANISM

Whether it is a matter of literature, philosophy, music, or the arts in general, for almost a century African discourse has been dominated by
three political-intellectual paradigms, which are not mutually exclusive.
First, there have been variants of anticolonial nationalism, which has had
a lasting influence on the spheres of culture, politics, economics, and religion. Second, there have been various rereadings of Marxism, which
have resulted, here and there, in figures of "African socialism." Finally,
there has been a Pan-African movement, which has given a special place
to two types of solidarity: a racial and transnational solidarity, and an
internationalist, anti-imperialist solidarity.

On the African side of the Atlantic, we can identify two key moments
of Afropolitanism. The first moment is properly postcolonial. This phase
was inaugurated by Ahmadou Kourouma at the beginning of the 1970s
with his work *The Suns of Independence*,[84] but especially by Yambo Ouologuem and his work *Bound to Violence*.[85] The writing of the self, which
for Senghor and the poets of Négritude consisted in the quest for a
lost name, and which for Cheikh Anta Diop coincided with the articulation of a debt to the future by virtue of a glorious past, becomes,

paradoxically, an experience of devouring time: chronophagy. This new sensibility is distinct from Negritude on at least three levels.

First, it relativizes the fetishism of origins by showing that every origin is bastard and that every origin rests on a heap of filth [*un tas d'immondices*]. Ouologuem, for example, is not satisfied with calling into question the very notions of origins, birth, and genealogy that are so central to the discourse of Négritude. He seeks, instead, to blur them, even to abolish them in the goal of making room for a new problematic: self-creation and *self-engendering*. But if it is possible to self-create, this means it is equally possible to self-destruct. Hence, the tension between self and Other, self and the world, so characteristic of the discourse of Négritude, becomes secondary, and is replaced by a problematic of disemboweling, in which the self, no longer able to "tell itself stories," is as if condemned to face itself, to confront itself: this is the problematic of *self-confrontation*.

Second, this new sensibility questions the status of what can be called "reality." The discourse of Négritude saw itself as a discourse on difference, a discourse of the community as difference. Difference was conceived as the means to recovering the community, considered to have been lost. It was thus necessary to convoke or reconvoke it, to bring it back to life, through mourning for a past raised up by signifying, ultimately, the truth of the subject. In this respect, it was a discourse of lamentation. Beginning with Ouologuem, the principle of loss and mourning was replaced by that of excess and immoderation. The community becomes by definition the site of immoderation, expenditure, and waste. Its function is to produce refuse. It comes into being and structures itself on the basis of the production of rubbish and the management of what it devours. There is a shift to a writing of surplus, of excess.[86] Reality (whether it is a matter of race, the past, tradition, or power) no longer appears only as what exists and can be represented, figured. It is also what covers up, surrounds, and exceeds what exists.

Due to this entanglement of the existent and what exceeds it, and because reality is not so much an assemblage as a coil, one cannot speak except in spirals, like a whirlwind. This space of whirlwind is precisely the point of departure of Sony Labou Tansi's writing, for example. It is not insignificant that his final (posthumous) book is titled *L'Autre monde: écrits inédits*.[87] Care for the self is thus transformed into care for the other world, into a way of scrutinizing the night, the domains of the nocturnal, thought to be the final resting place of sovereignty. This development is encouraged by the centrality, within the postcolony, of the failure represented by state violence and the increase in human suffering, by the entry into a new epoch characterized by crudeness and cruelty.[88]

This whirlwind writing is dominated by an aesthetics of transgression. To write the self, to write the world and the other world, is above all to *write in fusion*, to write rape and violation. The voice vanishes, replaced by the "cry."[89] Sony Labou Tansi thus writes in the preface to his novel *L'État honteux*: "The novel is, it seems, a work of imagination. However, this imagination must find its place somewhere in reality. I write, or I cry, a bit in order to force the world to come into the world."[90] There are three sites of this triple role (to write, to cry, to force the world to come into the world): religion, literature, and music (which includes dance and theater). It is through these three disciplines that African discourse concerning the suffering man, confronted with himself and his demon, obliged to create anew, is expressed in all its clarity. A doubling in fact takes place in these disciplines, by which the image of the self appears both as representation and as force of presentation. Thus, religion, literature, and music in many respects constitute sites where analytic practice takes place, whether this has to do with the manifestation of the unconscious, dynamics of repression and release [*refoulement et défoulement*], or the experience of cure itself (interpretation of dreams, séances against spells, treatment of the possessed, the struggle against what are called "demons" and other forces belonging to the "world of the night" and the "invisible").

The second moment of Afropolitanism corresponds to Africa's entry into a new age of dispersion and circulation. This new age is characterized by the intensification of migrations and the establishment of new African diasporas in the world. With the emergence of these new diasporas, Africa no longer constitutes a center in itself. It is now made up of poles between which there is constant passage, circulation, and trailblazing. These poles connect to and prolong each other. They form so many regions, layers, and cultural deposits from which African creation draws constantly. Whether in the domain of music or literature, the question is no longer knowing the essence of loss—it is knowing how to create new forms of the real, floating and mobile forms. It is no longer a matter of returning to some primal scene at all costs, or of re-creating the gestures of the past in the present. Though the past has disappeared, it is nevertheless not off-screen [*hors champ*]. It is still there, in the form of a mental image. One crosses out, erases, replaces, effaces, and re-creates both forms and contents. One proceeds by jump cuts [*faux raccords*], discordances, substitutions, and assemblages—the condition for achieving a new aesthetic force.

This is particularly the case in the new African novel and in music, dance, and the plastic arts, where creation takes place through encounters, some of which are ephemeral and others of which fail. The goal of artistic creation is no longer to describe a situation in which one has become a walking spectator of one's own life because one has been reduced to impotence as a consequence of historical accidents. To the contrary, it is a matter of bearing witness to the broken man who slowly gets up again and frees himself of his origins. For a long time, African creation concerned itself with the question of origins, while dissociating it from the question of movement. Its central object was firstness [*priméité*]: a subject that refers only to itself, a subject in its pure possibility. In the age of dispersion and circulation, this same creation is more concerned with the relation to an interval than to oneself or an other.[91] Africa itself is now imagined as an immense interval, an inexhaustible citation open to many forms of combination and composition. The reference is no longer to an essential singularity, but rather to a renewed capacity for bifurcation.

Important cultural reconfigurations are thus underway, even if a gap remains between the real life of culture and the intellectual tools by which societies apprehend their destiny. Of all the reconfigurations underway, two in particular are likely to have a singular influence on cultural life and on aesthetic and political creativity in the years to come. First, there are reconfigurations that have to do with new responses to the question of knowing who is "African" and who is not. There are many in whose eyes "Africans" are "black" and thus "not white," with degrees of authenticity being measured on the scale of brute racial difference. But it so happens that all sorts of people have some connection to or simply something to do with Africa—something that authorizes them ipso facto to claim "African citizenship." There are, naturally, those who are designated "Blacks." They are born and live within African states, and are nationals of these states. But, though black Africans form the majority of the continent's population, they are not its only inhabitants and are not the only ones to produce its art and culture.

Other population groups, from Asia, the Middle East, or Europe, have indeed established themselves in various parts of the continent during various periods of history and for various reasons. Some arrived as conquerors, merchants, or zealots, like the Arabs and the Europeans, fleeing all manner of hardship, seeking to escape persecution, either filled with hope for a peaceful life or moved by a thirst for riches. Others, like the Afrikaners and Jews, came as a result of more or less tragic historical circumstances. Still others—Malays, Indians, and Chinese in southern Africa—have put down roots as essentially servile labor within the context of migrations for work. More recently, Lebanese, Syrians, Indo-Pakistanis, and essentially hundreds or thousands of Chinese have appeared. All of them have arrived with their languages, customs, eating habits, styles of clothing, ways of praying—in short, with their arts of living and doing. Today, the relationships these various diasporas maintain with their societies of origin are very complex. Many of their members consider themselves full-fledged Africans, even if they also belong to an Elsewhere.

But, if Africa has long been a destination for all sorts of population movements and cultural flux, for several centuries it has also been a zone of departure toward other regions of the world. This centuries-long process of *dispersion* took place over the course of what is generally designated as the modern era, and it ran along three corridors: the Sahara, the Atlantic, and the Indian Ocean. The formation of African Negro diasporas in the New World, for example, is the result of this dispersion. Slavery, which as we know concerned not only European-American worlds, but also Arab-Asian worlds, played a decisive role in this process. Due to this circulation of worlds, traces of Africa can be found wherever capitalism and Islam spread. Other migrations, whose principal motor was colonization, took place in addition to the forced migrations of previous centuries. Today, millions of people of African origin are citizens of various countries of the globe.

When it comes to aesthetic creativity in contemporary Africa and the question of knowing who and what is "African," political and cultural critique is often silent on this historical phenomenon of the *circulation of worlds* in silence. Seen from Africa, this phenomenon of the circulation of worlds has at least two aspects: the *dispersion* I have just mentioned, and *immersion*. Historically, the dispersion of populations and cultures was not only a matter of foreigners coming to establish themselves in Africa. In fact, the precolonial history of African societies was entirely a history of people in constant movement across the whole continent. Once again, this is a history of cultures in collision, caught in the maelstrom of wars, invasions, migrations, and mixed marriages, full of various religions adopted, techniques exchanged, and merchandise peddled. The cultural history of the continent cannot be understood outside of the paradigm of roaming, mobility, and displacement.

It was, moreover, this culture of mobility that colonization in its time attempted to freeze via the modern institution of the border. To recall this history of roaming and mobilities is to speak of mixtures, amalgamations, superpositions—an *aesthetics of intertwining* [*entrelacement*]. Nothing—not Islam, Christianity, ways of dressing, doing business, speaking, or even eating habits—escaped the steamroller of *métissage* and *vernacularization*. This was the case well before colonization. There is indeed a *precolonial African modernity* that has not yet been sufficiently accounted for in contemporary creativity.

The other aspect of this circulation of worlds is *immersion*. Immersion, to various degrees, affected the minorities who came from afar and ended up putting down roots on the continent. With the passage of time, their connections to their origins (European or Asian) became uniquely complicated. Their members, through contact with geography, climate, and people, became cultural bastards—even if, due to colonization, Euro-Africans in particular continued to claim supremacy in the name of race and to mark their difference, even their contempt, with respect to anything seen as "African" or "indigenous."[92] This was in very large part the case with Afrikaners, whose very name means "Africans." The same ambivalence is found among Indians, Lebanese, and Syrians. The majority express themselves in local languages and are familiar with and practice certain customs of their countries of residence, but live within relatively closed communities and practice endogamy.

Thus, it is not only that there is a part of African history found elsewhere, outside of Africa. There is also a history of the rest of the world in which, through the force of circumstance, Africans are actors and of which they are guardians. At the same time, their way of being in the world, their manner of "being world," of inhabiting the world has always taken place under the sign of cultural *métissage* or the imbrication of worlds, in a slow and sometimes incoherent dance with signs that they did not have the luxury of choosing freely, but that they have managed, haphazardly, to domesticate and put to their own use. It is this cultural, historical, and aesthetic sensibility—the awareness of the imbrication of here and elsewhere, the presence of elsewhere here and vice versa, this relativization of roots and primary belongings and this manner of embracing, with full knowledge of the facts, the foreign, the foreigner, and the far-off, this capacity to recognize one's face in the face of the foreigner and to valorize the traces of the far-off in the nearby, to domesticate the unfamiliar, to work with what appear to be contradictions—that the term *Afropolitanism* indicates.

ONLINE ROUTES

Africa is going through a silent techno-computational revolution. Electronic and digital footprints are everywhere. People write blog posts. Many resort to credit card transactions. The visual and auditory landscape is fast changing. In music, we are witnessing an endless recombination and remix and mash-up of sounds and rhythms, the sampling and recombining of old and new material. Cut-up and collage practices extend well beyond music as such, as old and new creative practices keep generating innovative, useful content in almost every single domain of everyday life—in visual art, film, video, literature, culinary arts, fashion, and of course Internet applications.

Here like everywhere else in the world, life behind screens is fast becoming a fact of daily existence. People are exposed to, are producing, and are absorbing more images than ever before. They are increasingly surrounded by all kinds of devices, dream machines, and ubiquitous technologies—cell phones, the Web, videos, and films. Connection to the Internet is not simply a preoccupation for the middle class. It is increasingly in the interest of the urban poor to be connected too. Even before food, shelter, and access to electricity have been secured, the first thing the African urban poor strive for is a mobile phone, and then television and especially cable TV. And of course Internet access. It follows that as the boundaries of perception are being outstretched, more and more Africans are projected from one temporal regime to another. Time now unfolds in multiple versions. Its shapes are more protean than they have ever been. The struggles to capture these protean shapes of time have hardly been documented, and yet they are paving the way for an Afropolitan aesthetic sensibility we still need to map and properly study.

A most talked about—and as such prime—example of the ongoing Afrotechno revolution is the mobile phone. The introduction of the mobile phone on the continent has been a technological event of considerable singularity. Three comments in this regard are necessary. First, the mobile phone is not simply an object of use. It has become portable storage [*grenier*] of all kinds of knowledges and a crucial device that has changed the way people speak, act, and write, communicate, remember, and imagine who they are and how they relate to themselves, to others, and to the world at large.

Second, along with the advent of other computational media, the introduction of the mobile phone has also been a major *aesthetic and affect-laden event*. In Africa, this device is not only a medium of communication. It is also a medium of *self-stylization and self-singularization*. People spend a lot of time with their phones. It is as if they wear them. They have become an extension of one's being, a container of lives that they in turn shape. The way people treat their phones and the way they take care of these objects are themselves an indication of how they would like to be taken care of and, eventually, of the way they would like to be treated. Third, from a philosophical point of view, the biggest impact of the mobile phone—and of digital technologies more broadly—has been at the level of *the imaginary*. The interaction between humans and screens has intensified, and with it, the experience of life and the world as cinema—the cinematic nature of life.

The plasticity of digital forms speaks powerfully to the plasticity of African precolonial cultures and to ancient ways of working with representation and mediation, of folding reality. African precolonial cultures were obsessed with questioning the boundaries of life. As evidenced by their myths, oral literatures, and cosmogonies, among the most important human queries were those concerning the world beyond human perceptibility, visibility, and consciousness. The time of objects was not unlike the time of humans. Objects were not seen as static entities. Rather, they were like flexible living beings endowed with original and at times occult, magical, and even therapeutic properties.

Things and objects and the animal and organic worlds were also repositories of energy, vitality, and virtuality. As such, they constantly invited wonder and enchantment. Tools, technical objects, and artifacts facilitated the capacity for human cognition and language. They belonged to the world of interfaces and, as such, served as the linchpin for transgressing existing boundaries so as to access the Universe's infinite horizons. With human beings and other living entities, they entertained a relationship of reciprocal causation. This is what early anthropologists mistook for "animism." Indeed precolonial African ways of knowing have been particularly difficult to fit into Western analytical vocabularies. According to Jane Guyer, in her study of equatorial knowledge, such ways of knowing were not "specialist" "in the sense of a closed esoteric system with its classifications, propositions." Nor were they "controlled and monopolized by a small cadre of experts or a secret society hierarchy."[93]

Collectively, she tells us, "knowledge was conceptualized as an open repertoire and unbounded vista. Then, within collectivities the vista was divided up and quite widely distributed on the basis of personal capacity." "Adepts were many and varied," she says, "each pushing up against the outside limits of their own frontier of the known world, inventing new ways of configuring, storing and using" what must have been an ever-shifting spectrum of possibility. Citing Jan Vansina and James Fernandez in particular, she argues that these societies knew much more about their local habitats than they needed to know for utilitarian purposes—which means that knowledge for the sake of knowledge was a key feature of social existence. Whatever its origins, knowledge was something to be captured if necessary from outside as long as it could be mobilized for action or for performance. They showed "great receptivity to novelty," she argues. "Personal abilities existed first, but they could be augmented and actualized within the person, making that person a real person, singular to themselves" and recognized as such by others—the social process was about putting these singularities together.

It is as if the Internet was speaking unmediated to this archaic unconscious or to these societies' deepest and hidden brain. It is nowadays common sense to argue that the technological devices that saturate our lives have become extensions of ourselves. The novelty is that in the process, they have instituted a relationship between humans and other living or vital things that African traditions had long anticipated. Indeed in old African traditions, human beings were never satisfied simply being human beings. They were constantly in search of a supplement to their humanhood. Often, they added to their humanhood various attributes or properties taken from the worlds of animals, plants, and various objects. Modernity rejected such ways of being and their compositional logics, confining them to the childhood of Man. Clear distinctions between ourselves and the objects with which we share our existence were established. A human being was not a thing or an object. Nor was he or she an animal or a machine. This is precisely what human emancipation was supposed to mean.

Our own relationship to ourselves and to what surrounds us has changed as a result of our increasing entanglement with objects, technologies, or other living or animate things or beings. Today we want to capture for ourselves the forces and energies and vitalism of the objects that surround us, most of which we have invented. We think of ourselves as made up of various spare parts. This convergence, and at times fusion, between the living human being and the objects, the artifacts, or the technologies that supplement or augment us is at the source of the emergence of an entirely different kind of human being that we have not seen before.

With the advent of algorithmic thinking and various forms of automated reasoning, machines are increasingly endowed with decision-making capacities. The concretization of reasoning in machines—in other words the automation of reasoning—has cast a shadow on deductive reasoning and on the uniqueness of human reasoning. "Biologically bounded thought has been displaced by an abstract architecture of reasoning able to carry out tasks and make decisions by correlating data."[94]

In a global culture in which the footprints of social life are increasingly digitalized, software is becoming the engine of society and algorithmic reasoning a new form of thinking. To a large extent, software is remaking the human. The production of massive amounts of data at exponential rates has pushed us to the threshold of a different ontology of number. Numbers have become the engines not only of calculation and computation, but also of invention, imagination, and speculation. We can no longer rely entirely on dominant epistemological and ontological assumptions about numbers. New ways of theorizing measurement and quantification are more than ever required if we are to account for the ongoing computational reconfigurations of subjectivity and of the social.[95]

If, as Gerard Delanty and Aurea Mota argue, the emerging paradigm is that "the human societies and the Earth have now forged a tenuous unity as well as a consciousness of that unity" or that "the presuppositions of modernity are now once again called into question with the emergence of an entangled conception of nature and society, Earth and the world," then the question facing us is the following: What interpretive categories do we need for making sense of the world and of human societies, within a trajectory of time that encompasses planetary time?[96]

Let us take another example—the transformations that are affecting urban forms. These have been caused partly by the emergence, on the continent, of megacities and megaregions whose density, massive spatial expansion, sheer scale of population, high levels of risks, and great wealth disparities have been accompanied by dynamic and unexpected modes of urban growth. Major cities such as Lagos, Johannesburg, Kinshasa, Nairobi, Luanda, Dakar, and Abidjan have continued to expand in a relatively uncontrolled, decentralized, if not random, way since the 1980s. Today, such cities are better understood as largely deterritorialized megaregions with multiple urban enclaves.

Their myriad public spaces are increasingly privatized. Novel patterns of transregional migrations, settlement, and high consumption are transforming their economic and cultural fabric, paving the way for highly stylized and hybrid or creolized forms. Visible and invisible networks of social and economic exchange participate in, but are also separate from, the mainstream flows of global capital, real and fictitious. One of their defining features is not only their disjunctive social geography, but also the way in which humans and nonhumans are linked together in heterogeneous and often unrecognized assemblages that contribute to the making of a unique urban civilization. More than at any other time in their recent history, these megaregions are the direct outcome of new socioeconomic forms as well as a different politics of human/nonhuman/technoecological relations.

Let's consider, furthermore, what is going on in contemporary African art. In the Hegelian paradigm, there is obviously no such thing as "African contemporary art." Were it to exist, it would have neither authors nor concepts, only ethnicities and their fetishes. It is enough to place completely trivial domestic objects or ceremonial objects in a museum or a gallery for them to be transformed them into objects of art. In any case, the fact is that, since Duchamp, there are no longer works [*oeuvres*] as such in the West. Duchamp signed the death of the work of art in the classical sense of the term. There is no longer any image to isolate or to capture. There is no longer anything to interpret. There are only selections to be made and collections of objects to be assembled, curated, and exhibited. Since Duchamp, the act of giving form, of animation, has moved to the background. When the West "discovered" *l'art nègre* (Negro art) at the beginning of the twentieth century, it was above all else fascinated by what it had forgotten—that image and form did not need to be separated. In fact they could be reconciled in the object, and their reconciliation in the object is what endowed them both with a singular animating power. Thus the vitalist construction of African objects at the beginning of the twentieth century.

The magic of the arts of Africa and its diaspora has always come from its power [*puissance*] of dematerialization, its capacity to inhabit the sensible precisely with the aim of transforming it into an idea and an event. Historically it has come from an unambiguous recognition of the fact that the infinite cannot be captured in a form. The infinite exceeds every form even if, from time to time, it passes through form, that is, through the finite. But what fundamentally characterizes form is its own finitude. Form can only be ephemeral, evanescent, and fugitive. "To form" is to inhabit a space of essential fragility and vulnerability. This is the reason why caring, nurturing, and repairing life have been the three main functions of the arts in Africa.

The idea of art as an attempt to capture the forces of the infinite; an attempt to put the infinite in perceptible form, but a forming that consists in constantly doing, undoing, and redoing; assembling, disassembling, and reassembling—this idea is typically "African." It fully resonates with *the digital spirit of our times*. This is why there is a good chance that *the art of the twenty-first century will be Afropolitan*. Whatever the case, today, another cultural geography of the world is in the making. Whether one likes it or not, Africa is firmly writing itself within a new and decentered but global history of the arts. It is breaking with the ethnological paradigms that will have corseted it into primitivism or neoprimitivism.

More and more, the term *Africa* itself tends to refer to a *geoaesthetic category*. Africa being above all the body of a vast diaspora, it is by definition a body in motion, a deterritorialized body constituted in the crucible of various forms of migrancy. Its art objects too are above all objects in motion, coming straight out of a fluctuating imaginary. Such too is Afropolitanism—a migrant and circulatory form of modernity, born out of overlapping genealogies, at the intersections of multiple encounters with multiple elsewheres. Indeed if modern art is a response to the crisis of the image, it is possible that this crisis is at the point of being resolved by contemporary African and Afrodiasporic creation. African and Afrodiasporic creation is the vehicle that will allow us to escape from the crisis of the idea of the image opened up by modern art.

As we enter the twenty-first century, the Hegelian mythology—along with its multiple actualizations—manifestly no longer holds. It is now definitively unraveling. Something else is going on. It is being picked up both by Africans themselves and, curiously enough, by the world of high finance. Africa is a planetary laboratory at a time when history itself is being recast as an integrated history of the Earth system, technical systems, and the human world. Here, a technological revolution is taking shape at a time when *the continent is increasingly perceived as the last frontier of capitalism*. A vast amount of wealth has been extracted from Africa over centuries. This wealth has flowed out to every corner of the globe. To be sure, the continent's natural assets are in danger of being depleted. Waste and pollution have increased exponentially. But Africa remains the last territory on Earth that has not yet been entirely subjected to the rule of capital.

It is the last repository of a vast body of untapped wealth—minerals in the underground, plants and animals, water and sun, all the forms of energy latent in the Earth's crust. Its biosphere is still more or less intact. Its hydrographic power, its solar energy, its territorial immensities are hardly touched. It is the last major chunk of our planet that has not yet been entirely connected to its many different parts. This single gargantuan landmass can still support a huge number of people. It is the only place on Earth where people can still come and begin anew and where the potential for the human species is still high. The times, therefore, are propitious for big questions concerning the relation of human life to planetary life in a context of geological recasting of historical time. As a matter of fact, the destiny of our planet will be played out, to a large extent, in Africa. This planetary turn of the African predicament will constitute the main cultural and philosophical event of the twenty-first century.

EPILOGUE

The Politics of the Future World

C olonialism was far from a godsend. The giant figure before which the frightened or fascinated multitudes came to prostrate themselves in reality hid an enormous hollow. A metal carcass set with splendid jewels, colonialism also partook of the Beast and of manure.[1] A slow inferno dispersing its clouds of smoke everywhere, it sought to institute itself as both ritual and event: as word, gesture, and wisdom, story and myth, murder and accident. And it is in part because of its dreadful capacity for proliferation and metamorphosis that it caused such trembling in those whom it had enslaved, infiltrating their dreams, filling their most horrific nightmares, before wrenching atrocious laments from them.[2] As for colonization, the act of deploying colonialism, it was not only a technology, or a simple apparatus. It was not only ambiguities.[3] It was also a scaffold of certainties, each more illusory than the last: the power of the fake. It was a moving complex, of course, but in many regards, it was also a fixed, immobile, and sterile intercourse. Used to conquering without being in the right, colonization demanded not only that the colonized change their reasons for living, but also that they change reason itself and become beings in perpetual displacement.[4] And it is as such that the Thing and its representation provoked the resistance of those who lived under its yoke, causing indocility, terror, and seduction at once, as well as, here and there, a great number of insurrections.

This book has dealt with decolonization as a praxis of self-defense and as an experience of emergence and uprising. It is an inquiry into the *decolonized community*. In the conditions of the time, "uprising" consisted largely in a redistribution of languages. This was not only the case where it was necessary to use violence. The colonized at various levels, as if taken by the fire of the Paraclete, began to speak various languages in place of one single language. In this respect, decolonization represents a great moment of delinking and branching of languages within the history of our modernity. With decolonization, there is no longer a unique orator or mediator, no longer a master without a countermaster, no univocity. Everyone can express him- or herself in his or her own language. The knots having been undone, there is no longer anything but an immense bundle. In the minds of those who carried out decolonization, decolonizing never meant replaying the images of the Thing or its substitutes in a different time. The goal of the dénouement had always been to finally put an end to a world made up of two categories of humans: on one side, subjects who act and, on the other, objects that are acted on. The aim was a radical metamorphosis of relations. The ex-colonized would, from then on, create their own time, all the while constructing the time of the world. On the loam of their traditions and their imaginaries, drawing on their long past, they could henceforth reproduce within their own history—itself a manifest illustration of the history of all of humanity. From then on, the Event would be recognized by the way everything would begin anew. From then on, the power to engender would oppose the play of repetition without difference and the forces that since the time of servitude had sought to deplete or put an end to the duration of time. This is what, in Promethean language, Frantz Fanon called leaving the "dark night" [*grande nuit*] before life,[5] while Aimé Césaire spoke of the desire "for a more brilliant sun and purer stars."[6]

Coming out of the great darkness before life would require an approach conscious of the "provincialization of Europe." It was necessary, Fanon said, to turn one's back on this Europe, "which never stops talking of man yet massacres him at every one of its street corners, at every corner of the world." About this Europe that never stopped talking of man, he added that "today we know with what sufferings humanity has paid for every one of [its] triumphs of the mind."[7] Fanon did not just propose to not "follow" this Europe; he proposed "leaving" it because its game was up. The time had come to go on to "something else," he affirmed. Hence, the need to reexamine the "question of man." How? By walking "all the time, night and day, in the company of Man, in the company of all men."[8] For him, this is what made the decolonized community a walking community, a community of walkers, a vast, universal caravan. For others, this vast, universal caravan could be achieved not by dissociating oneself from Europe, but rather by looking upon Europe with solicitude and compassion, and breathing back into it the supplement of humanity it had lost.[9]

These primitive meanings of the Event are what we must be able to recover, beyond the compilation of historical details. They are found in the very substance of the colonial experience: in the language, words, writings, songs, acts, and consciousness of its protagonists, and in the history of the institutions they set up as well as in the memory they forged of their history.[10] It must be understood that the uprising (in particular the armed uprising) organized to end colonial domination and its pillar, the law of race, would scarcely have been possible without the conscious production of a strange power by the insurgents (sublime illusion or the power of dream?), an energetic and incendiary force, a structure of affects made of calculating reason and anger, faith and opportunism, desires and exaltations, messianism and madness, without the translation of this fire into praxis: the praxis of springing forth, of emergence.[11] On the horizon was the reversal of the old bonds of subjection and a new place in the time and structure of the world. And if, in the course of this ascent toward limits, confrontation with death became necessary, then, above all, it was important never to die like a rat or a domestic animal, trapped in the barnyard, the stables, the cowshed, on the auction block, or simply out in the open.[12]

For many of the protagonists of the time, decolonization was indeed a Manichean combat.[13] The struggle for decolonization, which was an interpretation of life and a preparation for death, many times took on the appearance of poetic procreation. It demanded from the heroes of the struggle—who are particularly well remembered in popular song—a relinquishment of the self, an astonishing capacity for asceticism, and, in certain cases, the trembling of drunkenness. Colonization had trapped a significant part of the globe in an immense web of dependence. The fight to end it, in return, took on a planetary dimension. It was a movement of repotentialization that some imagined as a festival of universal deliverance, humans' ascent to the highest degree of their symbolic faculties, beginning with the entire body, rhythmically shaken in its limbs and in its reason by song and dance—strident laugh and overabundance of life. This is what gave the anticolonial combat its oneiric and aesthetic dimension.

More than half a century later, what traces, what marks, what remains are left of this experience of uprising, of the passion that inhabited it, of this attempt to go from the state of thing to the state of subject, of the will to reexamine the "question of man" and that of the object? Is there really anything at all to commemorate, or, to the contrary, must everything be taken up again? Take up what, why, how, and in what conditions? In what new language, culture, and words, at the heart of the nebulous chaos of the present? If, as Frantz Fanon said, the decolonized community defines itself by its relation to the future—the experience of a new form of life and a new relation to humanity—who, then, will define anew the original content for which a new form must be created? If the extraordinary voyage toward a new world must be undertaken again, by means of what new knowledge will this be done? In short, how do we restore life to a way of being that is no more than a statue? Or must this apparently inert matter and henceforth cumbersome object simply be toppled?

Indeed, more than half a century later, instead of a true self-repossession, and in place of a foundational moment, what do we see?

An apparently lifeless block that testifies to everything except the form of a living and joyful body, disappearing under a double layer of rage and ressentiment. A few objects glittering in the middle of a river that is reversing its course. And at the bottom of the delta, illegible deposits awaiting excavation. Why is Africa—and the world—bored into and drilled? Why this plenitude in heaviness and this noise constantly outstripping the subject, seemingly drowning him or her in an unnamable state? And why this furor that envelops the apparent calm of things, only escaping its mute genealogy now and again to collapse with renewed vigor into stultifying emptiness? How long until we have the thing we have worked for? Where are we going?

Beyond its ambivalence and the extraordinary diversity of its forms and contents, modern colonization was a direct outcome of doctrines that consisted in sorting humans into groups: those who counted and who were counted, on the one hand, and, on the other hand, "the rest," those who were called "detritus of men" or "wastes of men." The first group, the masters, was the "last men." They sought to raise the conditions favorable to their own survival into a universal law. The "last man" was characterized by his will to dominate, enjoy, conquer, and command, by his propensity to dispossess and, if necessary, to exterminate. The "last man" constantly invoked law, reason, and civilization. But he operated precisely as if there were no law, reason, or civilization other than his own. This being the case, none of the crimes committed could be judged from any moral point of view. There was nothing that belonged to anyone else that he could not claim for himself, whether by force, ruse, or trickery. The last man was, finally, characterized by the weight he gave to self-preservation and the fear he cultivated with regard to any power great enough to protect the fruit of its work and its life autonomously.

The others, the "wastes of men" (incapable of engendering themselves), were called on to submit. After they had given up the struggle, their role was to bear the misfortune of the last men and to lament it endlessly. They espoused this role so well that they ended up wearing this

interminable lamentation and taking it as the last word on their identity. And, to the extent that the idea of universal equality and equivalence between men (the dogma of the weak) belonged in fact to religion
in the form of narcosis and pity, the very idea of morality had to be abolished. It had to make room for faith in one's own right—righteousness
not only that authorized force and predation but that, furthermore, was
comfortable in its ignorance and clear conscience.[14]

We are far from having left behind this era of righteousness, whose
apogee was colonialism and which sanctions force, ignorance, and the
right to a clear conscience. Our era is attempting to bring back into fashion the old myth that the West alone has a monopoly on the future.[15]
Under these circumstances, it is hardly surprising that some seek to deny
all paradigmatic meaning to the phenomena of colonialism and imperialism, and to bury the serious philosophical and ethical dilemmas that
came out of European expansion by consigning them to the register of
insignificant detail.

The rehabilitation of colonial righteousness in contemporary conditions rests on the conviction that real and effective freedom is not conferred by any contract between equal parties, or by any treaty. It is the
product of natural right (*jus naturale*). Ours is also an era in which the
only valid morality is a morality reduced to the instinct of pity, to a thousand forms of contempt masked by charity and good Samaritanism, to
the belief that the victor is, after all, right. And, in conditions where
might creates right and might and reason are united, why require justice and reparation? Moreover, according to this morality, there is no
place in our world for guilt, and even less for repentance, because both
the feeling of guilt and the desire for repentance are, ultimately, only cynical manifestations of the perversity of the weak.

Under these conditions, the major challenge facing our epoch is to
refound critical thinking: that is, thinking that thinks its possibility outside of itself, aware of the limits of its singularity, within the circuit that
always connects us to an Elsewhere. Such a refounding refers, by necessity, first to a certain disposition, which affirms the total, radical freedom of societies vis-à-vis their past and future. It is also thinking capable of confronting its world, which seeks to understand the history in

which we are stakeholders, and which makes it possible to identify the power of the future inscribed in the present.

If we must, together, walk anew the paths of humanity in companionship with all species, then it is perhaps necessary to begin by recognizing that at bottom there is no world or place where we are totally "at home," masters of the premises.[16] What is proper always arises at the same time as what is foreign. The foreign does not always come from elsewhere. It is always born out of an original and irreducible scission that requires, in return, detachment and appropriation. Obviously, the advent of such critical thinking capable of nourishing lateral universalism requires going beyond the radical opposition between the proper and the foreign, the human and the nonhuman.

Humanity is not given. It is pulled up and created over the course of struggles.

The aim of anticolonialism was to create a new form of reality: emancipation from what was most intolerable and unbearable in colonialism, its dead force, and then the constitution of a subject who, at the origin, would first refer to itself—and, in referring first to itself, to its pure possibility and free apparition, would inevitably relate to the world, to others, to an Elsewhere.

If there is an intellectual, moral, and political heritage of African nationalism worth our energy in contemporary conditions, it is in this direction that it must be sought—in the message of joy in a great universal future equitably open to all peoples, all nations, and all species.

The objective of the uprising was to be born into freedom. Its objective was to break the dead forces that limit the capacities for life. Becoming free was the equivalent of being by and for oneself, constituting oneself as a responsible human subject—before oneself, before others, and before nations. This is what I have referred to throughout this book as the politics of *ascent into humanity*.

I have also maintained that the uprising and organized struggle aimed to "make community." "Making community" is part of a will to life. The struggle aimed, ultimately, to produce life, to eliminate the forces that, in the colonial context, combined to mutilate, disfigure, and destroy life. This project for a full human life and for the future world was, at the origin, the political project of African nationalism. It remains the project of the Africa to come.

But the uprising also aimed to answer the threefold question: Who are we and where are we in the present? What do we want to become? And what must we hope for the world?

These questions of origin and destination, of will and hope, are still with us.

Today, the task is to turn these ideas into cultural acts capable of preparing the terrain for direct political practices, without which the future will be closed.

The invention of an alternative imaginary of life, power, and the planet requires renewing transversal solidarities—those that go beyond clan, race, and ethnic affiliations—mobilizing the religious resources of spiritualities of deliverance, consolidating and transnationalizing the institutions of civil society, renewing juridical activism, developing a capacity for swarming—notably in the direction of diasporas—and an idea of life and the arts that would be the foundation of radical democratic thought.

But inventing this new imaginary requires us, at the same time, to reflect on the question of revolutionary violence. This is an extremely complex political and ethical question that comes from our past and haunts our present, and that we must treat responsibly, for all the blood that has been and might still be spilled will not necessarily produce life, liberty, and community.

If Africans want to stand up and walk, sooner or later they must look elsewhere than to Europe. Europe is undoubtedly not a dying world. But, weary, it now represents the world of declining life and crimson sunsets. Here, the spirit has faded, eaten away by extreme forms of pessimism, nihilism, and frivolity.

Africa will have to turn its gaze toward the new. It will have to stage itself and, for the first time, accomplish what has never before been possible. It will have to do this with awareness that it is opening new ages for itself and for the planet.

NOTES

INTRODUCTION

Epigraph: Saint-Jean Perse, *Collected Poems* (Princeton: Princeton University Press, 1983), "Neiges" ("Snows"), trans. Denis Devlin, 207.

1. C. A. Bayly, "The First Age of Global Imperialism, c. 1760–1830," *Journal of Imperial and Commonwealth History* 26, no. 2 (1998): 30.

2. H. V. Bowen, "British Conceptions of Global Empire, 1756–83," *Journal of Imperial and Commonwealth History* 26, no. 3 (1998): 7.

3. See the synthesis by Prasenjit Duara, ed., *Decolonization: Perspectives Now and Then* (London: Routledge, 2004).

4. *Logique de Sens* is the French title of the book by Gilles Deleuze to which Mbembe later refers. It has been translated as *Logic of Sense* in English, so I have used that expression here.—TRANS.

5. Dilip P. Gaonkar, ed., *Alternative Modernities* (Durham: Duke University Press, 2001).

6. Fabien Éboussi Boulaga, *La Crise du Muntu* (Paris: Présence Africaine, 1977).

7. Jean-François Bayart, *The State in Africa* (London: Polity, 2009).

8. Ranajit Guha, *Dominance Without Hegemony* (Cambridge, MA: Harvard University Press, 1998); and Partha Chatterjee, *The Nation and Its Fragments* (Princeton: Princeton University Press, 1993).

9. Gilles Deleuze, *The Logic of Sense* (London: Athlone, 1990), 28–31.

10. Cf. Crawford Young and Thomas Turner, *The Rise and Decline of the Zairian State* (Madison: University of Wisconsin Press, 1985).

11. See Jane I. Guyer, "Africa Has Never Been 'Traditional,'" *African Studies Review* 50, no. 2 (2007): 183–202.

1. PLANETARY ENTANGLEMENT

1.   G. W. F. Hegel, *The Philosophy of History* (New York: Dover, 1956), 93.

2.   Hegel, 99.

3.   Francis Fukuyama, "The End of History?," *National Interest* (Summer 1989): 1.

4.   Fukuyama, 12.

5.   Robert Kaplan, "The Coming Anarchy," *Atlantic*, February 1994.

6.   "Hopeless Africa," *Economist*, May 11, 2000.

7.   See the introduction to Sarah Nuttall and Achille Mbembe, *Johannesburg: The Elusive Metropolis* (Durham: Duke University Press, 2008).

8.   V. Y. Mudimbe et al., *Africa and the Disciplines: The Contributions of Research in Africa to the Social Sciences and Humanities* (Chicago: University of Chicago Press, 1993).

9.   See, for instance, the account of a crucial category of Marxian and Freudian critique in William Pietz, "The Problem of the Fetish," *RES: Anthropology and Aesthetics* 9 (Spring 1985): 5–17; Pietz, "The Problem of the Fetish II: The Origin of the Fetish," *RES: Anthropology and Aesthetics* 13 (Spring 1987): 23–45; and Pietz, "The Problem of the Fetish IIIa: Bosman's Guinea and the Enlightenment Theory of Fetishism," *RES: Anthropology and Aesthetics* 16 (Autumn 1988): 105–124. See also the centrality of African material in Gilles Deleuze and Félix Guattari, *A Thousand Plateaus: Capitalism and Schizophrenia* (Minneapolis: University of Minnesota Press, 1987); and Deleuze and Guattari, *Anti-Oedipus* (New York: Penguin, 2009). More broadly, see Ernesto de Martino, *Magic: A Theory from the South* (Chicago: University of Chicago Press, 2015).

10.   G. W. F. Hegel, *Reason in History* (New York: Pearson, 1995).

11.   Arjun Appadurai, *The Future as Cultural Fact: Essays on the Global Condition* (New York: Verso, 2014).

12.   On the cultivation of strategic unknowns as perhaps the greatest resource for those in power, read Linsey McGoey, "Strategic Unknowns: Towards a Sociology of Ignorance," *Economy and Society* 41, no. 1 (2012): 1–16.

13.   Such challenges have been brought under the general umbrella of "development." For a critique of the production, transmission, and implementation of ideas of "development," see Fred Cooper and Randall M. Packard, eds., *International Development and the Social Sciences* (Berkeley: University of California Press, 1998); and Cooper and Packard, "Writing the History of Development," *Journal of Modern European History* 8 (2010): 5–23; Arturo Escobar, *Encountering Development: The Making and Unmaking of the Third World* (Princeton: Princeton University Press, 2011).

14.   To these should be added crucial issues such as the institutional organizations forming the social infrastructure of the field, the redistribution of academic authority across generations, the objects of inquiry that are privileged, and the cognitive tools and explanatory schemas that are used. On some of these issues, see Achille Mbembe, "At the Center of the Knot," *Social Dynamics* 38, no. 1 (2012): 8–14.

15.   See, for instance, Sara Berry, *Fathers Work for Their Sons: Accumulation, Mobility and Class Formation in an Extended Yoruba Community* (Berkeley: University of

California Press, 1985); Jane I. Guyer, *Marginal Gains: Monetary Transactions in Atlantic Africa* (Chicago: University of Chicago Press, 2004).

16. See, for example, John L. Comaroff and Jean Comaroff, *Chiefship, Capital, and the State in Contemporary Africa* (Chicago: University of Chicago Press, 2018); Jennifer Cole, ed., *Affective Circuits: African Migrations to Europe and the Pursuit of Social Regeneration* (Chicago: University of Chicago Press, 2016); Jane I. Guyer, *Marginal Gains: Monetary Transactions in Atlantic Africa* (Chicago: University of Chicago Press, 2004).

17. See "Thoughts on Theorizing from the South: An Interview with John Comaroff by Lisandro Claudio," *Johannesburg Salon* 10 (2015), www.jwtc.org.za.

18. See the introduction, Sara Berry, *No Condition Is Permanent: The Social Dynamics of Agrarian Change in Sub-Saharan Africa* (Madison: University of Wisconsin Press, 1993).

19. Adam Ashforth, *The Trials of Mrs K. Seeking Justice in a World of Witches* (Chicago: University of Chicago Press, 2018).

20. Cf. Jason de León, *The Land of Open Graves: Living and Dying on the Migrant Trail* (Berkeley: University of California Press, 2015); Charles Piot with Kodjo Nicolas Batema, *The Fixer: Visa Lottery Chronicles* (Durham: Duke University Press, 2019).

21. Sara Berry, *Chiefs Know Their Boundaries. Essays on Property, Power, and the Past in Asante, 1896–1996* (Portsmouth, NH: Heinemann; Oxford: James Currey; Cape Town, South Africa: David Philip, 2001); Jean Comaroff and John Comaroff, *Ethnicity, Inc.* (Chicago: University of Chicago Press, 2009).

22. Ato Quayson, *Oxford Street, Accra: City Life and the Itineraries of Transnationalism* (Durham: Duke University Press, 2014); Filip De Boeck and Marie-Francoise Plissart, *Kinshasa: Tales of the Invisible City* (Leuven: Leuven University Press, 2004).

23. Achille Mbembe, *Sortir de la grande nuit: essai sur l'Afrique décolonisée* (Paris: La Découverte, 2010); Denis Retaillé and Olivier Walther, "Rethinking Borders in a Mobile World: An Alternative Model," Working Paper no. 03/14, Department of Border Region Studies (2014); and Retaillé and Walther, "Conceptualizing the Mobility of Space Through the Malian Conflict," *Annales de Géographie* 6, no. 694 (2013): 595–618.

24. Jane Guyer, "Describing Urban 'No Man's Lands' in Africa," *Africa* 81, no. 3 (2011).

25. Cf. Arif Dirlik, "Transnationalization and the University: The Perspective of Global Modernity," *boundary 2* 39, no. 3 (2012): 47–73.

26. Anna Kosmutzky and Rahul Putty, "Transcending Borders and Traversing Boundaries: A Systematic Review of the Literature on Transnational, Offshore, Cross-Border, and Borderless Higher Education," *Journal of Studies in International Education* 20, no. 1 (2016): 8–33.

27. Anita Starosta, "Accented Criticism: Translation and Global Humanities," *boundary 2* 40, no. 3 (2013): 163–179; Mark Gamsa, "Cultural Translation and the Transnational Circulation of Books," *Journal of World History* 22, no. 3 (2011): 553–575.

28. Amy Allen, *The End of Progress: Decolonizing the Normative Foundations of Critical Theory* (New York: Columbia University Press, 2016); Chris Goto-Jones, "A Cosmos

Beyond Space and Area Studies: Toward Comparative Political Thought as *Political Thought*," *boundary 2* 38, no. 3 (2011): 87–118.

29.   Tom Looser, "The Global University, Area Studies, and the World Citizen: National Geography's Redistribution of the 'World,'" *Cultural Anthropology* 27, no. 1 (2012); Liu Xincheng, "The Global View of History in China," *Journal of World History* 23, no. 3 (2012): 491–511; Andrew J. Abalahin, "'Sino-Pacifica': Conceptualizing Greater Southeast Asia as a Sub-Arena of World History," *Journal of World History* 22, no. 4 (2011): 659–691; R. Hale, "Re-Visioning Latin American Studies," *Cultural Anthropology* (2011).

30.   Ahmet Davutoglu, *Alternative Paradigms: The Impact of Islamic and Western Weltanschauungs on Political Theory* (New York: University Press of America, 1994); Dipesh Chakrabarty, *Provincializing Europe* (Princeton: Princeton University Press, 1995); Kuan-Hsing Chen, *Asia as Method: Toward Deimperialization* (Durham: Duke University Press, 2010).

31.   See, for example, Donald Worster, *Shrinking the Earth: The Rise and Decline of American Abundance* (Oxford: Oxford University Press, 2016); Olivier Morton, *The Planet Remade: How Geoengineering Could Change the World* (Princeton: Princeton University Press, 2015); Fazal Sheikh and Eyal Weizman, *The Conflict Shoreline: Colonialism as Climate Change in the Negev Desert* (Göttingen: Steidl, 2015). More generally, cf. Kraig Schwartz, *Big History and the Future of Humanity* (London: Wiley-Blackwell, 2011); Roy Scranton, *Learning to Die in the Anthropocene* (San Francisco: City Lights, 2015).

32.   D. Chernilo, *The Natural Law Foundations of Modern Social Theory: A Quest for Universalism* (Cambridge: Cambridge University Press, 2013), 3. See also Seyla Benhabib, *Critique, Norm, and Utopia: A Study of the Foundations of Critical Theory* (New York: Columbia University Press, 1986).

33.   Boaventura de Sousa Santos, *The End of the Cognitive Empire: The Coming Age of Epistemologies of the South* (Durham: Duke University Press, 2018).

34.   On how this conception of reason operates including in psychoanalysis, see Alfred I. Tauber, "Freud's Dreams of Reason: The Kantian Structure of Psychoanalysis," *History of the Human Sciences* 22, no. 4 (2009): 1–29.

35.   On these cultural asymmetries and the replication of center-periphery dynamics including within Europe itself, see Stefan Nygard and Johan Strang, "Facing Asymmetry: Nordic Intellectuals and Center-Periphery Dynamics in European Cultural Space," *Journal of the History of Ideas* 77, no. 1 (2016): 75–97.

36.   Marc Redfield, *Theory at Yale: The Strange Case of Deconstruction in America* (New York: Fordham University Press, 2016), 1.

37.   Cf. Peter E. Gordon and John P. McCormick, *Weimar Thought: A Contested Legacy* (Princeton: Princeton University Press, 2013).

38.   Herbert Marcuse, *One-Dimensional Man: Studies in the Ideology of Advanced Industrial Society* (Boston: Beacon, 1964).

39.   "Criticism" consists in exposing the fundamental operations and conditions of possibility of particular systems or modes of inquiry. It seeks to reveal the extent to which

what initially appears to be beyond question and entirely obvious does, in fact, possess a complex history. "Criticism" is about following "the slipstream of the forever elusive signifier" while simultaneously attempting "to grasp the production of meaning in every medium, media and technologies included." On these issues, see Toril Moi, "How the French Read," *New Literary History* 44, no. 2 (2013): 309–317; Michael Chaouli, "Criticism and Style," *New Literary History* 44, no. 3 (2013): 323–344; Andrew H. Miller, "Implicating Criticism, or the Display of Thinking," *New Literary History* 44, no. 3 (2013): 345–360. As for "critique," see Michel Foucault, "What Is Critique?," in *The Politics of Truth*, ed. Sylvère Lotringer (Cambridge, MA: Semiotext[e], 2007), 41–81; Michel Foucault, "What Is Enlightenment?," in *The Foucault Reader*, ed. Paul Rabinow (New York: Pantheon, 1984), 32–50; Judith Butler, "What Is Critique? An Essay on Foucault's Virtue," in *The Political*, ed. David Ingram (London: Wiley-Blackwell, 2002).

40. Manuel DeLanda, *Philosophical Chemistry: Genealogy of a Scientific Field* (London: Bloomsbury, 2015). For calls for a synthesis, see Alain Caillé and Frédéric Vandenberghe, "Neo-Classical Sociology: The Prospects of Social Theory Today," *European Journal of Social Theory* 19, no. 1 (2016): 3–20.

41. Michael Hardt, "The Militancy of Theory," *South Atlantic Quarterly* 110, no. 1 (Winter 2011).

42. Jean Comaroff and John Comaroff, *Theory from the South* (New York: Paradigm, 2012), 47.

43. Jean Comaroff, "The Politics of Conviction: Faith on the Neo-Liberal Frontier," *Social Analysis* 53, no. 1 (2009): 17–38.

44. Nikolas Rose, "Reading the Human Brain: How the Mind Became Legible," *Body and Society* (January 12, 2016).

45. Suzanne R. Kirschner, "The Many Challenges of Theorizing Subjectivity," *Culture and Psychology* 19, no. 2 (2013): 225–236. See also Bernard E. Harcourt, *Exposed: Desire and Disobedience in the Digital Age* (Cambridge, MA: Harvard University Press, 2015).

46. Roger Smith, *Being Human: Historical Knowledge and the Creation of Human Nature* (Manchester: Manchester University Press, 2007).

47. Nikolas Rose, "The Human Sciences in a Biological Age," *Theory Culture and Society* 30, no. 1 (2013): 3–34, at 5, https://pdfs.semanticscholar.org/0d08/88b148a6138aa910f8 b723c575d2db02f78c.pdf.

48. Jerome Kagan, *On Being Human: Why Mind Matters* (New Haven: Yale University Press, 2016), 21.

49. Joelle M. Abi-Rached and Nikolas Rose, "The Birth of the Neuromolecular Gaze," *History of the Human Sciences* 23, no. 1 (2010): 11–36; and Jessica Pykett, "Neurocapitalism and the New Neuros: Using Neuroeconomics, Behavioural Economics and Picoeconomics for Public Policy," *Journal of Economic Geography* 13, no. 5 (2013): 845–869.

50. See Retaillé and Walther, "Conceptualizing the Mobility of Space Through the Malian Conflict."

51. For the most recent debates, see Robert C. Berwick and Noam Chomsky, *Why Only Us: Language and Evolution* (Cambridge, MA: MIT Press, 2016); Charles Taylor, *The*

Language Animal: The Full Shape of the Human Linguistic Capacity (Cambridge, MA: Belknap Press of Harvard University Press, 2016); Paolo Virno, *When the Word Becomes Flesh: Language and Human Nature* (Cambridge, MA: Semiotext[e], 2015).

52. Nikolas Rose, "The Human Sciences in a Biological Age," *Theory, Culture and Society* 30, no. 1 (2013): 3–34.

53. "The development of what we consider to be our uniquely human capacities is metaphysically realized in relationships that include continuously changing neural, corporeal, and sociocultural resources that are insensitive to putative boundaries between internal and external environments," argues Jennifer Greenwood in *Becoming Human: The Ontogenesis, Metaphysics, and Expression of Human Emotionality* (Cambridge, MA: MIT Press, 2015), 205. See also Katherine Isbister, *How Games Move Us: Emotion by Design* (Cambridge, MA: MIT Press, 2016).

54. Margrit Shildrick, "Estranged Bodies: Shifting Paradigms and the Biomedical Imaginary," *Body and Society* 21, no. 3 (2015): 3–19; and Rachel Alpha Johnston Hurst, *Surface Imaginations: Cosmetic Surgery, Photography, and Skin* (Montreal: McGill-Queen's University Press, 2015).

55. See Stacy Alaimo, *Bodily Natures: Science, Environment, and the Material Self* (Bloomington: Indiana University Press, 2010).

56. Tim Hodgkinson, *Music and the Myth of Wholeness: Toward a New Aesthetic Paradigm* (Cambridge, MA: MIT Press, 2016), 8.

57. Wendy Brown, "Resisting Left Melancholy," *boundary 2* 26, no. 3 (1999). See also Brown, "Untimeliness and Punctuality: Critical Theory in Dark Times," in *Edgework: Critical Essays on Knowledge and Politics* (Princeton: Princeton University Press, 2005).

58. Bruno Latour, "Why Has Critique Run out of Steam? From Matters of Fact to Matters of Concern," *CI* 30 (Winter 2004): 231.

59. Karen Barad, *Meeting the Universe Halfway: Quantum Physics and the Entanglement of Matter and Meaning* (Durham: Duke University Press, 2007).

60. Maria Puig de la Bellacasa, "Matters of Care in Technoscience: Assembling Neglected Things," *Social Studies of Science* 41, no. 1 (2010): 85–106.

61. See also Eben Kirksey, ed., *The Multispecies Salon* (Durham: Duke University Press, 2014).

62. For a Western-centric rendering of this history, cf. Rosi Braidotti, ed., *After Poststructuralism: Transitions and Transformations* (New York: Routledge, 2014).

63. Jane Bennett, *Vibrant Matter: A Political Ecology of Things* (Durham: Duke University Press, 2010); Levi Bryant, Nick Srnicek, and Greg Harman, eds., *The Speculative Turn: Continental Materialism and Realism* (Melbourne: re-press, 2011); Bruno Latour, *Reflections on Etienne Souriau's* Les différents modes d'existence, bruno-latour.fr.

64. Nigel Thrift, "Re-Inventing Invention: New Tendencies in Capitalist Commodification," *Economy and Society* 35, no. 2 (2006): 301. As shown by Christian Berndt, the increasing use of market-based propoor development policy in the global South has gone hand in hand with the rise of behaviorism and experimentalism as an influential policy script. The behavioral approach to poverty, he argues, shifts the focus from

the market to the market subject and engages in often thinly veiled attempts at behavioral engineering. See Berndt, "Behavioural Economics, Experimentalism and the Marketization of Development," *Economy and Society* 44, no. 4 (2015): 567–591.

65. See Arjun Appadurai, *Banking on Words: The Failure of Language in the Age of Derivative Finance* (Chicago: University of Chicago Press, 2015).

66. Andrew Leyson et al., "Accounting for E-Commerce: Abstractions, Virtualism and the Cultural Circuit of Capital," *Economy and Society* 34, no. 3 (2005): 431.

67. See, for instance, "A Questionnaire on Materialisms," *October* 155 (2016): 3–110.

68. See David Theo Goldberg, "The Afterlife of the Humanities" (2014), http://issuu.com /uchri/docs/afterlife. See also Ackbar Abbas, *Poor Theory: An Open Source Manifesto* (2009), www.humanities.uci.edu/critical/poortheory.pdf.

69. David J. Gunkel, *Of Remixology: Ethics and Aesthetics After Remix* (Cambridge, MA: MIT Press, 2016).

70. Dipesh Chakrabarty, "The Climate of History: Four Theses," *Critical Inquiry* 35 (2009); and Chakrabarty, "Postcolonial Studies and the Challenge of Climate Change," *New Literary History* 43, no. 1 (2012): 1–18.

71. Matthew Ritchie, in "A Questionnaire on Materialisms," 86.

72. Jedediah Purdy, *After Nature: A Politics for the Anthropocene* (Cambridge, MA: Harvard University Press, 2016).

73. Bruno Latour, "Agency at the Time of the Anthropocene," *New Literary History* 45, no. 1 (2014): 1–18; Ian Hodder, "The Entanglement of Humans and Things: A Long-Term View," *New Literary History* 45, no. 1 (2014): 19–36; and Graham Harman, "Entanglement and Relation: A Response to Bruno Latour and Ian Hodder," *New Literary History* 45, no. 1 (2014).

74. Eduardo Viveiros de Castro, *Cannibal Metaphysics* (Minneapolis: Univocal, 2014); and Viveiros de Castro, *The Relative Native: Essays on Indigenous Conceptual Worlds* (Chicago: HAU, 2016).

75. Daniel Black, "Where Bodies End and Artefacts Begin: Tools, Machines and Interfaces," *Body and Society* 20, no. 1 (2014): 31–60. On the extent to which interfaces are designed to affect user experience at a corporeal level and not only at a cognitive level, thereby reconfiguring the locus itself of our intimacy, see Antonio Casilli, "A History of Virulence: The Body and Computer Culture in the 1980s," *Body and Society* 16, no. 4 (2010).

76. André Gorz, *The Immaterial* (Chicago: Seagull, 2010).

77. Derek Gregory, "The Natures of War," *Antipode* 48, no. 1 (2016): 3–56; Isla Forsyth, "Designs on the Desert: Camouflage, Deception and the Militarization of Space," *Cultural Geographies* 21 (2014): 247–265.

78. See Krzystof Ziarek, "The Global Unworld: A Meditative Manifesto," in *Impasses of the Post-Global: Theory in the Era of Climate Change*, vol. 2, ed. Henry Sussman (London: Open Humanities Press, 2012).

79. Georg Simmel, *The Sociology of Georg Simmel*, trans. and ed. Kurt H. Wolf (New York: Free, 1950).

80. Jane I. Guyer, "Prophecy and the Near Future: Thoughts on Macroeconomic, Evangelical, and Punctuated Time," *American Ethnologist* 34, no. 3 (2007).

81. Maurizio Meloni, "A Postgenomic Body: Histories, Geneology, Politics," *Body and Society* 24, no. 3 (2018): 3–38.

82. Erik Brynjolfsson and Andrew McAfee, *The Second Machine Age: Work, Progress, and Prosperity in a Time of Brilliant Technologies* (New York: Norton, 2014).

83. Cf. Malcolm McCullough, *Ambient Commons: Attention in the Age of Embodied Information* (Cambridge, MA: MIT Press, 2016).

84. Cf. Lev Manovich, *Language of New Media* (Cambridge, MA: MIT Press, 2002); Anne Friedberg, *The Virtual Window: From Alberti to Microsoft* (Cambridge, MA: MIT Press, 2006); Andy Clark, *Being There: Putting Brain, Body and World Together Again* (Cambridge, MA: MIT Press, 1997).

85. See, for example, Jacob Arnoldi, "Computer Algorithms, Market Manipulation and the Institutionalization of High Frequency Trading," *Theory, Culture and Society* 33, no. 1 (2016): 29–52. On the extent to which social media is connecting human communicative spaces to automated computational spaces in ways that are affectively contagious and highly volatile, see Tero Karppi, "Social Media, Financial Algorithms and the Hack Crash," *Theory, Culture and Society* 33, no. 1 (2015): 73–92.

86. On digital power and critical theory, see David M. Berry, *Critical Theory and the Digital* (New York: Bloomsbury Academic, 2014).

87. See, at the interface of environmental studies, new media, and the history of technology, Carolyn L. Kane, *Chromatic Algorithms: Synthetic Color, Computer Art, and Aesthetics After Code* (Chicago: University of Chicago Press, 2014).

88. Wendy Brown, *Undoing the Demos: Neoliberalism's Stealth Revolution* (Cambridge, MA: Zone, 2015).

89. Jean-Luc Nancy, *The Truth of Democracy* (New York: Fordham University Press, 2010).

90. Wendy Brown, "We Are All Democrats Now," in *Democracy in What State?*, by Giorgio Agamben et al. (New York: Columbia University Press, 2010), 55.

91. Allen J. Scott, *The Cultural Economy of Cities* (London: Sage, 2000).

92. Comaroff and Comaroff, *Ethnicity, Inc.*

93. On other global histories of the South(s), see Antonio Gramsci, *The Southern Question* (New York: Bordhigera, 1995); Avery Craven, "The 'Turner Theories' and the South," *Southern Historical Association* 5, no. 3 (1939): 291–314; Klaus Eder, "Europe's Borders: The Narrative Construction of the Boundaries of Europe," *European Journal of Social Theory* 9, no. 2 (2006): 255–271; Marcelo C. Rosa, "Theories of the South: Limits and Perspectives of an Emergent Movement in Social Sciences," *Current Sociology* 62, no. 6 (2014): 851–867.

94. Comaroff and Comaroff, *Theory from the South*.

95. Cf. Achille Mbembe, *On the Postcolony* (Berkeley: University of California Press, 2001).

96. Jane I. Guyer, *Legacies, Logics, Logistics: Essays in the Anthropology of the Platform Economy* (Chicago: University of Chicago Press, 2016); Filip De Boek, *Suturing the City: Living Together in Congo's Urban Worlds* (London: Autograph ABP, 2016).

97. See in particular Jane I. Guyer and Samuel M. Eno Belinga, "Wealth in People as Wealth in Knowledge: Accumulation and Composition in Equatorial Africa," *Journal of African History* 36 (1995): 91–120. See also Guyer, *Marginal Gains: Monetary Transactions in Atlantic Africa* (Chicago: University of Chicago Press, 2004).

98. Abdoumaliq Simone, *For the City Yet to Come: Changing African Life in Four Cities* (Durham: Duke University Press, 2006).

99. See, for instance, Fabien Éboussi Boulaga, *La Crise du Muntu: authenicité africaine et philosophie* (Paris: Présence africaine, 1981); Jean Comaroff, *Body of Power, Spirit of Resistance: The Culture and History of a South African People* (Chicago: University of Chicago Press, 1985); Peter Geschiere, *Sorcellerie et politique en Afrique: la viande des autres* (Paris: Karthala, 1995); Jean-François Bayart, *L'État en Afrique: la politique du ventre* (Paris: Fayard, 1989); Mbembe, *On the Postcolony*; Mariane Ferme, *The Underneath of Things: Violence, History, and the Everyday in Sierra Leone* (Berkeley: University of California Press, 2001).

100. Jean Comaroff and John Comaroff, *Of Revelation and Revolution*, vol. 1, *Christianity, Colonialism, and Consciousness in South Africa* (Chicago: University of Chicago Press, 1991); Comaroff and Comaroff, *Of Revelation and Revolution*, vol. 2, *The Dialectics of Modernity on a South African Frontier* (Chicago: University of Chicago Press, 1997); Nancy Rose Hunt, *A Colonial Lexicon: Of Birth Ritual, Medicalization, and Mobility in the Congo* (Durham: Duke University Press, 1999); and later, Hunt, *Nervous State: Violence, Remedies, and Reverie in Colonial Congo* (Durham: Duke University Press, 2016).

101. Jeremy L. Jones, "'Nothing Is Straight in Zimbabwe': The Rise of the Kukiya-kiya Economy 2000–2008," *Journal of Southern African Studies* 36, no. 2 (2010): 285–299.

102. Arjun Appadurai, "Illusion of Permanence: Interview with Arjun Appadurai," *Perspecta* 34 (2003): 44–52.

103. Jane Guyer, "Prophecy and the Near Future: Thoughts on Macroeconomic, Evangelical, and Punctuated Time," *American Ethnologist* 34, no. 3 (2007): 409–421.

104. Mariane C. Ferme, *Out of War: Violence, Trauma, and the Political Imagination in Sierra Leone* (Berkeley: University of California Press, 2018).

105. Franco Barchiesi, *Precarious Liberation: Workers, the State, and Contested Social Citizenship in Postapartheid South Africa* (Albany: State University of New York Press, 2011); Rex A. McKenzie, "Financialization and Labour: What Does Marikana Tell Us About Inequality in South Africa?," Working Paper 05/2013, Department of Economics, New School for Social Research, 2013.

106. Naseem Badiey and Christian Doll, "Planning Amidst Precarity: Utopian Imaginings in South Sudan," *Journal of Eastern African Studies* 1 (2017).

107. Rosalind C. Morris, "Mediation, the Political Task: Between Language and Violence in Contemporary South Africa," *Current Anthropology* 58, supplement 15 (February 2017).

108. Cf. Deborah James, *Money from Nothing: Indebtedness and Aspiration in South Africa* (Stanford: Stanford University Press, 2014).

109. James Ferguson, *Give a Man a Fish: Reflections on the New Politics of Distribution* (Durham: Duke University Press, 2015).

110. On offshore extraction and the dynamics of petrocapital, see Hannah Apel, "Offshore Work: Oil, Modularity, and the How of Capitalism in Equatorial Guinea," *American Ethnologist* 39, no. 4 (2012): 692–709; Brenda Chalfin, "Governing Offshore Oil: Mapping Maritime Political Space in Ghana and the Western Gulf of Guinea," *South Atlantic Quarterly* 114, no. 1 (2015): 101–118.

111. For a case study, see Miles Larmer, Ann Laudati, and John F. Clark, "Neither War nor Peace in the Democratic Republic of Congo (DRC): Profiting and Coping Amid Violence and Disorder," *Review of African Political Economy* 40, no. 135 (2013):1–12. In the same issue, see also Ann Laudati, "Beyond Minerals: Broadening 'Economies of Violence' in Eastern Democratic Republic of Congo" (32–50) and Judith Verweijen, "Military Business and the Business of the Military" (67–82).

112. See Gorden Moyo, "The Curse of Military Commercialism in State Enterprises and Parastatals in Zimbabwe," *Journal of Southern African Studies* 42, no. 2 (2016): 351–364.

113. Jeffrey W. Mantz, "Improvisational Economies: Coltan Production in the Eastern Congo," *Anthropologie sociale* 16, no. 1 (2008): 34–50; James Smith, "Tantalus in the Digital Age: Coltan Ore, Temporal Dispossession, and 'Movement' in the Eastern Democratic Republic of the Congo," *American Ethnologist* 38, no. 1 (2011).

114. Smith, "Tantalus in the Digital Age"; Filipe Calvao, "Crypto-Miners: Digital Labor and the Power of Blockchain Technology," *Economic Anthropology* 6, no. 1 (2018): 123–134; Christoph Vogel, "Between Tags and Guns: Fragmentation of Public Authority Around Eastern Congo's Artisanal 3T Mines," *Political Geography* (2017).

115. Marx, *Capital: A Critique of Political Economy*, vol. 1 (New York: Vintage, 1976), chap. 25.

116. Cf. Michael McIntyre and Heidi J. Nast, "Bio(necro)polis: Marx, Surplus Populations, and the Spatial Dialectics of Reproduction and 'Race,' " *Antipode* 43, no. 5 (2011): 1465–1488.

117. The amount of capital the finance industry siphons off and manages far exceeds the amount of capital valorized in the real economy. The value of this capital is mostly fictitious, based as it is on debt and on expectations of future growth and profit. On some of these issues, see Arjun Appadurai, *Banking on Words: The Failure of Language in the Age of Derivative Finance* (Chicago: University of Chicago Press, 2015).

118. James Ferguson, *Global Shadows: Africa in the Neoliberal World Order* (Durham: Duke University Press, 2006).

119. Cf. Michelle Yates, "The Human-as-Waste, the Labor Theory of Value and Disposability in Contemporary Capitalism," *Antipode* 43, no. 5 (2011): 1679–1695; Yates, "The Afterlives of 'Waste': Notes from India for a Minor History of Capitalist Surplus," *Antipode* 43, no. 5 (2011): 1625–1658. More broadly, see Joshua Ozias Reno, "Toward a New Theory of Waste: From 'Matter out of Place' to Signs of Life," *Theory, Culture and Society* (January 24, 2014); and Brian Thill, *Waste* (New York: Bloomsbury Academic, 2015).

120. Ruth Gilmore, *The Golden Gulag: Prisons, Surplus, Crisis, and Opposition in Global-izing California* (Berkeley: University of California Press, 2007).

121. Oliver Morton, *The Planet Remade: How Geoengineering Could Change the World* (Princeton: Princeton University Press, 2016).

122. Wolgang Streeck, *Buying Time: The Delayed Crisis of Democratic Capitalism* (New York: Verso, 2014).

123. Stathis Kouvelakis, "The Greek Cauldron," *New Left Review* 72 (2011).

124. Wolfgang Streeck, "The Crisis of Democratic Capitalism," *New Left Review* 71 (September–October 2011).

125. Streeck, 29.

126. Janet Abu-Lughod, *Before European Hegemony* (Oxford: Oxford University Press, 1989); Andre Gunder Frank, *ReOrient: Global Economy in the Asian Age* (Berkeley: University of California Press, 1998); G. Arrighi, *Adam Smith in Beijing: Lineages of the Twenty-First Century* (London: Verso, 2007).

127. On some of these debates, see Gavin Menzies, *1421: The Year China Discovered America* (London: Transworld, 2002); Robert Finlay, "How Not to (Re)Write World History: Gavin Menzies and the Chinese Discovery of America," *Journal of World History* 15, no. 2 (2004): 229–242; Sebastian Conrad, "Enlightenment in Global History: A Historiographical Critique," *American Historical Review* 117, no. 4 (2012): 999–1027; Micol Seigel, "World History's Narrative Problem," *Hispanic American Historical Review* 84, no. 3 (2004): 431–446.

128. Giovanni Arrighi, "The Winding Paths of Capital. Interview by David Harvey," *New Left Review* 56 (March–April 2009).

129. See Giovanni Arrighi, "Labour Supplies in Historical Perspective: A Study of the Pro-letarianization of the African Peasantry in Rhodesia," *Journal of Development Studies* 6 (1970); Arrighi, "The Political Economy of Rhodesia," *New Left Review* 1, no. 39 (September–October 1966); Arrighi with John Saul, *Essays on the Political Economy of Africa* (New York: Monthly Review Press, 1973); Arrighi, "The African Crisis: World Systemic and Regional Aspects," *New Left Review* 15 (May–June 2002); and Arrighi with Nicole Ashoff and Ben Scully, "Accumulation by Dispossession and Its Limits: The Southern African Paradigm Revisited" (unpublished paper, 2009).

130. For a recent attempt, see Françoise Lionnet and Shu-mei Shih, *The Creolization of Theory* (Durham: Duke University Press, 2011).

131. During the last decade, Africa made its greatest ever contribution of "illicit" finan-cial outflows and net income payments to the rest of the world. Estimates suggest that at least $406 billion was lost to the continent over the last decade. In comparative terms, sub-Saharan Africa's net income payments are almost three times those of the Euro zone and five times greater than those of China or India. See Ndongo Samba Sylla, "From a Marginalized to an Emerging Africa? A Critical Analysis," *Review of African Political Economy* 41, no. 1 (2014).

132. Anthony P. D'Costa, "Compressed Capitalism and Development," *Critical Asian Studies* 46, no. 2 (2014).

133. Sarah Nuttall, *Entanglement* (Johannesburg: Wits University Press, 2006).

2. DISENCLOSURE

1. Frederick Cooper, *Decolonization and African Society* (Cambridge: Cambridge University Press, 1996).

2. See A. G. Hopkins, "Globalisation and Decolonisation," *Journal of Imperial and Commonwealth History* 45, no. 5 (2017):729–745; and Hopkins, "Rethinking Decolonization," *Past and Present* 200 (2008): 211–247.

3. Michael R. Broers, *Europe Under Napoleon, 1799–1815* (London: Hodder Arnold, 1996); Michael Broers, Peter Hicks, and Agustin Guimera, eds., *The Napoleonic Empire and the New European Political Culture* (New York: Palgrave Macmillan, 2012).

4. See, for example, Philip Buckner, ed., *Canada and the British Empire* (Oxford: Oxford University Press, 2008); Stuart Ward, *Australia and the British Embrace: The Demise of the Imperial Idea* (Melbourne: Melbourne University Press, 2001).

5. Els Bogaerts and Remco Raben, *Beyond Empire and Nation: The Decolonization of African and Asian Societies, 1930s–1970s* (Leiden: Brill, 2012), 2.

6. Fred Cooper, "Decolonization and Citizenship: Africa Between Empires and a World of Nations," in Bogaerts and Raben, *Beyond Empire and Nation*, 39–67.

7. David Strang, "Global Patterns of Decolonization, 1500–1987," *International Studies Quarterly* 35, no. 4 (1991): 429–454; Pat McGowan, "Pitfalls and Promise in the Quantitative Study of the World System: A Reanalysis of Bergesen and Schoenberg's 'Long Waves' of Colonialism," *Review* 8, no. 4 (1985): 177–200; A. Bergesen and R. Schoenberg, "The Long Waves of Colonial Expansion and Contraction, 1415–1970," in *Studies of the Modern World System*, ed. A. Bergesen (New York: Academic Press, 1980), 231–277.

8. Cf. Kwame Nkrumah, *Autobiography* (London: Nelson, 1957); Patrice E. Lumumba, *Speech on Independence Day*, June 30, 1960; Tom Mboya, *Freedom and After* (Boston: Little, Brown, 1963); Eduardo Mondlane, *The Struggle for Mozambique* (Baltimore: Penguin, 1969).

9. John Darwin, "Decolonization and the End of Empire," in *The Oxford History of the British Empire*, vol. 5, *Historiography*, ed. Robin W. Winks (Oxford: Oxford University Press, 1999).

10. Prosser Gifford and W. M. Roger Louis, eds., *The Transfer of Power in Africa: Decolonization, 1940–1960* (New Haven: Yale University Press, 1982).

11. Amilcal Cabral, *Unity and Struggle* (New York: PAIGC, 1979).

12. Karen E. Fields, *Revival and Rebellion in Colonial Central Africa* (Princeton: Princeton University Press, 1985).

13. Frantz Fanon, *Ecrits sur l'alienation et la liberte* (Paris: La Découverte, 2016).

14. See Gary Wilder, *Freedom Time: Negritude, Decolonization, and the Future of the World* (Durham: Duke University Press, 2015).

15. On the distinction between racism and racecraft, see Karen E. Fields and Barbara J. Fields, *Racecraft: The Soul of Inequality in American Life* (New York: Verso, 2012).

16. Terence O. Ranger, "Religious Movements and Politics in Sub-Saharan Africa," *African Studies Review* 29, no. 2 (1986): 1–69.

17. Ngugi Wa Thiong'o, *Decolonising the Mind* (Portsmouth, NH: Heinemann, 1986). Hereafter cited parenthetically in the text.

18. See, for example, Roland Burke, *Decolonization and the Evolution of International Human Rights* (Philadelphia: University of Pennsylvania Press, 2010).

19. Erik Gartzke and Dominic Rohner, "The Political Economy of Imperialism, Decolonization and Development," *British Journal of Political Science* 41, no. 3 (2011): 525–556.

20. J. A. Hobson, *Imperialism: A Study* (New York: James Pott, 1902); Vladimir Lenin, *Imperialism: The Highest Stage of Capitalism* (1917). See also David K. Fieldhouse, *The Theory of Capitalist Imperialism* (London: Longman, 1967); Patrick Wolfe, "History and Imperialism: A Century of Theory from Marx to Postcolonialism," *American History Review* 102 (1997): 388–420.

21. V. I. Lenin, "Imperialism, the Highest Stage of Capitalism," in *Essential Works of Lenin*, ed. Henry Christman (New York: Bantam, 1966).

22. John Gallagher and Ronald Robinson, "The Imperialism of Free Trade," *Economic History Review* 6 (1953): 1–15.

23. Samir Amin, *L'Échange inégal et la loi de la valeur* (Paris: Anthropos, 1988).

24. Andre Gunder Frank, "The Development of Underdevelopment," *Monthly Review* 18 (September 1966).

25. Immanuel Wallerstein, *The Capitalist World Economy* (Cambridge: Cambridge University Press, 1979); Joshua S. Goldstein, *Long Cycles: Prosperity and War in the Modern Age* (New Haven: Yale University Press, 1988); Christopher Chase-Dunn and Richard Rubinson, "Toward a Structural Perspective on the World-System," *Politics and Society* 7 (1979): 453–476.

26. David Strang, "From Dependency to Sovereignty: An Event History Analysis of Decolonization 1870–1987," *American Sociological Review* 55 (1990): 847.

27. See Immanuel Wallerstein, *The Modern World-System*, vols. 1–3 (San Diego, CA: Academic Press, 1989).

28. Albert Bergesen and Ronald Schoenberg, "The Long Waves of Colonial Expansion and Contraction, 1415–1970," in *Studies of the Modern World System*, ed. Albert Bergesen (New York: Academic Press, 1980), 231–278; Terry Boswell, "Colonial Empires and the Capitalist World-Economy: A Time-Series Analysis of Colonization, 1640–1960," *American Sociological Review* 54 (1989): 180–196.

29. Cf. Emerson Rupert, *From Empire to Nation* (Cambridge, MA: Harvard University Press, 1960).

30. Jacques Marseille, *Empire colonial et capitalisme francais: histoire d'un divorce* (Paris: Albin Michel, 1984).

31. On these debates, see Herschel Grossman and Murat Iyigun, "The Profitability of Colonial Investment," *Economics and Politics* 7 (1995): 229–241; Peter J. Cain and Anthony G. Hopkins, "The Political Economy of British Expansion Overseas, 1750–1914," *Economic History Review* 33 (1980): 463–490; Nicholas J. White, "The Business and the Politics of Decolonization: The British Experience in the Twentieth Century," *Economic History Review* 53 (2000): 544–564; Jeffrey A. Frieden, "International Investment and Colonial Control: A New Interpretation," *International Organization* 48 (1994): 559–593.

32. Kwame Nkrumah, *Neo-Colonialism: The Last Stage of Imperialism* (New York: International, 1965).

33. Miles Kahler, *Decolonization in Britain and France: The Domestic Consequences of International Relations* (Princeton: Princeton University Press, 1984); Roy Holland, *European Decolonization, 1918–1981: An Introductory Survey* (New York: St. Martin's, 1985); Henri Grimal, *Decolonization: The British, French, Dutch and Belgian Empires* (London: Routledge, 1978).

34. Fernand Braudel, *Civilization and Capitalism, 15th–18th Century*, vol. 3, *The Perspective of the World* (Berkeley: University of California Press, 1992).

     The French title of this volume is the expression Mbembe uses above: *Le Temps du monde* ("time of the world").—TRANS.

35. Cain and Hopkins, "The Political Economy of British Expansion Overseas," and Cain and Hopkins, "Gentlemanly Capitalism and British Expansion Overseas II: New Imperialism, 1850–1945," *Economic History Review* 39, no. 4 (November 1986): 501–525.

36. Cf. Timothy Anna, "The Independence of Mexico and Central America," in *The Cambridge History of Latin America*, vol. 3, *From Independence to c. 1870*, ed. L. Bethell (Cambridge: Cambridge University Press, 1985), 51–94. See also David Bushnell, "The Independence of Spanish South America," and J. H. Elliott, "Spain and America in the 16th and 17th Centuries," in *Cambridge History of Latin America*, vol. 1, *Colonial Latin America*, ed. L. Bethell (Cambridge: Cambridge University Press, 1984), 95–156, 149–206.

37. Lenin, "Imperialism, the Highest Stage of Capitalism"; John A. Hobson, *Imperialism* (Ann Arbor: University of Michigan Press, 1938); David K. Fieldhouse, *The Theory of Capitalist Imperialism* (London: Longman, 1967), and Fieldhouse, *Economics and Empire, 1830–1914* (Ithaca: Cornell University Press, 1973).

38. Laurent Dubois, *Avengers of the New World: The Story of the Haitian Revolution* (Cambridge, MA: Harvard University Press, 2004).

39. Blair Niles, *Black Haiti: A Biography of Africa's Eldest Daughter* (New York: Grosset and Dunlap, 1926).

40. René Depestre, "La France et Haïti: le mythe et la réalité," *Gradiva: Revue d'anthropologie et d'histoire des arts* 1 (2005): 28.

41. Aimé Césaire, *Toussaint Louverture: la révolution française et le problem colonial* (Paris: Présence africaine, 1981), 344.

42. Cf. John K. Thornton, "African Soldiers in the Haitian Revolution," in *Origins of the Black Atlantic*, ed. Laurent Dubois and Julius S. Scott (New York: Routledge, 2013).

43. G. W. F. Hegel, *Phenomenology of Spirit*, trans. A. V. Miller (New York: Oxford University Press, 1977), 114.

44. C. L. R. James, *The Black Jacobins: Toussaint Louverture and the San Domingo Revolution of 1791–1804* (London: Secker and Warburg, 1938).

45. Aimé Césaire, *La Tragédie du Roi Christophe* (Paris: Presence africaine, 1963).

46. See Howard Temperley, "African-American Aspirations and the Settlement of Liberia," *Slavery and Abolition* 21, no. 2 (2000).

47. W. E. B. DuBois, *Black Reconstruction in America, 1860–1880* (1935; New York: Free Press, 1999).

48. Edward W. Blyden, "'Ethiopia Stretching Out Her Hands Unto God or Africa's Service to the World,' Discourse Delivered Before the American Colonization Society, May 1880," in *Christianity, Islam, and the Negro Race* (1887; Edinburgh: Edinburgh University Press, 1967).

49. Edward W. Blyden, *The Jewish Question* (Liverpool: Lionel Hart, 1898).

50. Blyden, *Christianity, Islam, and the Negro Race.*

51. See in particular Edward W. Blyden, "'Our Origin, Dangers and Duties': Annual Address Before Mayor and Common Council of Monrovia, National Independence Day, 26 July 1865," in *Origins of West African Nationalism*, ed. Henry S. Wilson (London: MacMillan/St. Martin's, 1969), 94–104.

52. Andrew Diemer, "An African Republic: Black and White Virginians in the Making of Liberia," *Slavery and Abolition* 30, no. 3 (2009); W. Bryan Rommel Ruiz, "Colonizing the Black Atlantic: The African Colonization Movements in Postwar Rhode Island and Nova Scotia," *Slavery and Abolition* 27, no. 3 (2006).

53. Matthew Spooner, "'I Know This Scheme Is from God': Toward Reconsideration of the Origins of the American Colonization Society," *Slavery and Abolition* 35, no. 4 (2014).

54. Christine Whyte, "Between Empire and Colony: American Imperialism and Pan-African Colonialism in Liberia, 1820–2003," *National Identities* 18, no. 1 (2015).

55. Frantz Fanon, *The Wretched of the Earth*, trans. Constance Farrington (New York: Grove, 1963), 1. Hereafter cited parenthetically in the text.

56. See Clapperton C. Mavungha, *Transient Workspaces* (Cambridge, MA: MIT Press, 2014); and Paulin Hountondji, ed., *Endogeneous Knowledge: Research Trails* (Dakar: CODESRIA, 1997).

57. For a critique, see Jean Comaroff and John Comaroff, *Ethnicity Inc.* (Chicago: University of Chicago Press, 2004).

58. Paulin Hountondji, "Knowledge of Africa, Knowledge by Africans: Two Perspectives on African Studies," *RCCS* 80 (March 2008).

59. Cf. Hountondji.

60. Cf. Walter D. Mignolo, *Local Histories/Global Designs: Coloniality, Subaltern Knowledges, and Border Thinking* (Princeton: Princeton University Press, 2000); Mignolo, "Delinking: The Rhetoric of Modernity, the Logic of Coloniality and the Grammar of Decoloniality," *Cultural Studies* 21, nos. 2–3 (2007); Nelson Maldonado-Torres, "On the Coloniality of Being: Contributions to the Development of a Concept," *Cultural Studies* 21, nos. 2–3 (2007): 240–270; Annibal Quijano, "Coloniality and Modernity/Rationality," *Cultural Studies* 21, nos. 2–3 (2007): 168–178.

61. For a synthesis, see Maxim Silverman, *Deconstructing the Nation: Immigration, Racism, and Citizenship in Modern France* (New York: Routledge, 1992).

62. Laurent Dubois, *Les Esclaves de la république: l'histoire oubliée de la première emancipation, 1789–1794* (Paris: Calmann-Lévy, 1998).

63. See in particular Alexis de Tocqueville, *Écrits et discours politiques*, in *Oeuvres complètes*, vol. 3 (Paris: Gallimard, 1992).

64. On the idea of the "French race," see Robert Soucy, *Fascism in France: The Case of Maurice Barrès* (Berkeley: University of California Press, 1972); and Zeev Sternhell, *Maurice Barrès et le nationalisme français* (Paris: Fayard, 2000).

65. Gregory Mann, "What Was the Indigenat?: The Empire of Law in French West Africa," *Journal of African History* 50 (2009): 331–353.

66. Concerning Algeria in particular, see Pierre Nora, *Les Français d'Algérie* (Paris: Julliard, 1961); David Prochaska, *Making Algeria French: Colonialism in Bône, 1870–1920* (Cambridge: Cambridge University Press, 1990); and Alain Lardillier, *Le Peuplement français en Algérie de 1830 à 1900* (Versailles: Atlanthrope, 1992).

67. Tyler Stovall, "Universalisme, différence et invisibilité: essai sur la notion de race dans l'histoire de la France contemporaine," *Cahiers d'histoire* 96–97 (2005).

68. Jean-Luc Nancy, *Dis-Enclosure: The Deconstruction of Christianity* (New York: Fordham University Press, 2008), 6.

69. Frantz Fanon, *Black Skin, White Masks*, trans. Charles Lam Markmann (London: Pluto, 1986), 180.

70. Vincent Descombes, *Le Complément de sujet: enquête sur le fait d'agir de soi-même* (Paris: Gallimard, 2004), 383.

71. Fanon, *Black Skin, White Masks*, 2.

    In the English translation of Fanon, *surgissement* is translated as "upheaval" which seems less suited to what Mbembe is describing than "rising" or "surging up," which are used in the present translation.—Trans.

72. Fanon, 3.

73. Fanon, 180 ["Le nègre n'est pas. Pas plus que le Blanc," p. 228 in the French]; p. 48 ["'le nègre est un homme pareil aux autres, un homme comme les autres,'" p. 79 in the French]; p. 85 ["un homme parmi d'autres hommes," p. 121 in the French].

74. Léopold Sédor Senghor, Conference de Léopold Sédor Senghor, "L'Esprit de la civilization ou les lois de la culture négro-africaine," *Présence Africaine* 8-9-10 (June–November 1956): 51–64.

75. Paul Gilroy, *The Black Atlantic: Modernity and Double Consciousness* (Cambridge, MA: Harvard University Press, 1993); and Gilroy, *Against Race: Imagining Political Culture Beyond the Color Line* (Cambridge, MA: Harvard University Press, 2000).

76. Paul Gilroy, *Postcolonial Melancholia* (New York: Columbia University Press, 2005).

77. Jan Patocka, *L'Europe après l'Europe* (Lagrasse: Verdier, 2007), 13. (Translation mine.—Trans.)

78. Patocka, 235. (Translation mine.—Trans.)

79. Jean-Luc Nancy, *Dis-Enclosure: The Deconstruction of Christianity* (New York: Fordham University Press, 2008), 142.

80. Paul Valéry, "La Crise de l'esprit," in *Variétés, Ouevres*, vol. 1 (Paris: Bibliotheque de la Pleiade, 1919), 98–1014.

81. Marc Crépon, "Penser l'Europe avec Patocka: Réflection sur l'altérité," *Esprit* (December 2004). (Translation mine.—Trans.)

82. Jacques Derrida, "Le Souverain bien—ou l'Europe en mal de souveraineté," *Cités* 30 (2007).

83. Derrida.

84. Edward Said, *Orientalism* (New York: Vintage, 1979).

85. Edward Said, *The World, the Text, the Critic* (Cambridge, MA: Harvard University Press, 1983).

86. Edward Said, *Culture and Imperialism* (New York: Vintage, 1993).

87. Aijaz Ahmed, *In Theory: Classes, Nations, Literatures* (London: Verso, 1994).

88. Chandra Talpade Mohanty, *Third World Women and the Politics of Feminism* (Bloomington: Indiana University Press, 1991).

89. Dipesh Chakrabarty, *Provincializing Europe* (Princeton: Princeton University Press, 2000).

90. W. E. B. Du Bois, *The Souls of Black Folk* (New York: Dover, 1994).

91. Du Bois, 155.

92. Paul Gilroy, *Darker Than Blue* (Cambridge, MA: Harvard University Press, 2010).

93. Leopold Sédar Senghor, *Songs of Shadow*, in *Poems of a Black Orpheus*, trans. William Oxley (London: Menard, 1981).

94. Bernard Mouralis, *L'Europe, l'Afrique et la folie* (Paris: Présence Africaine, 1993).

95. Aimé Césaire, *Discourse on Colonialism*, trans. Joan Pinkham (New York: Monthly Review Press, 2001).

96. Léopold Sédar Senghor, *Oeuvre poétique* (Paris: Editions du Seuil, 1990).

97. Peter Linebaugh and Marcus Rediker, *The Many-Headed Hydra: Slaves, Sailors, Commoners and the Hidden History of the Revolutionary Atlantic* (New York: Beacon, 2001).

98. Claude McKay, *Banjo: A Story Without a Plot* (New York: Harcourt, Brace, Jovanovich, 1970).

99. See Tebello Letsekha, "Revisiting the Debate on the Africanisation of Higher Education: An Appeal for a Conceptual Shift," *Independent Journal of Teaching and Learning* 8 (2013).

100. See Steven Feierman, *Peasant Intellectuals: Anthropology and History in Tanzania* (Madison: University of Wisconsin Press, 1990).

101. Boaventura de Sousa Santos, *Another Knowledge Is Possible: Beyond Northern Epistemologies* (London: Verso, 2008); and de Sousa Santos, *Epistemologies of the South* (New York: Routledge, 2014).

102. See de Sousa Santos, "The University in the Twenty-First Century: Towards a Democratic and Emancipatory University Reform," *Eurozine* (July 1, 2010).

103. See Holger Potzsch, "Posthumanism, Technogenesis, and Digital Technologies: A Conversation with N. Katherine Hayles," *Fibreculture Journal* 23 (2014).

104. Patrik Svensson and David Goldberg, *Between Humanities and the Digital* (Cambridge, MA: MIT Press, 2015); and Cathy Davidson and David Goldberg, *The Future of Learning Institutions in a Digital Age* (Cambridge, MA: MIT Press, 2009).

105. George Steiner, ed., *Is Science Nearing Its Limits?* (Manchester, UK: Carcanet, 2008), xxii–xxiv.

106. Elizabeth A. St. Pierre et al., "New Empiricisms and New Materialisms: Conditions for New Inquiry," *Cultural Studies* 16, no. 2 (2016).

107. Yinon M. Bar-On, Rob Phillips, and Ron Milo, "The Biomass Distribution on Earth," *Proceedings of the National Academy of Sciences* 115, no. 25 (June 2018): 6506–6511.

108. N. Katherine Hayles, "Computing the Human," *Theory, Culture and Society* 22 (2005): 143.

109. Des Fitzgerald and Felicity Callard, "Social Science and Neuroscience Beyond Interdisciplinarity: Experimental Entanglements," *Theory, Culture and Society* 32 (2016).

110. Maurizio Meloni, "How Biology Became Social and What It Means for Social Theory," *Sociological Review* 62 (2014): 594.

111. Lisa Blackman, "The Challenges of New Biopsychosocialities: Hearing Voices, Trauma, Epigenetics and Mediated Perception," *Sociological Review* 64, no. 1 (March 2016): 256–273, at 7.

112. Lisa Blackman, "The New Biologies: Epigenetics, the Microbiome and Immunities," *Body and Society* 22, no. 4 (2016): 3–18, at 4.

113. Blackman, 8.

114. Fitzgerald and Callard, "Social Science and Neuroscience Beyond Interdisciplinarity."

115. Cf. Nikolas Rose, "Reading the Human Brain: How the Mind Became Legible," *Body and Society* 22, no. 2 (2016).

116. See N. Katherine Hayles, "The Cognitive Nonconscious: Enlarging the Mind of the Humanities," *Critical Inquiry* 42, no. 4 (2016).

117. Y. Citton, "Fictional Attachments and Literary Weavings in the Anthropocene," *New Literary History* 47 (2016): 309.

118. Cf. Bernard Stiegler, "The New Conflict of the Faculties and Functions: Quasi-Causality and Serendipity in the Anthropocene," *Qui Parle?* 26, no. 1 (2017).

119. Cf. Dipesh Chakrabarty, "Postcolonial Studies and the Challenge of Climate Change," *New Literary History* 43, no. 1 (2012): 1–18; Ian Baucom, "History 4: Postcolonial Method in Anthropocene Time," *Cambridge Journal of Postcolonial Literary Inquiry* 1 (2014): 123–142; and Baucom, " 'Moving Centers': Climate Change, Critical Method, and the Historical Novel," *Modern Language Quarterly* 76, no. 2 (2015): 137–157.

3. PROXIMITY WITHOUT RECIPROCITY

1. See *La Démocratie à venir: Autour de Jacques Derrida* (Paris: Galilée, 2004). This book collects papers from the 2002 Cerisy-la-Salle Conference.

2. On this subject, see Étienne Balibar, *Europe, Constitution, Frontière* (Paris: Éditions du Passant, 2005).

3. See Christopher L. Miller, *The French Atlantic Triangle: Literature and Culture of the Slave Trade* (Durham: Duke University Press, 2008).

4. Jocelyne Dakhlia, *Islamicités* (Paris: PUF, 2005), 8.

5. Jacques Hassoun, *L'Obscur object de la haine* (Paris: Aubier, 1997), 14.

6. Oxfam France, *L'Afrique à Biarritz: mise en examen de la politique française, Biarritz 8-9 novembre 1994* (Paris: Karthala, 1995); François-Xavier Verschave, *La*

Françafrique: le plus long scandale de la république (Paris: Stock, 1998); John Chipman, *French Power in Africa* (Oxford: Blackwell, 1989).

7. Alexis de Tocqueville, "Essay on Algeria," in *Writings on Empire and Slavery*, ed. and trans. Jennifer Pitts (Baltimore: Johns Hopkins University Press, 2001), 69.

8. De Tocqueville, 69.

9. See Jean-François Bayart, "Réflexions sur la politique africaine de la France," *Politique africaine* 58; and, Bayart, "*Bis repetita*: La Politique africaine de François Mitterand," in *Mitterand et la sortie de la guerre froide*, ed. Samy Cohen (Paris: PUF, 1998).

10. Achille Mbembe, "On Private Indirect Government," in *On the Postcolony*, trans. A. M. Barrett et al. (Berkeley: University of California Press, 2001), 66–101.

11. Léopold Sédar Senghor, *Liberté*, vol. 5, *Le Dialogue des cultures* (Paris: Seuil, 1992).

12. Didier Gondola, "La Crise de la formation en histoire africaine en France vue par les étudiants africains," *Politique africaine* 64 (1997).

13. Gina Dent, ed., *Black Popular Culture* (Seattle: Bay, 1992).

14. Paul Gilroy, *The Black Atlantic: Modernity and Double Consciousness* (Cambridge, MA: Harvard University Press, 1993).

15. Didier Fassin, Alain Morice, and Catherine Quiminal, eds., *Les Lois de l'inhospitalité* (Paris: La Découverte, 1997).

16. Une Malgache, "La 'Grandeur' de la France à l'aune d'un consulat: témoignage," *Politique africaine* 67 (1997). See also the entire special dossier "La France et les migrants africains" in the same issue.

17. Ngugi Wa Thiong'o, *Decolonising the Mind* (Portsmouth, NH: Heinemann, 1986); and Paulin Hountondji, ed., *Endogenous Knowledge: Research Trails* (Dakar: CODESRIA, 1997).

18. Fernand Braudel, *The Identity of France*, vol. 1, *History and Environment*, trans. Siân Reynolds (New York: Harper and Row, 1988).

19. Michel Foucault, *The Order of Things* (1966; London: Routledge, 2010).

20. Michael Hénaff, *The Price of Truth: Gift, Money, and Philosophy*, trans. Jean-Louis Morhange (Stanford: Stanford University Press, 2010).

21. Simone Weil, "New Facts About the Colonial Problem in the French Empire," in *Simone Weil on Colonialism*, ed. and trans. J. P. Little (Oxford: Rowman and Littlefield, 2003), 66.

22. De Tocqueville, "Essay on Algeria," 70.

23. De Tocqueville, 78.

24. Olivier Le Cour Grandmaison, *Coloniser, exterminer* (Paris: Fayard, 2005).

25. Hannah Arendt, *The Origins of Totalitarianism* (New York: Harcourt, Brace, Jovanovich, 1973).

26. Simone Weil, "The Colonial Question and the Destiny of the French People," in Little, *Simone Weil on Colonialism*, 110.

27. Ann Stoler and Frederick Cooper, eds., *Tensions of Empire: Colonial Cultures in a Bourgeois World* (Berkeley: University of California Press, 1997), 1–56.

28. Herbert Frankel, *Capital Investment in Africa, Its Course and Effects* (London: Oxford University Press, 1938).

29. Catherine Coquery-Vidrovitch, *Le Congo au temps des compagnies concessionnaires, 1898–1930* (Paris: Éditions de l'EHESS, 1972).

30. Frederick Cooper, *Decolonization and African Society* (Cambridge: Cambridge University Press, 1996).

31. Julia Kristeva, *Strangers to Ourselves*, trans. Leon S. Roudiez (New York: Columbia University Press, 1994), 154.

32. Édouard Glissant, *Poetics of Relation*, trans. Betsy Wing (Ann Arbor: University of Michigan Press, 1997); and Glissant, *Tout-Monde: Roman* (Paris: Gallimard, 1993); and Paul Gilroy, *After Empire: Melancholia or Convivial Culture?* (London: Routledge, 2004).

33. Paul Gilroy, *Against Race* (Cambridge, MA: Harvard University Press, 2002).

34. Nancy, *The Experience of Freedom*, trans. Bridget McDonald (Stanford: Stanford University Press, 1993), 71.

35. Laurent Dubois, *A Colony of Citizens: Revolution and Slave Emancipation in the French Caribbean, 1787–1804* (Durham: University of North Carolina Press, 2004); Sue Peabody, *"There Are No Slaves in France": The Political Culture of Race and Slavery in the Ancien Régime* (Oxford: Oxford University Press, 1996); and Sue Peabody and Tyler Stovall, eds., *The Color of Liberty: Histories of Race in France* (Durham: Duke University Press, 2003).

36. Vincent Descombes, *Le Complément de sujet: enquête sur le fait d'agir de soi-même* (Paris: Gallimard, 2004).

37. See Pierre Rosanvallon, *Le Peuple introuvable: histoire de la représentation démocratique en France* (Paris: Gallimard, 1998).

38. Véronique de Rudder, ed., *L'Inégalité raciste: l'universalité républicaine à l'épreuve* (Paris: PUF, 2000).

39. Nancy, *The Experience of Freedom*, 72.

40. Nancy, 71.

41. Nancy, 73, emphasis added.

42. Maurice Merleau-Ponty, *Phenomenology of Perception*, trans. Donald A. Landes (London: Routledge and Kegan Paul), 406.

43. Jean-Luc Nancy, *The Creation of the World, or, Globalization*, trans. François Raffoul and David Pettigrew (Albany: State University of New York Press, 2007), 73.

4. THE LONG FRENCH IMPERIAL WINTER

1. As an example of this diversity, see Mabel Morana, Enrique Dussel, and Carlos A. Jauregui, eds., *Coloniality at Large: Latin America and the Postcolonial Debate* (Durham: Duke University Press, 2008). See also Fernando Coroni, "Latin American Postcolonial Studies and Global Decolonization," in *Penser le postocolonial*, ed. Neil Lazarus (Paris: Éditions Amsterdam, 2006); and Vinayak Chaturvedi, ed., *Mapping Subaltern Studies and the Postcolonial* (New York: Verso, 2000).

2. See, for example, Simon During, "Postcolonialism and Globalization: Towards a Historicization of the Interrelation," *Cultural Studies* 14, nos. 3–4 (2000): 385–404;

Harry D. Harootunian, "Postcoloniality's Unconscious/Area Studies' Desire," *Postcolonial Studies* 2, no. 2 (1999): 127–147. See, more recently, *New Formations* 59 (2006); *PMLA* 122, no. 3 (2007). See also the special issue of *Social Text* 10, nos. 2–3 (1999); special issue of the *American Historical Review* 99 (1994). See also Aijaz Ahmad, *In Theory: Classes, Nations, Literatures* (New York: Verso, 2008), and Arif Dirlik, *The Postcolonial Aura: Third World Criticism in the Age of Global Capitalism* (Boulder, CO: Westview, 1997).

3. See, in particular, Robert J. C. Young, *Postcolonialism: An Historical Introduction* (Oxford: Blackwell, 2001); and David Ludden, ed., *Reading Subaltern Studies: Critical History, Contested Meaning, and the Globalization of South Asia* (New Delhi: Permanent Black, 2001).

4. Jacques Pouchepadass, "Les *Subaltern Studies* ou la critique postcoloniale de la modernité," *L'Homme* 156 (2000): 161–186. See, from the middle of the first decade of the twenty-first century, Marie Claude Smouts, ed., *La Situation postcoloniale: les postcolonial studies dans le débat français* (Paris: Fondation Nationale des Sciences Politiques, 2007).

5. See, however, the texts by subaltern studies authors brought together in Mamadou Diouf, ed., *L'Historiographie indienne en débat: colonialisme, nationalisme, et societies postcoloniales* (Paris: Karthala, 1999).

6. See Sophie Dulocq, Catherine Coquery-Vidrovich, Jean Frémigacci, Emmannuelle Sibeud, and Jean-Louis Triaud, "L'Écriture de l'histoire de la colonization en France depuis 1960," *Afrique et Histoire* 2, no. 6 (2006): 243. See also Jean-François Bayart's arguments on the "specific historicity of African societies" in *The State in Africa: The Politics of the Belly* (New York: Polity, 2009).

7. Alain Finkielkraut, *The Defeat of the Mind*, trans. Judith Friedlander (New York: Columbia University Press, 1996), 64.

8. Luc Ferry and Alain Renaut, *French Philosophy of the Sixties: An Essay on Anti-Humanism*, trans. Mary Schnackenberg Cattani (Amherst: University of Massachusetts Press, 1990), foreword.

9. See the critical assessment by Gérard Chaliand, *Revolution in the Third World: Myths and Prospects*, trans. D. Johnsone (New York: Viking, 1989); Pascal Bruckner, *The Tears of the White Man: Compassion as Contempt*, trans. William Beer (New York: Free, 1986); Carlos Rangel, *Third World Ideology and Western Reality: Manufacturing Political Myth*, trans. Vladimir Tismăneanu, María Helena Contreras, and Ralph Van Roy (New Brunswick, NJ: Transaction, 1986).

10. Régis Debray, *A Critique of Arms*, trans. Rosemary Sheed (New York: Penguin, 1977).

11. Jean-Paul Sartre, *Colonialism and Neocolonialism* (New York: Routledge, 2001).

12. Aimé Césaire, *The Tragedy of King Christophe: A Play*, trans. Ralph Manheim (New York: Grove, 1970); Césaire, *A Season in Congo*, trans. Gayatri Chakravorty Spivak (New York: Seagull, 2010).

13. Michel Foucault, *"Society Must Be Defended": Lectures at the Collège de France, 1975–1976*, trans. David Macey, ed. Mauro Bertani and Alessandro Fontana (New York: Picador, 2003).

14. Regarding this phenomenon, W. E. B. Du Bois wrote, "I have walked in Paris with
     [Blaise] Diagne who represents Senegal—all Senegal, white and black—in the French
     parliament. But Diagne is a Frenchman who is accidentally black. I suspect Diagne
     despises his own black Wolofs. I have talked with Candace, black deputy of Guadeloupe.
     Candace is virulently French. He has no conception of Negro uplift, as apart from
     French development." W. E. B. Du Bois, "The Negro Mind Reaches Out," in *The New
     Negro: Voices of the Harlem Renaissance* (New York: Simon and Schuster, 1925), 397.

15. Mbembe uses the term *tirailleur* here, which comes from the French word for "to
     shoot" and means "infantryman," but the term is commonly used to refer to North
     African (*tirailleurs nord-africains*), and especially Senegalese (*tirailleurs sénégalais*)
     colonial infantrymen who served in the French army.—TRANS.

16. See his journal, *Peuples noirs, peuples africains* (1978–1991), http://mongobeti.arts.uwa
     .edu.au/.

17. Mongo Beti, *Main basse sur le Cameroun* (Paris: François Maspero, 1972).

18. Concerning the paradoxes of criticism of "68 thought" in general, see Serge Audier,
     La Pensée anti-68: essai sur les origines d'une restauration intellectuelle (Paris: La
     Découverte, 2009).

19. See, for example, the special edition of the journal *Esprit* from January–February 1934;
     Boris Souvarine, *La Critique sociale, 1931–1934* (Paris: La Différence, 1983); and Dan-
     iel Guérin, *Fascism and Big Business*, trans. Frances and Mason Merr (New York:
     Pathfinder, 2000).

20. See, for example, Maurice Merleau-Ponty, *Humanism and Terror: An Essay on the
     Communist Problem*, trans. John O'Neill (1947; Boston: Beacon, 2000); and Maurice
     Merleau-Ponty, *Adventures of the Dialectic*, trans. Joseph Bien (1955; Evanston, IL:
     Northwestern University Press, 1973).

21. Raymond Aron, *Democracy and Totalitarianism* (New York: Praeger, 1965).

22. Michael Christofferson, *Les Intellectuels contre la gauche: l'idéologie antitotalitaire
     en France, 1968–1981* (Marseille: Agone, 2009). See also Julian Bourg, *From Revolu-
     tion to Ethics: May 68 and Contemporary French Thought* (Montreal: McGill-Queen's
     University Press, 2007).

23. See Cornelius Castoriadis, *The Imaginary Institution of Society*, trans. Kathleen
     Blamey (Cambridge, MA: MIT Press, 1987), in particular, chap. 1, "Marxism: A Pro-
     visional Assessment."

24. Cornelius Castoriadis, *La Société bureaucratique* (Paris: Bourgois, 1990); Claude
     Lefort, *Complications: Communism and the Dilemmas of Democracy*, trans. Julian
     Bourg (New York: Columbia University Press, 2007); Claude Lefort, *L'Invention
     démocratique: les limites de la domination totalitaire* (Paris: Fayard, 1981).

25. Pierre Singaravélou, *L'Empire des géographes: géographie, exploration et colonisation,
     XIX–XX siècle* (Paris: Belin, 2008).

26. See Lewis Pyenson, *Civilizing Mission: Exact Sciences and French Overseas Expan-
     sion, 1830–1940* (Baltimore: Johns Hopkins University Press, 1993); Michael A.
     Osborne, *Nature, the Exotic, and the Science of French Colonialism* (Bloomington:
     Indiana University Press, 1994).

27. On their paradoxes and ambiguities, see Emmanuelle Sibeud, *Une Science impériale pour l'Afrique?: la construction des saviors Africanists en France, 1878–1930* (Paris: Éditions de l'EHESS, 2002).

28. Isabelle Poutrin, ed., *Le XIXe siècle: Science, politique, et tradition* (Paris: Berger-Levrault, 1995).

29. Daniel Rivet, "Le Fait colonial et nous: histoire d'un éloignement," *Vingtième siècle* 33 (January–March 1992): 127–138; Catherine Coquery-Vidrovitch, "Plaidoyer pour l'histoire du monde dans l'Université française," *Vingtième siècle* 61 (1999): 111–125.

30. A sign of this anachronism in this moment of so-called "world literature": the prestigious Gallimard publishing house—unlike Seuil—has found nowhere better than an editorial ghetto called "Black Continents" (!) to stick the majority of their non-white authors.

31. For more on the views of American historians on the contemporary history of France, see, for example, the special issue of *Cahiers d'histoire: Revue d'histoire critique* 96–97 (2005). See also the articles brought together in the special issue of *French Politics, Culture and Society* 18, no. 3 (2000), and in *Yale French Studies* 100 (2001).

32. Arjun Appadurai, *Modernity at Large* (Minneapolis: University of Minnesota Press, 1996).

33. Dilip P. Gaonkar, ed., *Alternative Modernities* (Durham: Duke University Press, 2001).

34. Heike Raphael-Hernandez, ed., *Blackening Europe: The African-American Presence* (New York: Routledge, 2003).

35. On this period, see Tyler Stovall, *Paris Noir: African-Americans in the City of Light* (New York: Houghton Mifflin, 1996). For what followed, see Dominic Thomas, *Black France: Colonialism, Immigration, and Transnationalism* (Bloomington: Indiana University Press, 2007); and Bennetta Jules-Rosette, *Black Paris: The African Writers' Landscape* (Urbana: University of Illinois Press, 2000).

36. Manuel Boucher, *Rap, expression des lascars: significations et enjeux du Rap dans la société française* (Paris: L'Harmattan, 1999); and A. J. M. Prévos, "Two Decades of Rap in France: Emergence, Development, Prospects," in *Black, Blanc, Beur: Rap Music and Hip-Hop Culture in the Francophone World*, ed. Alain-Phillippe Durand (Oxford: Scarecrow, 2002), 1–21.

37. Laurent Dubois, *Soccer Empire: The World Cup and the Future of France* (Los Angeles: University of California Press, 2010); and Lilian Thuram, *Mes Étoiles noires* (Paris: Philippe Rey, 2010).

38. This corresponds more or less with Paul Gilroy's observations in *Darker Than Blue* (Cambridge, MA: Harvard University Press, 2010). See also A. J. M. Prévos, "In It for the Money: Rap and Business Culture in France," *Popular Music and Society* 26, no. 4 (2003): 445–461.

39. Didier Fassin, Alain Morice, and Catherine Quiminal, eds., *Les Lois de l'inhospitalité* (Paris: La Découverte, 1997).

40. See Anne-Isabelle Barthélémy et al., eds., *Cette France-là* (Paris: La Découverte, 2009).

41. See, in particular, Olivier Le Cour Grandmaison, *La République imperial: politique et racism d'état* (Paris: Fayard, 2009).

42. Pierre Rosanvallon, *Le Peuple introuvable: histoire de la représentation démocratique en France* (Paris: Gallimard, 1998), 13.

43. Concerning these discussions, see Alain Renaut, *Un Humanisme de la diversité: essai sur la décolonisation des identités* (Paris: Flammarion, 2009).

44. Nacira Guénif-Souilamas and Éric Macé, *Les Féministes et le garçon arabe* (Paris: L'Aube, 2004).

45. On this point, see Elsa Dorlin, "Le Grand strip-tease: féminisme, nationalisme, et burqa en France," in *Ruptures postcoloniales: les nouveaux visages de la société française*, ed. Nicolas Bancel et al. (Paris: La Découverte, 2010).

46. See the articles by Frederick Cooper, "From Imperial Inclusion to Republican Exclusion?: France's Ambiguous Postwar Trajectory," and by Didier Gondola, "Transient Citizens: The Othering and Indigenization of Blacks and Beurs Within the French Republic," in *Frenchness and the African Diaspora: Identity and Uprising in Contemporary France*, ed. Charles Tshimanga (Bloomington: Indiana University Press, 2009).

47. Elizabeth Badinter, "Mission d'information sur la pratique du port du voile intégral sur le territoire national," September 9, 2009, www.assemblee-nationale.fr/13/cr -miburqa/08-09/c0809004.asp.

48. Eric Macé, "Postcolonialité et francité dans les imaginaires télévisuels de la nation," in Bancel et al., *Ruptures postcoloniales*, 398.

49. Macé, 399.

50. Isabelle Rigoni, ed., *Qui a peur de la télévision en couleurs?: la diversité culturelle dans les médias* (Montreuil: Aux lieux d'être, 2007); and Wayne Brekhus, "Une Sociologie de l'invisibilité: réorienter notre regard," *Réseaux* 129–130 (2005).

51. Nicolas Bancel, Pascal Blanchard, and Francis Delabarre, eds., *Images d'empire: 1930– 1960, trente ans de photographies officielles sur l'Afrique française* (Paris: Éditions de la Martinière, 1997).

52. Nicolas Bancel, Pascal Blanchard, and Françoise Vergès, *La République coloniale* (Paris: Albin Michel, 2003); and Nicolas Bancel, Pascal Blanchard, and Sandrine Lemaire, *La Fracture coloniale* (Paris: La Découverte, 2005).

53. Achille Mbembe, *On the Postcolony* (Berkeley: University of California Press, 2001). See in particular the preface to the second edition.

54. Jean-Marc Moura, *Littératures francophones et théorie postcoloniale* (Paris: PUF, 1999); Jacqueline Bardolph, *Études postcoloniales et littérature* (Paris: Champion, 2002); Michel Beniamiano and Lise Gauvin, *Vocabulaire des études francophones: les concepts de base* (Limoges: Presses universitaires de Limoges, 2005).

55. Elsa Dorlin, *La Matrice de la race: généalogie sexuelle et coloniale de la nation française* (Paris: La Découverte, 2006).

56. Françoise Vergès, *Abolir l'esclavage: une utopie coloniale* (Paris: Albin Michel, 2001).

57. See the study by Pap Ndiaye, *La Condition noire: essai sur une minorité française* (Paris: Calmann-Lévy, 2008).

58. See in particular Didier Fassin and Éric Fassin, *De la Question sociale à la question raciale?: représenter la société française* (Paris: La Découverte, 2010).

59. See the translations into French of Homi Bhabha, *Les Lieux de la culture*, trans. Françoise Bouillot (Paris: Payot, 2008); and of Neil Lazarus, ed., *Penser le postcolonial*,

trans. Marianne Groulez, Christophe Jaquet, and Hélène Quiniou (Paris: Éditions Amsterdam, 2006).

60. See Catherine Coquery-Vidrovitch, *Les Enjeux politiques de l'histoire coloniale* (Marseille: Agone, 2009).

61. Jean-Loup Amselle, *L'Occident décroché: enquête sur les postcolonialismes* (Paris: Stock, 2008).

62. Jean-François Bayart, *Les Études postcoloniales: un carnaval académique* (Paris: Karthala, 2010).

63. For an attempt at a philosophical formulation of these stakes, see Alain Renaut, *Un Humanisme de la diversité*.

64. Paul Ricoeur, *History and Truth*, trans. Charles A. Kelbley (Evanston, IL: Northwestern University Press, 1992), 11.

65. This is a mode of investigation that consists in starting from forms of resistance to three types of power characteristic of colonial imperialism: the power to conquer and dominate, the power to exploit, and the power to subject. For an evaluation, see Barbara Bush, *Imperialism and Postcolonialism* (London: Longman, 2006); Patrick Wolfe, "History and Imperialism: A Century of Theory from Marx to Postcolonialism," *American History Review* 2, no. 102 (1997): 388–420. In the historical-literary field, see also Elleke Boehmer, *Empire, the National, and the Postcolonial, 1890–1920* (New York: Oxford University Press, 2001).

66. For a sometimes caricatural and polemic formulation of this position, see Jane Burbank and Frederick Cooper, " 'Nouvelles' colonies et 'vieux' empires," *Mil Neuf Cent* 27 (2009); and Bayart, *Les Études postcoloniales*.

67. Bayart, *Les Études postcoloniales*; Pierre Grosser, "Comment écrire l'histoire des relations internationales aujourd'hui?: quelques réflexions à partir de l'empire britannique," *Histoire @Politique* 10 (January–April 2010).

68. Husserl had already called into question this attraction in the middle of the 1930s. See Edmund Husserl, *The Crisis of European Sciences and Transcendental Phenomenology* (1935; Evanston, IL: Northwestern University Press, 1970).

69. Michel de Certeau, *The Writing of History*, trans. Tom Conley (1975; New York: Columbia University Press, 1988); and Paul Ricoeur, *Time and Narrative*, vol. 1, trans. Kathleen McLaughlin and David Pellauer (Chicago: University of Chicago Press, 1984), in particular chap. 2.

70. Paul Veyne, *Writing History: Essay on Epistemology*, trans. Mina Moore-Rinvolucri (1971; Middletown: Wesleyan University Press, 1984).

71. Jacques Revel, *Jeux d'échelles: la micro-analyse à l'éxperience* (Paris: Gallimard/Seuil, 1996).

72. For a broader understanding of the real and of practices, see Michel Foucault, *Dits et écrits*, vol. 4, *1980–1988* (Paris: Gallimard, 1994), 15: "It is necessary to demystify the *global instance* of the real as a totality to be restored. There is no 'real' that could be reached if we were to speak of everything or of certain things that are more 'real' than others, and that we would miss—to the profit of unsound abstractions—if we were to limit ourselves to bringing out other elements and other relations. We must perhaps also question the principle, which is often accepted implicitly, that

the only *reality* that history should lay claim to is *society* itself." (Translation mine.—TRANS.)

73. See, for example, Dipesh Chakrabarty, *Rethinking Working-Class History: Bengal, 1980–1940* (Princeton: Princeton University Press, 1989); Gyan Prakash, *Bonded Histories: Genealogies of Labor Servitude in Colonial India* (Cambridge: Cambridge University Press, 1990).

74. Max Weber, *Economy and Society*, vol. 1 (Berkeley: University of California Press, 1978), in particular the first part of chapter 1.

75. On this kind of argument, see Bernard Lepetit, *Les Formes de l'expérience: une autre histoire sociale* (Paris: Albin Michel, 1995).

76. Here, I am using the term *citoyenneté en souffrance* in the sense in which one speaks of a *lettre restée en souffrance*: a letter that has not reached its destination and has thus remained without response.

77. Jean Birnbaum, *Les Maoccidents: un néoconservatisme à la française* (Paris: Stock, 2009).

78. Arjun Appadurai, *Fear of Small Numbers: An Essay on the Geography of Anger* (Durham: Duke University Press, 2006).

79. On this question of the border, see in particular Étienne Balibar, *We, the People of Europe?: Reflections on Transnational Citizenship* (Princeton: Princeton University Press, 2004).

80. Michel Agier, Rémy Bazenguissa-Ganga, and Achille Mbembe, "Mobilités africaines, racisme français," *Vacarme* 43 (2008): 1–8.

81. See "L'Europe des camps: la mise à l'écart des étrangers," special issue of *Cultures et Conflits* 57 (2005).

82. Decree Number 2007-999 of May 31, 2007, relative to the duties and functions of the Ministry of Immigration, Integration, National Identity, and Co-Development. www .legifrance.gouv.fr.

83. M. Agier, "L'Encampement comme nouvel espace politique," *Vacarme* 44 (2008): 2–3.

84. Elsa Dorlin, "Pas en notre nom!," www.lautrecampagne.org/article.php?id=132.

85. See Pierre Tévanian, *La République du mépris: les métamorphoses du racisme dans la France des années Sarkozy* (Paris: Découverte, 2007); and S. Bouamama, *L'Affaire du foulard islamique: la production d'un racisme respectable* (Roubaix: Geai bleu, 2004).

86. See Nilüfer Gôle's piece in Charlotte Nordmann, ed., *Le Foulard islamique en questions* (Paris: Éditions Amsterdam, 2004).

87. Sylvie Tissot, "Bilan d'un féminisme d'État," *Plein Droit* 75 (December 2007): www .gisti.org/spip.php?article1072. See also Éric Fassin, "La Démocratie sexuelle et le conflit des civilisations," *Multitudes* 26 (Fall 2006): http://multitudes.samizdat.net/La -Democratie-sexuelle-et-le.

88. This is, moreover, the internal economy of the Stasi Report. See Bernard Stasi, *Laïcité et république: rapport de la commission de réflexion sur l'application du principe de laïcité dans la république remis au président de la république le 11 décembre 2003* (Paris: Documentation française, 2003), www.ladocumentationfrancaise.fr/var/storage /rapports-publics/034000725/0000.pdf.

89. Cécile Laborde, *Critical Republicanism: The Hijab Controversy and Political Philosophy* (Oxford: Oxford University Press, 2008).

90. Cécile Laborde, "Virginity and Burqa: Unreasonable Accomodations?," September 16, 2008, www.booksandideas.net/Virginity-and-Burqa-Unreasonable.html?lang=fr.

91. Fassin and Fassin, *De la Question sociale à la question raciale*; and Robert Castel, *La Discrimination négative: citoyens ou indigènes* (Paris: Seuil, 2007).

92. Hervé Lemoine, *La Maison de l'histoire de France: pour la création d'un centre de recherché et de collections permanentes dédié à l'histoire civile et militaire de la France: Rapport à Monsieur le Ministre de la Défense et Madame la Ministre de la Culture et de la Communication* (April 2008), www.culture.gouv.fr/culture/actualites/rapports /rapporthlemoine.pdf. See also Jean-Pierre Azéma, "Guy Môquet, Sarkozy et le roman national," *L'Histoire* 323 (September 2007); Suzanne Citron, *Le Mythe national: l'histoire de la France revisitée* (Paris: L'Atelier, 2008); Sylvie Aprile, "L'Histoire par Nicholas Sarkozy: le rêve passéiste d'un futur national-libéral" (April 30, 2007), http:// cvuh.free.fr/spip.php?article82.

93. Paul Aussaresses, *The Battle of the Casbah: Terrorism and Counter-Terrorism in Algeria, 1955–1957*, trans. Robert Miller (New York: Enigma, 2010).

94. Marc Michel, *Essai sur la colonisation positive: affrontements et accommodements en Afrique noire, 1830–1930* (Paris: Perrin, 2009).

95. Alain Griotteray, *Je ne demande pas pardon: La France n'est pas coupable* (Monaco: Le Rocher, 2001); Daniel Lefeuvre, *Pour en finir avec la repentance coloniale* (Paris: Flammarion, 2006); Paul-François Paoli, *Nous ne sommes pas coupables: assez de repentances!* (Paris: La Table Ronde, 2006); Max Gallo, *Fier d'être Français* (Paris: Fayard, 2006); Pascal Bruckner, *The Tyranny of Guilt: An Essay on Western Masochism*, trans. Steven Rendall (Princeton: Princeton University Press, 2012).

96. Nicholas Sarkozy, speech made on May 7, 2007, in Toulon. Full text (in French) at http://sites.univ-provence.fr/veronis/Discours2007/transcript.php?n=Sarkozy&p= 2007-02-07.

97. On the episode of slavery in particular and the paradoxes of race and citizenship, see Laurent Dubois, *A Colony of Citizens: Revolution and Slave Emancipation in the French Caribbean, 1787–1804* (Chapel Hill: University of North Carolina Press, 2004).

98. Dror Mishani and Aurelia Smotriez, "What Sort of Frenchmen Are They?," interview with Alain Finkielkraut, *Haaretz*, November 17, 2005, www.haaretz.com/what-sort -of-frenchmen-are-they-1.174419.

99. Mishani and Smotriez.

100. Mishani and Smotriez.

101. On all the preceding, see the original interview as well as Sylvain Cypel, "La Voix 'très déviante' d'Alain Fienkielkraut au quotidien Haaretz," *Le Monde* (November 24, 2005).

102. Alain Finkielkraut, *Au Nom de l'autre: refléxions sur l'antisémitisme qui vient* (Paris: Gallimard, 2003). On fairly closely related themes, see Pierre André Taguieff, *Rising from the Muck: The New Anti-Semitism in Europe* (Chicago: Ivan R. Dee, 2004); and

Taguieff, *La Judéophobie des modernes, des lumières au jihad mondial* (Paris: Odile Jacobs, 2008).

103. Pierre Nora, ed., "Introduction," in *Les Lieux de mémoire*, vol. 1 (Paris: Gallimard, Quarto, 1997), 560.

104. On these perils, see Nora, 560. On this compartmentalization, see Fernand Braudel, *The Identity of France*, vol. 1, *History and Environment*, trans. Siân Reynolds (New York: Harper and Row, 1988); Theodore Zeldin, *France, 1848–1945* (Oxford: Oxford University Press, 1979); and Eugen Weber, *Peasants Into Frenchmen: The Modernization of Rural France, 1870–1914* (Stanford: Stanford University Press, 1976).

105. For a general approach to these relations, see Paul Ricoeur, *Memory, History, Forgetting*, trans. Kathleen Blamey and David Pellauer (Chicago: University of Chicago Press, 2006).

106. This was, for example, the case between 1789 and 1795. One need only think of the public executions of Louis XVI, Marie-Antoinette, and Madame Élisabeth, of the guillotined and exhibited heads of Launey (governor of the Bastille) and Flesselles (provost-marshall of Paris merchants), Foulon's mouth stuffed with straw, Berthier de Sauvigny's (the intendant of Paris's) heart ripped out, the head of the deputy Féraud cut off and displayed in the middle of the Convention of 1795, or of the congestion of the cemeteries and charnel houses of Madeleine, Picpus, Errancis, or Sainte-Marguerite. On this subject, see Emmanuel Fureix, *La France des larmes: Deuils politiques à l'âge romantique, 1814–1840* (Paris: Champ Vallon, 2009).

107. Ernest Renan, lecture delivered at the Sorbonne, March 11, 1882. "Qu'est-ce qu'une nation?," *Œuvres Complètes*, vol. 1, ed. Henriette Psichari (Paris: Calmann-Lévy, 1947), 907.

108. Nicholas Bancel and Pascal Blanchard, "Colonisation: Commémorations et mémoriaux," in Bancel et al., *Rupture Postcoloniales*.

109. Anne-Emmanuelle Demartini and Dominique Kalifa, eds., *Imaginaire et sensibilités au XIX siècle* (Paris: Créaphis, 2005).

110. On the preceding, see Bancel and Blanchard, "Colonisation."

111. Laurence de Cock, Fanny Madeline, Nicolas Offenstadt, and Sophie Wahnich, *Comment Nicolas Sarkozy écrit l'histoire de France* (Marseille: Agone, 2008).

112. See the *Rapport de la commission sur la modernisation des commémorations publiques*, overseen by André Kaspi, November 2008, www.ladocumentationfrancaise.fr/rapports-publics/084000707/index.shtml.

113. Guy Perville, *Pour une histoire de la guerre d'Algérie, 1954–1962* (Paris: Picard, 2002); Mohammed Harbi and Benjamin Stora, eds., *La Guerre d'Algérie* (Paris: Robert Laffont, 2004). See also Pascal Blanchard and Isabelle Veyrat-Masson, eds., *Les Guerres de mémoire: la France et son histoire* (Paris: La Découverte, 2008).

114. According to the demographer Kamel Kateb, the conflict resulted in four hundred thousand deaths, including the combatants on both sides and civil victims.

115. Todd Shepard, *The Invention of Decolonization: The Algerian War and the Remaking of France* (Ithaca: Cornell University Press, 2006).

116. Benjamin Stora, "Guerre d'Algérie: 1999–2003, les accélérations de la mémoire," *Hommes et Migrations* 1244 (July–August 2003).

117. Jean-François Bayart, "Les Études postcoloniales, une invention politique de la tradition?," *Sociétés politiques comparées* 12 (April 2009), www.fasopo.org.

118. See Benjamin Stora, "Entre la France et l'Algérie, le traumitisme (post)colonial des années 2000," in Bancel et al., *Ruptures postcoloniales*.

119. Wendy Brown, *States of Injury: Power and Freedom in Late Modernity* (Princeton: Princeton University Press, 1995).

120. Judith Butler, *Precarious Life: The Powers of Mourning and Violence* (New York: Verso, 2004).

121. Nietzsche, *Beyond Good and Evil*, trans. Walter Kaufmann (New York: Random House, 1966), 22.

122. See Derek Gregory, *The Colonial Present: Afghanistan, Palestine, Iraq* (London: Blackwell, 2005); Eyal Weizam, *Hollow Land: Israel's Architecture of Occupation* (London: Verso, 2008); Adi Ophir, Michal Givoni, and Sari Hanefi, eds., *The Power of Inclusive Exclusion* (New York: Zone, 2009).

123. Nietzsche, *Beyond Good and Evil*, §23, p. 31.

124. Friedrich Nietzsche, *On the Genealogy of Morals*, trans. Walter Kaufmann (New York: Vintage, 1989), §26, p. 158.

5. THE HOUSE WITHOUT KEYS

1. The idea of African "objects" or "artifacts" is the idea of a general set, or an entire population of "things" or material productions, whether or not these latter take on an aesthetic function or call for an investment of the same kind. On these discussions in the European context, see Jean-Marie Schaeffer, "Objets esthetiques?," *L'Homme* 170 (2004): 25–45.

2. Engelbert Mveng, *L'Art et l'artisanat africains* (Yaounde: CLE, 1980); Léopold Sédar Senghor, "Standards critiques de l'art africain," *African Arts* 1, no. 1 (1967): 6–9, 52; Aimé Césaire, "Discours prononcé à Dakar le 6 avril 1966," *Gradhiva* 10 (2009): 1–7.

3. D. Lopes and F. Pigafetta, *Description du royaume de Congo et des contrées environnantes*, trans. and annotation Willy Bal (Louvain: Nauwelaerts, 1965), 81–82; J. Cuvelier, *L'Ancien royaume du Congo: fondation, découverte et première évangélisation de l'ancien royaume du Congo* (Bruges: Desclée De Brouwer, 1946); and O. Dapper, "Description de l'Afrique," in *Objets interdits*, ed. A. Van Dantzig (Paris: Fondation Dapper, 1989), 89–367; on Dahomey in the seventeenth century, see Jean Bonfils, "La Mission catholique en République populaire du Benin aux XVIIe et XVIIIe siècles," *Nouvelle Revue de sciences missionnaires* (1986): 161–174.

4. In the register of exceptions, see, for example, Martine Balard, "Les Combats du père Aupiais (1877–1945), missionnaire et ethnographe du Dahomey pour la reconnaissance africaine," *Histoire et Missions Chrétiennes* 2, no. 2 (2007): 74–93.

5. See Robert Muchembled, *Une histoire du diable: XIIe–XXe siècle* (Paris: Points, 2002).

6. See "Le Diable en procès: démonologie et sorcellerie à la fin du Moyen-Âge," special issue, *Medievales* 44 (2003).

7. Alain Boureau, *Satan hérétique: Naissance de la démonologie dans l'Occident médiéval, 1280–1330* (Paris: Odile Jacob, 2004).

8. Guy Bechtel, *La Sorcière et l'Occident: la destruction de la sorcellerie en Europe des origines aux grands buchers* (Paris: Plon, 1997).

9. Michael McCabe, "L'Évolution de la théologie de la mission dans la Société des Missions Africaines de Marion Bresillac à nos jours," *Histoire et Missions Chrétiennes* 2, no. 2 (2007): 1–22.

10. By way of example, see Kevin Carroll, *Yoruba Religious Carving: Pagan and Christian Sculpture in Nigeria and Dahomey* (London: Geoffrey Chapman, 1967).

11. On these debates, see Lucien Lévy-Bruhl, *Primitive Mentality* (1922; Los Angeles: HardPress, 2013); Lévy-Bruhl, *How Natives Think*, trans. Lilian A. Claire (1927; London: Routledge, 2019); and Lévy-Bruhl, *The "Soul" of the Primitive* (1928; London: Routledge, 2016). For more on debates from the time, see O. Leroy, *La Raison primitive: essai de réfutation de la théorie du prélogisme* (Paris: Guethner, 1927); and Raoul Allier, *Les Non-civilisés et nous: différence irréductible ou identité foncière* (Paris: Payot, 1927).

12. Jan Assmann, *Le Monothéisme et le langage de la violence: les débuts bibliques de la religion radicale* (Paris: Bayard, 2018), 75.

13. Cécile Fromont, *The Art of Conversion: Christian Visual Culture in the Kingdom of Kongo* (Chapel Hill: University of North Carolina Press, 2017).

14. On this topic, see Jean Comaroff and John Comaroff, *Of Revelation and Revolution*, vol. 1 (Chicago: University of Chicago Press, 1991); and John Comaroff and Jean Comaroff, *The Dialectics of Modernity on a South African Frontier*, vol. 2 (Chicago: University of Chicago Press, 1997). See also Achille Mbembe, *Afriques indociles: Christianisme, pouvoir et état en société postcoloniale* (Paris: Karthala, 1988).

15. J. E. Bouche, "La Religion des nègres africains, en particulier des Djedjis et des Nagos," *Le Contemporain*, 2nd ed. (1874): 57–875.

16. B. Salvaing, *Les Missionnaires à la rencontre de l'Afrique au XIXe siècle (Cote des Esclaves et pays yoruba, 1840–1891)* (Paris: L'Harmattan, 1995), 261–299.

17. Paule Brasseur, "Les Missionnaires catholiques à la côte d'Afrique pendant la deuxième moitié du XIX siècle," *Mélanges d'Ecole française de Rome, Italie et Méditerranée* 109, no. 2 (1997): 723–745.

18. Laurick Zerbini, "La Construction du discours patrimonial: les musées missionnaires à Lyon (1860–1960)," *Outre-Mers* 95, no. 356–357 (2007): 125–138.

19. Pedro Descoqs, "Métaphysique et raison primitive," *Archives de philosophie* 5, no. 3 (1928): 127–165.

20. See the works of Laurick Zerbini, "Les Collections africaines des Oeuvres Pontificales: l'objet africain sous le prisme du missionnaire catholique," in *Objets des terres lointaines*, ed. Essertel Yannick (Milano: Silvana Editoriale Spa, 2011), 31–51; as well as Zerbini, "L'Exposition vaticane de 1925: affirmation de la politique missionnaire de Pie XI," in *Le Gouvernement pontifical sous Pie XI: pratiques romaines et gestion de l'universel 1922–1939*, ed. Laura Pettinaroli (Rome: Collection EFR, 2013), 649–673.

21. Cited in Michel Bonemaison, "Le Musée Africain de Lyon d'hier à aujourd'hui," *Histoire et Missions Chrétiennes* 2, no. 2 (2007): 2.

22. For a notorious case, see Pierre Duviols, *La Lutte contre les religions autochtones dans le Perou colonial: l'extirpation de l'idolatrie entre 1532 et 1660* (Toulouse: Presses Universitaires du Mirail, 2008); and Fabien Eboussi Boulaga, *Christianisme sans fétiches: révélation et domination* (Paris: Présence africaine, 1981).

23. See, for example, José Sarzi Amade, "Trois missionnaires capucins dans le Royaume de Congo de la fin du XVIIe siècle: Cavazzi, Merolla et Zucchelli: force et prose dans les récits de spectacles punitifs et de châtiments exemplaires," *Veritas* 139 (2018): 137–160.

24. See James Schmidt and Amélie Oksenberg Rorty, eds., *Kant's "Idea for a Universal History with a Cosmopolitan Aim": A Critical Guide* (Cambridge: Cambridge University Press, 2009).

25. G. W. F. Hegel, *Lectures on the Philosophy of History*, trans. Ruben Alvarado (Aalten, Netherlands: WordBridge, 2013); and Hegel, *Philosophy of Right*, trans. S. W. Dyde (Mineola, NY: Dover, 2005).

26. Ernst Cassirer, *The Myth of the State* (New Haven: Yale University Press, 2009).

27. Achille Mbembe, *Critique of Black Reason*, trans. Laurent Dubois (Durham: Duke University Press, 2017).

28. Cassirer, *The Myth of the State*, 273.

29. Hegel, *Elements of the Philosophy of Right*, trans. Hugh Barr Nisbet (Cambridge: Cambridge University Press, 1991), 374.

30. Eric Voegelin, *Race and State*, trans. Ruth Hein (Colombia: University of Missouri Press, 1997).

31. Catherine Coquery-Vidrovitch, "La Fête des coutumes au Dahomey: historique et essai d'interprétation," *Annales* 4 (1964): 696–716.

32. Georges Bataille, *Theory of Religion*, trans. Robert Hurley (New York: Zone, 1989), 52–54.

33. Sigmund Freud, *On Sexuality: Three Essays on the Theory of Sexuality and Other Works*, trans. James Strachey (London: Penguin, 1991).

34. Carl Einstein, *Negerplastik* (Leipzig: Verlag der Weissen Bucher, 1915). In this work, Einstein endeavors to study the formal qualities of "black objects," whereas in *Afrikanische plastic* (Berlin: E. Wasmuth, 1921), he is more interested in their functions and meaning within their societies of origin.

35. See Coline Bidault, "La Présentation des objets africains dans DOCUMENTS (1929/1930), magazine illustre," *Les Cahiers de l'Ecole du Louvre* 3, no. 3 (2013): 5–13.

36. André Bréton, *L'Art magique* (Paris: Club français du livre, 1957).

37. Here I am partially drawing on Carlo Severi's analysis in *L'Objet-personne: une anthropologie de la croyance visuelle* (Paris: Editions de la Rue d'Ulm, 2017), 49–53.

38. Aimé Césaire, *Discourse on Colonialism* (1952; New York: Monthly Review Press, 2000).

39. "Those who invented neither gunpowder nor compass / those who could not ever tame steam or electricity / those who have not explored either seas or sky / but without whom the earth would not be the earth." Aimé Césaire, *Journal of a Homecoming/ Cahier d'un retour au pays natal*, trans. N. Gregson Davis (1939; Durham: Duke University Press, 2017), 47.

40. By way of illustration, read *Le Rapport Brazza: mission d'enquête du Congo: rapport et documents, 1905–1907* (Paris: Le Passager clandestin, 2014).

41. Lotte Arndt, "Vestiges of Oblivion: Sammy Baloji's Works on Skulls in European Museum Collections," *darkmatter*, www.darkmatter101.org/site/2013/11/18.

42. See Julien Bondaz, "L'Ethnograhie comme chasse: Michel Leiris et le animaux de la mission Dakar-Djibouti," *Gradhiva* 13 (2011): 162–181; and Bondaz, "L'Ethnographie parasitée?: anthropologie et enthomologie en Afrique de l'Ouest (1928–1960)," *L'Homme* 206 (2013): 121–150. See also Nancy J. Jacobs, "The Intimate Politics of Ornithology in Colonial Africa," *Comparative Studies in Society and History* 48, no. 3 (2006): 564–603.

43. J. MacKenzie, *The Empire of Nature: Hunting, Conservation and British Imperialism* (Manchester: Manchester University Press, 1988).

44. See Nelia Dias, "L'Afrique naturalisée," *Cahiers d'études africaines* 39, nos. 155–156 (1999): 590.

45. Allen F. Roberts, *A Dance of Assassins: Performing Early Colonial Hegemony in the Congo* (Bloomington: Indiana University Press, 1998); Ricardo Roque, *Headhunting and Colonialism: Anthropology and the Circulation of Human Skulls in the Portuguese Empire, 1870–1930* (Cambridge: Cambridge University Press, 2011); and Andrew Zimmerman, *Anthropology and Antihumanism in Imperial Germany* (Chicago: University of Chicago Press, 2001).

46. See Julien Bondaz, "Entrer en collection: pour une ethnographie des gestes et des techniques de collecte," *Les Cahiers de l'Ecole du Louvre* 4, no. 4 (2014).

47. Dominique Zahan, *La Graine et la viande: mythologie dogon* (Paris: Présence africaine, 1969).

48. Severi, *L'Objet-personne*, 267.

49. Joyce Cheng, "Georges Braque et l'anthropologie de l'image onirique de Carl Einstein," *Gradhiva* 14 (2011): 107.

50. Amos Tutuola, *My Life in the Bush of Ghosts* (London: Faber and Faber, 2014).

51. On this topic, see the works of Pierre Bonnafé, "Une Force, un objet, un champ: le *buti* des Kukuya au Congo," *Systèmes de pensée en Afrique noire* 8 (1987): 25–67; Bonnafé, "Une Grande fête de la vie et de la mort: le *miyali* des Kukuya," *L'Homme* (June 1973): 97–166; and Bonnafé, *Le Lignage de la mort, Nzo lipfu* (Paris: Nanterre, 1978).

52. Not only the making but also the conservation and restoration of objects required a host of technical knowledges about the botanical, vegetal, mineral, and organic worlds. The use of wood, for example, demanded a minimum of knowledge about its components, notably what made it moisture- and weather-resistant. Similarly for animal oils and fats, as well as various pigments and elements such as fire, which was used to make objects nonputrescible. On this subject, read Pol Pierre Gossiaux, "Conserver, restaurer: écrire le temps en Afrique," *CeROArt* 1 (2007).

53. For Johannes Fabian, it is precisely this practice of "decontextualization" that is specific to ethnographic collection. See "On Recognizing Things: The 'Ethnic Artefact' and the 'Ethnographic Object,'" *L'Homme* 170 (2004): 47–60.

54. See Gaetano Speranza, "Sculpture africaine: Blessures et altérité," *CeROArt* 2 (2008).

55. See Gossiaux, "Conserver, restaurer."

56. Kwame Anthony Appiah, "Comprendre les réparations: réflexion préliminaire," *Cahiers d'études africaines* 1, nos. 173–174 (2004): 25–40.

57. See Placide Tempels, *Bantu Philosophy*, trans. Colin King (Paris: Présence africaine, HBC, 1969), 80.

58. Édouard Glissant, *Une Nouvelle region du monde: esthetique 1* (Paris: Gallimard, 2006).

6. AFROPOLITANISM

1. See, for example, Julius Nyerere, *Freedom and Socialism* (New York: Oxford University Press, 1968); and Nyerere, *Essays on Socialism* (New York: Oxford University Press, 1972).

2. Julius Nyerere, *Freedom and Development* (New York: Oxford University Press, 1974).

3. Anthea Jeffrey, "Spectre of the New Racism," in *Frontiers of Freedom* (Johannesburg: Fourth Quarter, 2000), 3–12.

4. René Lemarchand, "Hate Crimes: Race and Retribution in Rwanda," *Transition* 81–82 (1999): 114–132.

5. John Boye Ejobowah, "Who Owns the Oil? The Politics of Ethnicity in the Niger Delta of Nigeria," *Africa Today* 37 (1999): 29–47.

6. Mamadou Diouf, "The Murid Trade Diaspora and the Making of a Vernacular Cosmopolitanism," *CODESRIA Bulletin* 1 (2000).

7. Robert Launay, "Spirit Media: The Electronic Media and Islam Among the Dyula of Northern Côte d'Ivoire," *Africa* 67, no. 3 (1997): 441–453.

8. See Ambra Formenti, "Holy Strangers: Transnational Mobility and Moral Empowerment Among Evangelical Guineans in Lisbon, Portugal," *African Diaspora* 10, nos. 1–2 (2018): 46–71; and Niewke Pruiksma, "Making a 'Home Away from Home': Home-Making Practices in the Celestial Church of Christ in Amsterdam, the Netherlands," *African Diaspora* 10, nos. 1–2 (2018): 139–162.

9. Ruth Marshall, *Political Spiritualities: The Pentecostal Revolution in Nigeria* (Chicago: University of Chicago Press, 2009).

10. Achille Mbembe, "À Propos des écritures africaines de soi," *Politique africaine* 77 (2000).

11. Jean Comaroff, "The Politics of Conviction: Faith on the Neo-Liberal Frontier," *Social Analysis* 53, no. 1 (2009): 17–38.

12. Asonzeh Ukah, "Redeeming Urban Spaces: The Ambivalence of Building a Pentecostal City in Lagos, Nigeria," in *Global Prayers: Contemporary Manifestations of the Religious in the City*, ed. Jochen Becker et al. (Zurich: Lars Muller, 2014), 178–197.

13. L. B. Landau and I. Freemantle, "Tactical Cosmopolitanism and Idioms of Belonging: Insertion and Self-Exclusion in Johannesburg," *Journal of Ethnic and Migration Studies* 36, no. 3 (2010): 375–390.

14. See Mbembe, "À Propos des écritures africaines de soi."

15. See Njabulo S. Ndebele, "Of Lions and Rabbits: Thoughts on Democracy and Reconciliation," *Pretexts: Literary and Cultural Studies* 8, no. 2 (1999): 147–158.

16. On the latter, see C. Ryan, "New Nollywood: A Sketch of Nollywood's Metropolitan New Style," *African Studies Review* 58, no. 3 (2015): 55–76.

17. Nic Cheesenen et al., "Decentralization in Kenya: The Governance of Governors," *Journal of Modern African Studies* 54, no. 1 (2016): 1–35.

18. Peter Geschiere and Francis Nyamnjoh, "Capitalism and Autochthony: The Seesaw of Mobility and Belonging," *Public Culture* 12, no. 2 (2000): 423–452. See also Peter Geschiere, *The Perils of Belonging: Autochthony, Citizenship and Exclusion in Africa and Europe* (Chicago: University of Chicago Press, 2009); and John L. Comaroff and Jean Comaroff, *Ethnicity, Inc.* (Chicago: University of Chicago Press, 2009).

19. Thomas Bierschenk and Jean-Pierre Olivier de Sardan, eds., *Les Pouvoirs au village* (Paris: Karthala, 1998).

20. Comaroff and Comaroff, *Ethnicity Inc.*; John L. Comaroff and Jean Comaroff, *The Politics of Custom: Chiefship, Capital, and the State in Contemporary Africa* (Chicago: University of Chicago Press, 2018).

21. Cf. Anneli Ekblom et al., "Conservation Through Biocultural Heritage: Examples from Sub-Saharan Africa," *Land* 8, no. 5 (2019).

22. Jocelyn Alexander and JoAnn McGregor, "Wildlife and Politics: CAMPFIRE in Zimbabwe," *Development and Change* 31 (June 2000): 605–607.

23. François Ekoko, "Balancing Politics, Economics, and Conservation: The Case of the Cameroon Forestry Law Reform," *Development and Change* 31 (June 2000): 131–154.

24. See Émile LeBris, Étienne LeRoy, and Paul Mathieu, eds., *L'Appropriation de la terre en Afrique noire* (Paris: Karthala, 1991); and Étienne LeRoy, ed., *La Sécurisation foncière en Afrique: pour une gestion viable des ressources renouvelables* (Paris: Karthala, 1996).

25. Cf. Louise Lombard, "Denouncing Sovereignty: Claims to Liberty in Northeastern Central African Republic," *Comparative Studies in History and Society* 60, no. 4 (2018): 1066–1095; Geschiere, *The Perils of Belonging*.

26. See John Boye Ejobowah, "Who Owns the Oil? The Politics of Ethnicity in the Niger Delta of Nigeria," *Africa Today* 37 (2000): 29–47.

27. Jean-Pierre Chauvau, "Question fonciere, ethnicite, autochtonie et crise de la ruralite dans l'Ouest foretier ivoirien," www.researchgate.net/publication/322758260.

28. See the studies by Philippe Antoine, Dieudonné Ouédraogo, and Victor Piché, *Trois générations de citadins au Sahel: trente ans d'histoire sociale à Dakar et à Bamako* (Paris: L'Harmattan, 1999); and Philippe Antoine et al., *Les Familles dakaroises face à la crise* (Dakar: ORSTOM-IFAN-CEPED, 1995).

29. See, for example, Michael W. Yarbrough, "Something Old, Something New: Historicizing Same-Sex Marriage Within Ongoing Struggles Over African Marriage in South Africa," *Sexualities*, September 12, 2017.

30. Jeremy L. Jones, "'Nothing Is Straight in Zimbabwe': The Rise of the Kukiya-kiya Economy 2000–2008," *Journal of Southern African Studies* 36, no. 2 (2010): 285–299.

31. R. Sooryamoorthy and Mzwandile Makhoba, "The Family in Modern South Africa: Insights from Recent Research," *Journal of Comparative Family Studies* 47, no. 3 (2016): 309–321.

32. Jeanne Bisilliat, ed., *Femmes du Sud, chefs de famille* (Paris: Karthala, 1996).

33. See Luc Sindjoun, ed., *La Biographie sociale du sexe: genre, société et politique au Cameroun* (Paris: Karthala, 2000).

34. C. J. Van Aardt, "The Changing Income Demographics of South Africa, 1996–2006," *Southern African Journal of Demography* 12 (2011): 5–36.

35. See the collective work *The Art of African Fashion* (Trenton, NJ: Africa World, 1999); and Dominique Malaquais, ed., "Cosmopolis," special edition, *Politique africaine* 100 (2005).

36. Didier Gondola, "Dream and Drama: The Search for Elegance Among Congolese Youth," *African Studies Review* 42, no. 1 (1999); and Adam Ashforth, "Weighing Manhood in Soweto," *CODESRIA Bulletin* 3–4 (1999).

37. S. Ziehl, "Divorce Statistics: A Case of the Wool Being Pulled Over Our Eyes?," *Southern African Journal of Demography* 8 (2000): 9–22.

38. Jacob Wale Mobolaji et al., "Household Structure and Living Arrangements Among Older Persons in Selected West African Countries," *African Population Studies* 32, no. 3 (2018).

39. Louise Vincent and Simon Howell, "'Unnatural,' 'Un-African' and 'Ungodly': Homophobic Discourse in Democratic South Africa," *Sexualities* 17, no. 4 (2014): 472–483.

40. Cf. Tabona Shoko, "'Worse Than Dogs and Pigs?': Attitudes Toward Homosexual Practice in Zimbabwe," *Journal of Homosexuality* 57, no. 5 (2010); Adriaan S. van Klinken, "Gay Rights, the Devil and the End of Times: Public Religion and the Enchantment of the Homosexuality Debate in Zambia," *Religion* 43, no. 4 (2013).

41. Daniel Yaw Fiaveh, "Phallocentrism, Female Penile Choices, and the Use of Sex Toys in Ghana," *Sexualities*, November 21, 2018; Rachel Spronk, "Invisible Desires in Ghana and Kenya: Same-Sex Erotic Experiences in Cross-Sex Oriented Lives," *Sexualities* 21, nos. 5–6 (2017): 883–898.

42. Sony Labou Tansi, *Life and a Half*, trans. Alison Dundy (1979; Bloomington: Indiana University Press, 2011).

43. Sony Labou Tansi, *The Shameful State*, trans. Dominic Thomas (1981; Bloomington: Indiana University Press, 2016).

44. Cf. Achille Mbembe, *On the Postcolony* (Berkeley: University of California Press, 2001).

45. Parfait Akana, "Note sur la denudation publique du corps feminin au Cameroun: a propos d'une explication mediatique," *L'Autre* 14, no. 2 (2013).

46. Thomas Hendriks, "'Erotiques Cannibales': A Queer Ontological Take on Desire from Urban Congo," *Sexualities*, March 30, 2017, https://doi.org/10.1177/13634607 16677283.

47. Deborah Posel, "Sex, Death and the Fate of the Nation: Reflections on the Politicization of Sexuality in Post-Apartheid South Africa," *Africa* 75, no. 2 (2005): 125–153.
48. Veena Das, *Words and Life: Exploring Violence and Descent Into the Ordinary* (Berkeley: University of California Press, 2006).
49. See Fatima Mernissi, *Beyond the Veil: Male–Female Dynamics in Muslim Society* (London: Al Saqi, 1975), and Mernissi, *Scheherazade Goes West* (New York: Washington Square Press, 2001). See, for a more general treatment, Fethi Benslama and Nadia Tazi, eds., *La Virilité en Islam* (Paris: Éditions de L'Aube, 2004).
50. Suzanne Preston Blier, *African Vodun: Art, Psychology, and Power* (Chicago: University of Chicago Press, 1995).
51. Preston Blier, 149–150.
52. Hachem Foda, "L'Ombre portée de la virilité," in Benslama and Tazi, *La Virilité en Islam*, 163–164.
53. Henri Rey-Flaud, *Le Démenti pervers: le refoulé et l'oublié* (Paris: Aubier, 2002), 119.
54. See the contributions in Signe Arnfred, ed., *Re-Thinking Sexualities in Africa* (Uppsala, Sweden: Nordic Africa Institute, 2004).
55. Preston Blier, *African Vodun*, chap. 4.
56. See, for example, Patrick Vandermeersch, *La Chair de la passion* (Paris: Éditions du Cerf, 2002).
57. Aziz Al-Azmeh, "Rhetoric for the Senses: A Consideration of Muslim Paradise Narratives," *Journal of Arabic Literature* 26 (1995).
58. Francesca Bray, *Technology and Gender: Fabrics of Power in Late Imperial China* (Berkeley: University of California Press, 1997), 281.
59. See Dominique Zahan, *La Viande et la graine* (Paris: Présence africaine, 1969).
60. Evans-Pritchard, "L'Inversion sexuelle chez les Azande," *Politique africaine* 126 (2012): 109–119.
61. See, in particular, Marcel Griaule, *Conversations with Ogotemmeli: An Introduction to Dogon Religious Ideas* (Oxford: Oxford University Press, 1965); and Griaule, *Masques Dogons* (Paris: Institut d'ethnologie, 1938).
62. Mariane C. Ferme, *The Underneath of Things: Violence, History, and the Everyday in Sierra Leone* (Berkeley: University of California Press, 2001), 61–74.
63. Ferme, 78–79.
64. Cited by Claude Lévesque, *Par-delà le masculin et le féminin* (Paris: Aubier, 2002), 105.
65. Thomas Hendriks, "Race and Desire in the Porno-Tropics: Ethnographic Perspectives from the Postcolony," *Sexualities*, February 5, 2014, https://doi.org/10.1177/1363460713511100.
66. Preston Blier, *African Vodun*, 150.
67. Peter Geschiere, *The Modernity of Witchcraft: Politics and the Occult in Postcolonial Africa* (Charlottesville: University of Virginia Press, 1997).
68. See Stephen O. Murray and Will Roscoe, eds., *Boy-Wives and Female Husbands: Studies of African Homosexualities* (New York: St. Martin's, 1998). On the practice of

"thigh-sex" between adult men and boys, see Dunbar Moodie, "Black Migrant Mine Labourers and the Vicissitudes of Male Desire," in *Changing Men in Southern Africa*, ed. Robert Morell (London: Zed, 2001). On sexual relations between women, see Kathryn Kendall, "Women in Lesotho and the (Western) Construction of Homophobia," in *Female Desires: Transgender Practices Across Cultures*, ed. E. Blackwood and S. Wieringa (New York: Columbia University Press, 1999).

69. More so than social-scientific literature, African literary fiction takes account of this imaginary. See, for example, the work of Sony Labou Tansi, or, more recently, Samy Tchak, *Place des fêtes* (Paris: Gallimard, 2000).

70. Georges Bataille, *Visions of Excess: Selected Writings, 1927–1939* (Minneapolis: University of Minnesota Press, 1999), 94.

71. This expression was used by Lacan in the seminar of March 6, 1963 (*L'Angoisse*, unpublished).

72. Callixthe Beyala, *Femme nue, femme noire* (Paris: Albin Michel, 2003).

73. On this subject of this distinction, see Oyewùmí Oyèrònké, "Family Bonds/Conceptual Binds: African Notes on Feminist Epistemologies," *Signs* 25 (2000); and Oyèrònké, "Conceptualizing Gender: The Eurocentric Foundations of Feminist Concepts and the Challenge of African Epistemologies," *Jenda* 2 (2002). Concerning the circulation of women in relation to ideology and maternity, see Jane Guyer and her concept of "polyandrous motherhood" in "Lineal Identities and Lateral Networks: The Logic of Polyandrous Motherhood," in *Nuptiality in Sub-Saharan Africa: Contemporary Anthropological and Demographic Perspectives*, ed. Caroline H. Bledsoe and Gilles Pison (Oxford: Clarendon, 1994).

74. Michel Foucault, *"Society Must Be Defended": Lectures at the Collège de France, 1975–1976*, trans. David Macey, ed. Mauro Bertani and Alessandro Fontana (New York: Picador, 2003), 255–256.

75. Ida B. Wells, quoted in D. Roberts, *Killing the Black Body: Race, Reproduction, and the Meaning of Liberty* (New York: Vintage, 1997), 30.

76. See Roberts, *Killing the Black Body*.

77. Frederick Douglass, *Life and Times of Frederick Douglass* (New York: Crowell, 1966), 188–189.

78. Roberts, *Killing the Black Body*, 28.

79. Todd L. Savitt, *Medicine and Slavery: The Diseases and Health Care of Blacks in Antebellum Virginia* (Urbana: University of Illinois Press, 1981).

80. Gilles Deleuze and Félix Guattari, *A Thousand Plateaus: Capitalism and Schizophrenia* (Minneapolis: University of Minnesota Press, 2002), 116.

81. Robert Carr, *Black Nationalism in the New World: Reading the African American and West Indian Experience* (Durham: Duke University Press, 2002), esp. chap. 5.

82. Cf. Tshikala K. Biaya, " 'Crushing the Pistachio': Eroticism in Senegal and the Art of Ousmane Ndiaye Dago," *Public Culture* 12 (2000).

83. Monique Schneider, *Généalogie du masculin* (Paris: Aubier, 2000), 127.

84. Ahmadou Kourouma, *The Suns of Independence*, trans. Adrian Adams (1968; New York: Africana, 1981).

85. Yando Ouologuem, *Bound to Violence*, trans. Ralph Manheim (1968; New York: Harcourt Brace, 1971).

86. In addition to the writings of Sony Labou Tansi, see, for example, Ahmadou Kourouma, *Allah Is Not Obliged*, trans. Frank Wynne (New York: Anchor, 2007).

87. Sony Labou Tansi, *L'Autre monde: écrits inédits* (Paris: Éditions Revue Noire, 1997).

88. Mbembe, *On the Postcolony*.

89. Patricia Célérier, "Engagement et esthétique du cri," *Notre Librairie* 148 (September 2002); Jean-Marc Éla, *African Cry* (1980; Maryknoll, NY: Orbis, 1986); Sony Labou Tansi, *Le Commencement des douleurs* (Paris: Éditions du Seuil, 1995).

90. Sony Labou Tansi, *L'État honteux* (Paris: Éditions du Seuil, 1981).

91. Alan Mabanckou, *Black Bazar* (Paris: Éditions du Seuil, 2009).

92. See George E. Brooks, *Eurafricans in Western Africa* (Athens: Ohio University Press, 2003).

93. Jane I. Guyer and Samuel M. Eno Belinga, "Wealth in People and Wealth in Knowledge: Accumulation and Composition in Equatorial Africa," *Journal of African History* 36, no. 1 (1995).

94. Luciana Parisi, "Automated Thinking and the Limits of Reason," *Cultural Studies* 16, no. 5 (2016): 471–481.

95. See Elizabeth de Freitas et al., "Alternative Ontologies of Number: Rethinking the Quantitative in Computational Culture," *Cultural Studies* 16, no. 5 (2016): 431–434.

96. Gerard Delanty and Aurea Mota, "Governing the Anthropocene: Agency, Governance, Knowledge," *European Journal of Social Theory* 20, no. 1 (2017): 9.

EPILOGUE

1. Yambo Ouologuem, *Bound to Violence*, trans. Ralph Manheim (1971; New York: Harcourt Brace Jovanovich, 1986).

2. Achille Mbembe, *La Naissance du maquis dans le Sud-Cameroun, 1920–1960: histoire des usages de la raison en colonie* (Paris: Karthala, 1996).

3. Caroline Elkins, *Imperial Reckoning: The Untold Story of Britain's Gulag in Kenya* (New York: Henry Holt, 2005); and David Anderson, *Histories of the Hanged: The Dirty War in Kenya and the End of Empire* (New York: Norton, 2005).

4. Cheikh Hamidou Kane, *Ambiguous Adventure* (London: Heinemann, 1972).

5. Frantz Fanon, *The Wretched of the Earth*, trans. Constance Farrington (New York: Grove, 1963), 311. ["We must shake off the heavy darkness (*grande nuit*) in which we were plunged, and leave it behind."]

6. Aimé Césaire, *Les Armes miraculeuses* (Paris: Gallimard, 1970), 15.

7. Fanon, *The Wretched of the Earth*, 312.

8. Fanon, 315.

9. Léopold Sédar Senghor, *Chants d'ombre* (Paris: Seuil, 1956); and Gary Wilder, "Race, Reason, Impasse: Césaire, Fanon, and the Legacy of Emancipation," *Radical History Review* 90 (Autumn 2004).

10. Achille Mbembe, "Pouvoir des morts et langages des vivants," *Politique africaine* 22 (1982).

11. David Lan, *Guns and Rains: Guerillas and Spirit Mediums in Zimbabwe* (Berkeley: University of California Press, 1985).

12. On the theme of a freely accepted death, see Nelson Mandela, *Long Walk to Freedom* (London: Little, Brown, 1995).

13. Ho Chi Minh, *Down with Colonialism* (London: Verso, 2007).

14. On the historical antecedents of this, see Jennifer Pitts, *A Turn to Empire: The Rise of Liberal Imperialism in Britain and France* (Princeton: Princeton University Press, 2006).

15. See Yuk Hui, "On the Unhappy Consciousness of Neoreactionaries," *e-flux* 81 (2017).

16. Bernard Waldenfels, *Études pour une phénoménologie de l'étranger*, vol. 1, *Topographie de l'étranger* (Paris: Van Dieren, 2009).